O9-BTM-552

great spiritual leaders and guides who some-how, somewhere, managed to move so many others to joy and ecstasy often seemed to struggle with melancholy and at times even with the darkest despair. What was this sad-ness they had to engage in combat—and why?''

It is Elie Wiesel's unique gift to make the lives and tales of these great teachers as com-pelling now as they were in a different time and place. In the great tradition of Hasidism itself, he leaves us to struggle with questions of morality and commitment and provides truths that can be pondered for a lifetime.

PHOTOGRAPH © BY ARNOLD NEWMAN

Elie Wiesel, author of twenty books, is Uni-versity Professor and Andrew Mellon Profes-sor in the Humanities at Boston University. He and his family live in New York City.

Translated from the French

by Marion Wiesel

SUMMIT BOOKS

NEW YORK

Somewhere a Master

Further Hasidic
Portraits and Legends

Elie Wiesel

10 9 8 7 6 5 4 3 2 1
First Edition

Library of Congress Cataloging in Publication Data

Wiesel, Elie, date.
    Somewhere a master.

    Contents: Pinhas of Koretz—Aharon of Karlin
—Wolfe of Zbarazh—[etc.]
    1. Hasidim—Biography. 2. Hasidim—Legends.
I. Title.
BM750.W54   1982   296.8'33[B]   82–10370
ISBN 0–671–44170–1

CONTENTS

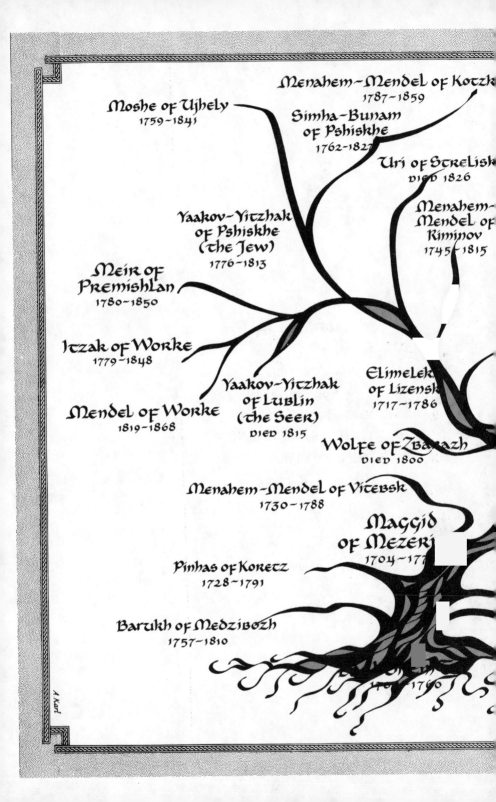

Menahem–Mendel of Kotzk
1787–1859

Moshe of Ujhely
1759–1841

Simha–Bunam
of Pshiskhe
1762–1827

Uri of Strelisk
died 1826

Yaakov–Yitzhak
of Pshiskhe
(the Jew)
1776–1813

Menahem–
Mendel of
Riminov
1745–1815

Meir of
Premishlan
1780–1850

Itzak of Worke
1779–1848

Elimelek
of Lizensk
1717–1786

Yaakov–Yitzhak
of Lublin
(the Seer)
died 1815

Mendel of Worke
1819–1868

Wolfe of Zbarazh
died 1800

Menahem–Mendel of Vitebsk
1730–1788

Maggid
of Mezeri
1704–177

Pinhas of Koretz
1728–1791

Barukh of Medzibozh
1757–1810

A Karl

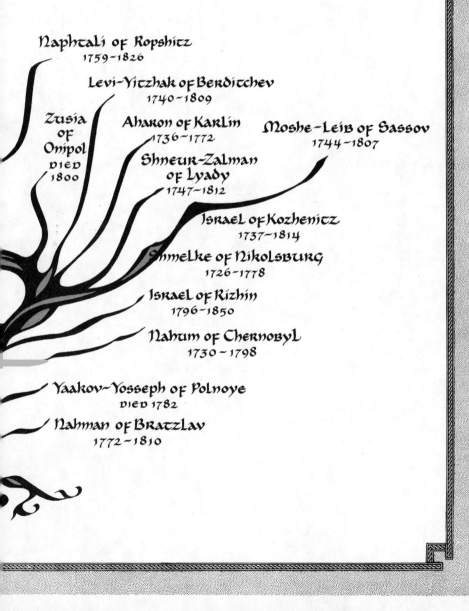

Naphtali of Ropshitz
1759–1826

Levi-Yitzhak of Berditchev
1740–1809

Zusia
of
Onipol
died
1800

Aharon of Karlin
1736–1772

Moshe-Leib of Sassov
1744–1807

Shneur-Zalman
of Lyady
1747–1812

Israel of Kozhenitz
1737–1814

Shmelke of Nikolsburg
1726–1778

Israel of Rizhin
1796–1850

Nahum of Chernobyl
1730–1798

Yaakov-Yosseph of Polnoye
died 1782

Nahman of Bratzlav
1772–1810

PINHAS
OF KORETZ

ONE DAY, a young Hasid came to see
Rebbe Pinhas of Koretz, known for his wisdom and compassion.

"Help me, Master," he said. "I need your advice, I need your
support. My distress is unbearable; make it disappear. The
world around me, the world inside me, are filled with turmoil
and sadness. Men are not human, life is not sacred. Words are
empty—empty of truth, empty of faith. So strong are my doubts
that I no longer know who I am—nor do I care to know. What
am I to do, Rebbe? Tell me, what am I to do?"

"Go and study," said Rebbe Pinhas of Koretz. "It's the only
remedy I know. Torah contains all the answers. Torah *is* the
answer."

"Woe unto me," said the disciple. "I am unable even to
study. So shaky are my foundations, so all-pervasive my uncertainties, that my mind finds no anchor, no safety. It wanders
and wanders, and leaves me behind. I open the Talmud and
contemplate it endlessly, aimlessly. For weeks and weeks I remain riveted to the same page, to the same problem. I cannot go
farther, not even by a step, not even by a line. What must I do,
Rebbe, what can I do to go on?"

When a Jew can provide no answer, he at least has a tale to
tell. And so Rebbe Pinhas of Koretz invited the young man to
come closer, and then said with a smile, "You must know, my
friend, that what is happening to you also happened to me.

When I was your age I stumbled over the same obstacles. I, too, was filled with questions and doubts. About man and his fate, creation and its meaning. I was struggling with so many dark forces that I could not advance; I was wallowing in doubt, locked in despair. I tried study, prayer, meditation. In vain. Penitence, silence, solitude. My doubts remained doubts. Worse: they became threats. Impossible to proceed, to project myself into the future. I simply could not go on. Then one day I learned that Rebbe Israel Baal Shem Tov would be coming to our town. Curiosity led me to the *shtibl*, where he was receiving his followers. I entered just as he was finishing the *Amida* prayer. He turned around and saw me, and I was convinced that he was seeing me, me and no one else. The intensity of his gaze overwhelmed me, and I felt less alone. And strangely, I was able to go home, open the Talmud, and plunge into my studies once more. You see," said Rebbe Pinhas of Koretz, "the questions remained questions. But I was able to go on. . . ."

What did Pinhas of Koretz try to teach his young visitor? One: Not to give up. Even if some questions are without answers, go on asking them. Two: Doubts are not necessarily destructive—provided they bring one to a Rebbe. Three: One must not think that one is alone and that one's tragedy is exclusively one's own; others have gone through the same sorrow and endured the same anguish. Four: One must know where to look, and to whom. Five: God is everywhere, even in pain, even in the search for faith. Six: A good story in Hasidism is not about miracles, but about friendship and hope—the greatest miracles of all.

A variation of the same story: Fearing that his faith would be weakened by doubts, Rebbe Pinhas decided to go to Medzibozh to see Rebbe Israel Baal Shem Tov, the founder of the Hasidic movement. By coincidence, that day the Besht,* as he was known, happened to be visiting Koretz. Rebbe Pinhas quickly returned to Koretz and ran to the inn where the Baal Shem was staying. There he heard the Master explaining to his followers

* From the Hebrew acronym of his name.

the passage in Scripture describing how Moses stood with his arms raised in prayer, giving his people the strength to do battle against the Amalekites.

"It happens," said the Master, "that a person can feel troubled; it happens that a person's faith can waver. What does one do then? One turns to God in prayer and implores God to help one recapture one's true faith."

And Rebbe Pinhas understood that the Besht had meant him too.

Though he was one of the Besht's closest companions, Rebbe Pinhas never formally joined the Hasidic movement. He chose to remain on the sidelines, watching with interest and amusement what was happening onstage.

After the death of the Founder, his peers wanted Rebbe Pinhas to at least assume the role of mediator in the power struggle between the two factions representing the two contenders for the succession: Rebbe Dov-Ber of Mezeritch and Rebbe Yaakov-Yosseph of Polnoye. But Rebbe Pinhas refused.

Actually, he himself would have made an excellent candidate to succeed the Besht. He was respected and celebrated by scholars and disciples alike. The Besht's affection for him was well known. Once the Besht was asked to give his opinion of his friends, and he did. When he came to Rebbe Pinhas he stopped: and said nothing. Rebbe Pinhas was a case apart. The famous "Grandfather of Shpole" admired him; so did the legendary Reb Leib, son of Sarah, who called him "the brain of the world." Hasidic tradition has it that the Besht left his knowledge to the Maggid of Mezeritch, his saintliness to Reb Mikhel of Zlotchov and his wisdom to Rebbe Pinhas of Koretz. In Hasidic literature, Rebbe Pinhas is called "the Sage."

Withdrawn, reserved, modest, an individualist, he refused to be crowned Rebbe. He held no court, proposed no doctrine, promised no miracles, established no dynasty, declined honors and privileges. He had five sons but only one disciple: Rebbe Raphael of Barshad, a former beadle and gravedigger whom he had pulled out of anonymity. When Rebbe Pinhas died on his way to the Holy Land, he was succeeded by this disciple. That day at the Wall in Jerusalem, a Tzaddik saw the Shekhina—Divine Presence—in mourning.

Rebbe Pinhas: the most human, the most gracious and beautiful character among the Elders of Hasidism.

Who was he?

As is the case with most of his illustrious contemporaries, not much is known of Rebbe Pinhas' childhood and formative years. Born in 1728 in Shklov into a poor rabbinic family, of ancestors who had died as martyrs of the faith, he studied Talmud and Kabbala; he also showed an unusual interest in the exact sciences and philosophy.

He rarely spoke of his father. Instead, he frequently referred to his grandfather—also Rebbe Pinhas—who had made it his lifework to roam around Eastern Europe seeking out Jewish converts to Christianity to bring them back to the fold.

Rebbe Pinhas married young and led an austere life. For a while he taught small children and was nicknamed "the dark teacher," perhaps because of his dark complexion, perhaps because of his taste for solitude and meditation.

Unlike the Besht, he quickly gained a wide reputation as a rabbinic and mystical scholar. His teachings contain commentaries on the Bible, the Zohar, the Talmud and even on the Code of Ethics, the *Shulkhan Arukh*.

Also unlike the Besht, it had been his wish to be able to stay in one place and do his work there—but he could not. He fled Shklov to avoid harassment and took refuge in Miropol in Volhynia. From there he moved to Koretz, then to Ostraha, where he settled. He remained there until he decided to leave for the Holy Land in 1791. On his way, he stopped in Shipitovke, unaware that death was waiting for him there.

He was kind and generous. He once overheard his wife shouting at their servant and promptly admonished her, "Please—please never raise your voice at any human being; a human being is precious, so precious." He himself spoke softly, patiently. A devoted husband, a good father, he rarely lost his temper. "I don't think I succeeded in defeating vanity," he once remarked. "But I did succeed in controlling my anger. I simply put it into my pocket and I pull it out only when I absolutely need to."

Contemplative by nature, he would gaze at his visitors and say nothing—thereby causing his visitors to look at him and say nothing. He prayed quietly, meditatively, shunning all visible demonstrations of ecstasy.

At the death of the Besht in 1760, Rebbe Pinhas was barely thirty-two, so he must have been quite young when they first met. The Besht treated him as an equal and went out of his way to win him over, although, unlike the Besht's other companions —such as Reb Gershon of Kitev, Reb Nahman of Kossov, and Reb Mikhel of Zlotchov—Rebbe Pinhas did not belong to any existing esoteric group. He represented no potential ally, no influential clan whose adherence was important to the new movement. No, the Besht wanted Rebbe Pinhas for what he was and not for what he possessed: he wanted him for himself and not for the movement. Perhaps he needed him more as a friend than as a follower.

"Man is not alone," the Besht told him when they first met. "God makes us remember the past so as to break our solitude. Our forefathers stand behind us, some of them tested or chosen by God. Whatever they did, they did for us. Whatever we do, we do for them. Long ago, in Egypt, every one of us strove for the preservation of the holy tongue, the names of our ancestors and their descendants, and the memory of the Covenant. Every one of us sat at the Prophets' feet to receive their teachings. Every one of us marched through the desert, to Sinai and from Sinai. Every one of us watched the splendor and the desolation of Jerusalem. Every one of us followed Reb Yohanan Ben-Zakkai into exile; and every one of us shared his anguish and pride. And that is why we must stay together."

There was something delicate, reticent and yet warm, in their relationship. Their mutual respect and affection went so far as to prevent the one from trying to change the other.

Legend has it that Rebbe Pinhas visited the Besht twice—and

that the Besht visited him twice. Another Hasidic tradition claims that Rebbe Pinhas learned three things from the Besht. We do not know what they were. But we do know that, in exchange, Rebbe Pinhas taught the Besht three things. Could they have been the same things?

The two friends were together on the last Shavuot they were to spend together, when the Besht was lying on his deathbed. Most of the disciples had obeyed the Master's wish and returned home. Rebbe Pinhas had stayed. At one point he began to pray, quietly but fervently, interceding with heaven on behalf of the old Master. "Too late," the Besht whispered, "too late, Pinhas. What is done is done; what is done will not be undone."

In the dispute over who was to be the Besht's successor, Rebbe Pinhas, characteristically, felt closer to the losers—in particular to the dead Master's son, Reb Tzvi-Hersh, whose name is frequently mentioned in his sayings. Rebbe Pinhas was Reb Tzvi-Hersh's ever-present and affectionate confidant and protector.

He also maintained cordial relations with another loser, Reb Yaakov-Yosseph of Polnoye, who had aspired to succeed the Besht after serving him faithfully. Feeling rejected and bitter, Reb Yaakov-Yosseph often chose to celebrate Shabbat alone. Only Rebbe Pinhas sometimes came to keep him company.

Once Rebbe Pinhas tried to console his unhappy friend with the following parable: "When the king retires at night, his crown rests on a nail fastened to the wall. Why on a nail, a common object used by common people for common purposes, and not on the head of a minister especially selected for such a distinct honor? I shall tell you why: After a while, with the crown resting on his head, the minister might take himself seriously. No such danger with a nail. . . ."

From this we may conclude that there probably was some tension in his relations with the winner, Rebbe Dov-Ber, the great Maggid of Mezeritch. Not that Rebbe Pinhas had objected to the Maggid's election, or that he lacked consideration for his virtues and talents. No. He had high regard for the new leader of the movement. But in his own gentle way, Pinhas distrusted all leaders. That is why he refused to become one himself. For a long time he wore no rabbinic garment, accepted no crown and discouraged all manifestations of admiration. He would wear shabby clothes and sit with beggars and strangers near the stove, far from the limelight. Was it that he felt unworthy or unable to guide others toward truth? Perhaps he worried too much about the perils of vanity inherent in leadership —perhaps he was afraid of fame.

The Grandfather of Shpole told the following story: "For years and years I lived the life of a wanderer. In the company of beggars, I went from town to town, from village to village. Once we happened to arrive in Koretz on Shabbat eve. So we went to attend services conducted by Rebbe Pinhas. When the services were over, he greeted every one of us. When my turn came to shake his hand, he looked at me—and embraced me; he knew who I was. Years later, when I was no longer anonymous, I came to visit him again. Again it was Shabbat eve. Again Rebbe Pinhas greeted all the strangers. Then came my turn. He looked at me and said, 'Who are *you?* Where do *you* come from?' "

How typical of Rebbe Pinhas. When *nobody* knew the Grandfather of Shpole, he recognized him. Now that *everybody* knew him, he did not.

As for the Grandfather of Shpole, he concluded the story by saying, "It is not good to be famous, no, it is not good, I am telling you."

Among Rebbe Pinhas' numerous aphorisms, all reflecting common sense and wisdom, many relate to the pitfalls of vanity —how to unmask it, how to fight it and vanquish it.

"If someone finds it necessary to honor me," he said, "that means he is more humble than I. Which means he is better and saintlier than I. Which means that I should honor him. But then, why is he honoring me?"

His disciple, Rebbe Raphael of Barshad, said: "When I shall appear before the heavenly tribunal, its members will question me on my various sins, and I, naturally, shall do my best to invent all kinds of excuses. Why didn't I study enough? I had neither the talent nor the time. Why didn't I pray with greater concentration? I was too busy making a living. And fasting, did I do some fasting? No, no, I was too weak. What about charity? No, no, I was too poor. But then they will ask me, 'If *this* is how it was—if you didn't study and didn't pray, if you lacked both compassion and charity, if you were too busy with yourself —how did it come about that you exuded such vanity?' And to this I shall have no answer, no excuse."

Rebbe Pinhas said: "Every sin is linked to a reason, good or bad—with the sole exception of vanity, which needs no reason to grow and grow. One can easily lie in rags on the ground and be hungry; one could lack all virtues and all knowledge, and still think endlessly, I am great, I am learned, I am just."

He also said: "Everything I know I learned earlier, when I sat in the last row, out of sight. Now I am here, occupying a place of honor, and I don't understand. . . ."

Of course, all Masters were aware of the spiritual threat inherent in their position. It is difficult to claim to possess powers and not fall into the trap of believing that one deserves them. From the Maggid on, most Hasidic leaders stressed the absolute and constant need to fight pride and complacency. Except that he, Rebbe Pinhas, refused even to be tempted.

What, then, attracted him to Hasidism? Only the Besht and his friendship? No. He stayed attached to the movement some thirty years after the death of its founder. His motives were not only personal; they were linked to the conditions inside the Jewish communities in Eastern Europe.

Hasidism was then the most revolutionary movement in Judaism. It excited the young, stimulated the dreamers, the poor, the desperate, the defeated. The elite came to join; this can be seen by the quality of the Besht's early companions. They were all great, renowned scholars. They, too, had felt that Hasidism was accomplishing something vital and necessary for Jewish continuity: it was offering hope to the hopeless and a sense of belonging to those who needed it. The uprooted, isolated, impoverished and uneducated villagers who, due to conditions not of their making, lived on the edge of history, and even outside its boundaries, suddenly felt linked to the people and the destiny of Israel. The force of the movement lay not in ideology but in life: the Besht literally changed the climate and the quality of Jewish life in hundreds and hundreds of towns and villages; his victories meant survival for their dispersed communities.

For those were cruel times for Eastern European Jewry. While Washington and his generals fought for American independence and the French revolutionaries proclaimed the reign of reason and liberty, Jews in Russia and Poland were isolated and miserable. Polish Jews were still accused—regularly—of ritual murder. A Polish author wrote: "Just as freedom cannot be conceived without the right to protest, Jewish matzoth for Passover cannot be made without Christian blood. . . ."

In Britain, Parliament rejected proposals granting civil rights to Jews. In Rome, Pope Pius VI condemned seven thousand Jews of his own city to public disgrace. In Russia, Jews were persecuted and massacred. Voltaire and Rousseau, Kant and Goethe, Mozart and Goya, Danton and Robespierre—all were contemporaries of the Besht and the Maggid of Mezeritch and Rebbe Pinhas of Koretz, and it was as though they lived in different worlds. Jewish history seems to have unfolded in the margin of history. In the so-called Age of Enlightenment, Jews were still relegated to subhuman status, not only by Christian fanatics but by enlightened secularists as well.

Thus the Jews had good reason to doubt society's wisdom and justice. They had good reason to doubt the absolute power of rationalism. Therefore they turned inward and became mystical. They turned to the Rebbe, for only he knew how to comfort them, how to impart to them a sense of sacredness. Suddenly, and for the first time in centuries, they realized that they were not useless creatures. In the Rebbe's eyes, every one of their gestures, every one of their prayers, no matter how awkward, counted and made a difference. The shepherd who played his pipe on Yom Kippur performed an action that had its reverberations in the highest spheres. The beggar's blessing compelled God to offer His own.

God is everywhere, said the Besht. In pain too? Yes, in pain too—especially in pain. God *is*, and that means that He dwells in every human being. In the unlearned too? Yes, in the unlearned too. In the sinner too. In the humble, in the humble most of all, He can be found. And He can be perceived by everyone. As he sits on His throne, said Rebbe Pinhas, He can be approached both through the tears of the penitent and the fervor of the worshiper. God *is*, God is *one*; and that means He is the same to people who turn to Him in different ways.

This offer of consolation was, at the same time, an appeal for unity. Within the Hasidic framework, Jews were told that they could fulfill themselves—as Jews—in more ways than one: the learned through their learning, the poor through their piety. God is not indifferent and man is not His enemy—this was the substance of the Hasidic message. It was a message against despair, against resignation; it sensitized the individual Jew to his own problems and made him aware of his ability to solve them. It taught him that hope must be derived from his own history, and joy from within his own condition.

Hasidism's concern for the wretched, for the victimized and forgotten Jew, induced many distinguished scholars to change their milieu, their way of life, and join the movement, and after the passing of the Maggid of Mezeritch in 1772, they became its leaders. They responded to a need, hence their inevitable success.

Rebbe Pinhas, too, became popular, much to his chagrin. Too many people visited him for too many reasons, taking too much of his time away from study and meditation. One Yom Kippur he addressed this plea to God:

"Master of the Universe, forgive my audacity. I know I should thank You for the gifts You have bestowed upon me, thank You for making me so liked by Your children. But do understand, please, that I have no time left for You. Do something, anything. Make people like me less. . . ."

His wish was granted. People stopped visiting him at home, no longer greeted him on the street. And he was happy. But then came the Succoth holiday. As was the custom, he recited the *Ushpizin* prayer with true fervor, inviting the shepherds of our people to enter his tent and be his guests. The first one to appear was Abraham; he stood at the entrance but refused to step inside, explaining: "If nobody comes to you, I must stay away too. A Jew must live with his people, not only for his people. . . ." Next day Rebbe Pinhas addressed another plea to God. And people sought him out once more.

This, too, is part of the Hasidic message: There is a solution to loneliness—and loneliness is no solution. What is the significance of *Tikkun*—mystical reparation? Rebbe Pinhas would ask. It is to be concerned not only with yourself but with everything that goes on around you; help others and you will help yourself. You want to serve God? Start with serving His children. Knowledge is to be shared, as is faith, and everything else.

People brought him money, which he promptly distributed among the poor. Once he remarked: "I only desire what I already possess." How simple and how wise—better to desire what one has than to have what one desires.

Often students would turn to him for help in matters of faith. To one he said, "True, God may be hiding, but you know it. That ought to be sufficient." Did the student suffer less? No, but he suffered differently.

Having been told that atheists were demanding proof of God's existence, he rushed to the House of Study, opened the Holy Ark, seized the sacred scrolls and shouted, "I swear, I swear that God exists; isn't that proof enough?"

A student suffered from such anguish that he did not dare speak about it. Rebbe Pinhas looked at him and smiled. "I know, I know how you feel . . . but tell me, if *I* know, don't you think that *He* also knows?"

. . .

Speaking on grave and urgent topics, he would display a subtle sense of humor.

"All that is important is rare," he once remarked. "Millions and millions of people inhabit the earth, but only a few are Jewish. Among the Jews, only a few are learned. Among the learned, only a few are pious. And even fewer are those who know how to pray properly."

Another time: "God created Eve to serve as Adam's *ezer kenegdo*, according to Scripture: to help him—against him. What does that mean? Well, imagine you visit a rich man, asking for charity. He welcomes you warmly and says: 'Oh, I wish I could, I so wish I could give as much as you need, as much as you deserve, but you see, I cannot; my wife is against it.' "

A student asked him, "What am I to do? I am pursued by evil temptations." And he answered, "Are you sure? Are you sure it is not the other way around?"

Perceptive and sharp-minded, Rebbe Pinhas was nevertheless also naïve. He was convinced, for instance, that all sickness originates in lies: a person who does not lie shall not be ill. Also: When a Jew answers a question, he defeats the enemy of Israel; if his answer is correct, all his enemies are defeated. Also: When telling lies shall be considered as grave a transgression as adultery, the Messiah will appear.

On Judgment Day, he would say, even the lectern will be judged, and sentenced.

Also: After his death a Tzaddik ascends from one level to another, higher and higher, until he becomes first a sacred letter, then a sacred thought, and finally a sacred name.

And this advice he loved to repeat in the name of the Besht: If you feel the urge to praise, praise God; if you feel the urge to blame, blame yourself.

Rebbe Pinhas' posthumously published book—*Midrash Pinhas*—contains aphorisms, parables and insights, combining the written tradition with the oral one, sealed secrets with revealed intentions. He loved the Book of Splendor; he "sought refuge" in the Zohar.

Redemption occupied his thoughts and dreams. What Hasid does not wait for the Messiah? What Rebbe does not try to hasten his coming? To be Jewish is to link one's fate to that of the Messiah—to that of all those who are waiting for the Messiah. How is one to accelerate events? Never mind the Kabbalistic methods. They are too complicated and inaccessible; and then, they have not proved too successful in the past. No, better try simpler ways. Better appeal to simpler people. Every human being may change the course of history; it is in the power of every individual to shorten exile.

Therein lies Rebbe Pinhas' originality. In his teachings, he assigns no important role to the Tzaddik, and certainly not as mediator between heaven and earth, as the instrument chosen by God to make His will known and implemented. Instead he stresses the importance of each individual, no matter how saintly or how ignorant. Every one of us can open the gates and thus enable the Redeemer to appear in our midst.

"If I so desired," said Rebbe Pinhas, "I could bring the Messiah as easily as I can lift a straw; but I prefer to rely on the Almighty. And He relies on man. If all Jews would give charity, redemption would occur."

On another occasion he said: "If all men would speak the truth, there would be no further need to bring the Messiah; he would be here already. Just as the Messiah brings truth, truth brings the Messiah." Truth: Rebbe Pinhas' total obsession and all-consuming passion.

"I broke all my bones while working on myself to attain truth," he said. "This lasted twenty-one years: seven years to discover what truth is; another seven years to expel falsehood from my being; and the last seven years to receive truth and live it."

Respect for truth was so profound among his friends and followers that they dared not repeat his comments for fear of misquoting him.

His heir, Rebbe Raphael of Barshad, was once stopped in the street by a man who asked him, "Aren't you Reb Raphael of Barshad?" "Yes . . . I think so," replied the Rebbe.

Summoned to testify on behalf of a man whose innocence he doubted, the same Rebbe Raphael spent all night weeping: he could not bring himself to tell a possible lie. He cried and cried. And died at dawn.

Once, during *Maariv* services, Rebbe Pinhas let out a cry so full of pain that his followers were anguished. The countess who owned much of Koretz happened to pass by his window just then. "I have never heard a cry filled with such truth," she told her retinue. When Rebbe Pinhas was informed of her comment, he smiled; he liked it. "Everybody can find truth," he remarked, "even Gentiles." On another occasion he emphasized: "We must love even the wicked among the Gentiles and pray for them; only then will redemption materialize."

But, of course, his main concern was for his own community —his own people—on whose behalf he pleaded with God Himself. "If only I knew how to sing," he once whispered, "I would force Him to come down and be with His children, witness their suffering, and save them." Another time he exclaimed: "Why do You leave Your people in exile? Why must it last so long? Only because we did not—and do not—observe Your laws? But tell me, tell me, who compelled You to give them to us? Did we ask for them, did we want them? It was You who made us receive them. Furthermore, Master of the Universe, tell me: Didn't You know even then that we would not comply with all Your laws? Still You chose us—then why are You angry?"

Like his celebrated contemporary Rebbe Levi-Yitzhak of Berditchev, he would speak to God on Yom Kippur—in Yiddish—and plead the cause of Israel with such strength and conviction that whoever heard him trembled with emotion.

Another passion that dominated Rebbe Pinhas' life was friendship.

He was a friend both to his peers and to his pupils; his role was forever that of a friend. He understood that Hasidism, in order to justify its ideals in human terms, would have to grow into a center radiating friendship—which it did. *Dibuk-haverim* —closeness among friends—was among Hasidism's cardinal precepts. People came to Mezeritch, and later to Lizensk, Rizhin and Lublin, not only to see the Master but also to make friends, to share joys and sorrows, and help one another be it with a gesture, a word, a smile, a song or a tale.

Said Rebbe Raphael of Barshad, "Our Master and teacher Rebbe Pinhas of Koretz invited me once to join him in his coach. Unfortunately there was not enough room. 'Do not worry,' our Master said reassuringly. 'Do not worry; let us be close friends and there will be room.' "

Rebbe Raphael also recalled, "Rebbe Pinhas loved to speak of friendship; often he referred to God, blessed be He and blessed be His Name, as a friend, a true friend. And as he spoke about this at length his face would be shining with love."

This tale alone would be sufficient to make us love and admire Rebbe Pinhas of Koretz. We have known God to be a father, a judge, a king; we never saw Him in the role of friend to man, a role eagerly attributed to Him by Rebbe Pinhas.

Yet Rebbe Pinhas, who sought friendship in every person, everywhere, even in heaven, spent his last months on earth in sadness. Like most great Masters of that period, he somehow sank into melancholy—just what he had desperately sought to avoid.

No definite facts about his change of mood and outlook are available. We must rely on allusions, many based on intuition rather than facts. But intuition in Hasidic literature is as important as facts.

An unexpected event took place in the year 1791—the last year of Rebbe Pinhas' life. Suddenly he left Ostraha, where he had served as Rebbe, and went to Shipitovke to bid farewell to his father-in-law. His plan: to go and settle in the Holy Land. This was not the first time he had felt the urge to go there. Years before, he had been tempted by the dream and had been about to set out on his journey when he fell sick. "You do not want me to go," he said to God. "Good, I shall stay."

He stayed, but kept on dreaming. His love for Jerusalem was such that he tried to imagine the city, but without success; it transcended his imagination. All he could manage to do was to imagine someone who had been in Jerusalem.

Now he was ready for the journey. He was determined to break with his familiar surroundings in Eastern Europe—and turn his back on the suffering in the Diaspora.

The last years of his life were clouded by anxiety. He often spoke of unfulfilled wishes: "If only I could sing . . ." Or: "If only I could write down what my mouth is saying . . ." And also: "I am so afraid of being more wise than pious, but," he added cryptically, "I am too ill."

Often, too often, he was overwhelmed by gloom. "I study Zohar," he confided to Rebbe Raphael; "I explore its depths and sometimes I feel frightened. I sit there staring at the Book of Splendor in front of me. I look and look and I keep silent—and that is all I do."

Once he revealed certain secrets to his companions—only to forbid them later to disclose those secrets to others. Still later, he expressed regret at having revealed them in the first place.

Rebbe Pinhas began to say strange things. As he reminisced about his visit to Zaslav twenty-two years earlier, he said it was "to drive a certain great power" out of Poland—with his prayers. He wrote a mysterious letter to a mysterious Reb Yeshayahu who "had difficulties in *kabalat ol malkhut shamayim*—accepting the yoke of heaven."

He had become a changed man; perhaps he had been struck by some secret tragedy, some personal ordeal. What could it have been? What could have made him, the consoler, become so inconsolable?

His illness? His despair? The state of affairs in the world and at home? Violent battles were raging between the Hasidim and their opponents, the Mitnagdim. Excommunications and denunciations followed one another. Numerically the movement was blooming—in some thirty years it had prevailed in most of the deprived communities in Eastern Europe—yet the possible spiritual decline represented a real danger. Suddenly there were too many schools, too many courts, too many Rebbes—and some of their followers had begun fighting among themselves. Clans were formed; sectarian loyalties were encouraged. These were still heroic times, with great Masters such as Rebbe Elimelekh of Lizensk, the Berditchever and the Bratzlaver kindling flames everywhere. But the impetus and purity of the beginning were gone, or at least forgotten, in many quarters.

Rebbe Pinhas of Koretz must have been aware of all this: the attacks on Rebbe Nahman of Bratzlav; the dissension between Lizensk and Lublin. He must have agonized over the realization that Jews too—and even Hasidim—were capable of rejecting friendship; that Jews too—and even Hasidim—could, on occasion, lack compassion. And he must have remembered the early days, the vision of the Besht, the sobriety of the Maggid, the intensity of their disciples. He had witnessed three generations of leaders and followers. Did he foresee the decline of the movement? Was that the reason for his sadness? Or was it that, like the other Masters, he had heard too many tales of sorrow and pain? People were forever coming to him with their doubts and regrets, sharing with him their anguish and misery. Was it that at one point he could take no more? Or did he have a premonition of what would be the end of Koretz?

Was it Reb Pinhas' tragic intuition, or tragic imagination, that prompted him to set the example and move away—away from Gentile hate and Jewish laxity, away from quarreling factions and their leaders, away from unfulfilled dreams? Or did he simply want to leave everything behind and go—go to the land of promise and prophecy, go to weep in Jerusalem over Jerusalem and for Jerusalem—and weep as one weeps only in Jerusalem?

But it was written that, like his good friend the Besht, he would never reach the Holy City. It was written that he would die on the way.

In Shipitovke, shortly before he was to leave, he began to tremble with fever. He was in pain, terrible pain, and his mind was on fire. He spoke of death with great anguish. He did not want to die—not then, not there. He was afraid to die alone, without any friends. He asked that his disciple Reb Raphael be called. When Reb Raphael arrived, he felt better. They talked and talked—and when they stopped talking, Rebbe Pinhas refused to address anyone else in the room. For two days he lay motionless and mute. Then he began calling for his old friend Reb Haim of Krasna, who was not there. On the following Shabbat his condition worsened; the end was near. Rebbe Pinhas was heard whispering, "Haim, Haim, my friend, my brother —come stay with me . . . I am afraid. . . . Save me from the Angel of Death, Haim. . . . If you stay with me, my friend, I won't die."

A rabbinical council, convened urgently by Rebbe Shimshon of Shipitovke, authorized the dispatch of a special messenger to summon Reb Haim of Krasna, who was spending Shabbat in a nearby village. The messenger carried a letter dated *Hayom Shabbat kodesh*—on this day of Shabbat. It was a race against time, a race against death.

Time won. Death won. Hasidism lost. When Reb Haim of Krasna arrived, it was too late. His friend already belonged to another world.

His mystery remains intact. We don't know what happened to him at the end of his life—we never will. He who was always lucid, calm and serene—why was he possessed by such fear at the end? What had he glimpsed? What visions did he have—and about whom? What were the questions? Were there any answers? Did he suddenly fully understand that the Jews had no friends—anywhere? Did it become clear to him that the Messiah would be late in coming—much later than he had anticipated, much later than he had feared?

He died—and Koretz died with him. And now he has become a sacred letter, a mysterious tale, an evocative name: a key to wisdom and compassion.

His quest is our quest, his questions remain our questions . . . and we must go on.

AHARON
OF KARLIN

LITTLE IS KNOWN about his life and less about his death; but much is known—and remembered—about his personality. In Hasidic literature he is, to this day, referred to as the great Rebbe Aharon of Karlin.

We are told that he was a handsome man of great vitality, endowed with an irresistible power of persuasion. His energy and enthusiasm were such that he could never stay in one place for long. And so he traveled through towns big and small, spreading the Hasidic message, igniting sparks and setting crowds of listeners aflame. He and Rebbe Mendel of Vitebsk jointly confronted the Mitnagdim at the first public disputation —which took place in Shklov—between Hasidim and their vocal opponents. Practically alone, he stormed the traditional rabbinic fortress in Lithuania, shaking its very foundations. Faithful in friendship, loyal to his teachers and disciples, fearless in his undertakings, he was the spearhead of the new movement.

All this is known. What is not known is how and why he died—and at such an early age.

Here is a word of advice which he was fond of repeating: When Hasidim meet, he said, they would do well to study the Zohar, the Book of Splendor, in which creation's primary secrets are waiting to be uncovered. If that should prove too difficult, let them open the Talmud and study together—be it only one page, one problem. Thus they would go back in time to the sages, the scribes, the Prophets, and finally to Moses. If the Talmud, too, should prove inaccessible to them, let them open the Bible and read the portion of the week and its commentaries, and thus be in touch with eternal truth. If that also should be too difficult, let them simply tell one another Hasidic tales about great Masters and their saintly ways; and if, heaven forbid, they don't even know or remember any such stories, then let them sing a Hasidic *Niggun* which, as everyone knows, is the key to higher spheres and sanctuaries. But what if, woe unto us, they don't know a *Niggun*? Well, in that case, let them . . . love one another.

This advice—more than any saying uttered by any Master—summarizes the attitude of the Hasidic movement: Ask the utmost of man, but accept him as he is.

Surely it is better to know the Zohar and to master the Talmud; but if you were neither fortunate enough nor gifted enough to spend years on study—if all you possess is the *desire* to pray—then that too will be enough.

In other words, prayer and study are important, but no one ought ever to despair of being unable to do either. Every person has his own path to follow, his own rhythm; every sorrow has its own remedy. True, God does demand much, sometimes even the impossible—but He leaves it up to man to choose the means by which to attain perfection.

What is a true Hasid? Beneath a torn overcoat, inside a hovel, a heart broken but yearning for perfection. And that yearning in itself is enough.

Man's goal is to be worthy of God—but God accepts him even when he is not, provided he truly wants to be; provided, too, that he love his friend and neighbor. There is no tragedy or sin in not knowing how to decipher an obscure passage of Zohar, provided the Hasid is aware of his limitations and is dedicated to seeking truth. Not everybody is capable of *Ahavat-*

Hashem, love of God; or of *Ahavat-Torah,* love of Torah; but everyone must be capable of *Ahavat-Israel,* love for one's fellow man.

No wonder that Hasidism was so successful with economically impoverished and spiritually neglected Jews—and that it met such determined opposition among those for whom study was an absolute priority. For poor and uneducated Jews, many of whom lived in remote villages, it was vitally important to be told that not only were they worthy of being loved but that they were expected to give love to others. And that their love, too, carried weight both on earth and above. So simplistic a philosophy, however, could only arouse antagonism among the scholars.

And since the Jews of Lithuania and White Russia were dominated by their scholars, it was to be expected that among those Jews the opposition to Hasidism would be more violent than elsewhere. And that was precisely why Rebbe Aharon was sent by the great Maggid of Mezeritch to establish a Lithuanian center. And indeed, he overcame the hostility of the local leadership and succeeded in building a first bridgehead—so much so that for a time the Mitnagdim called all Hasidim "Karliner."

Thus, when we evoke Karlin we do so in an astonishing context, for we must turn our attention, at the same time, to its fierce and pitiless opponents, headed by the great and unique Rebbe Eliyahu, the Gaon of Vilna.

Today, in retrospect, their quarrels—so violent and so intolerant—seem somewhat absurd and surely exaggerated. Their fanaticism strikes us as extreme: Really—what was the wisdom, where was the need to fight with words, and sometimes even with fists, over which prayers were to be said or omitted, what gestures were to be made or avoided, what tales were to be repeated or condemned? How is one to explain *today* the hate that existed on both sides? The ancient sages Shammai and Hillel differed in most areas of Jewish life and yet they maintained relations of mutual esteem and affection. Why was it that no authoritative voice was heard, eighteen centuries after Shammai and Hillel, to proclaim that the words of *both* the Besht and the Gaon of Vilna reflected God's living truth? Actually, the Besht and his disciples did say it—but the Gaon and his followers did not—to Rebbe Aharon's great regret, as we shall see.

Born in 1736—the year the Besht revealed himself to his followers—Rebbe Aharon died thirty-six years later, shortly before the emergence of the great Maggid Reb Dov-Ber of Mezeritch.

Aharon's father, Reb Yaakov, was a beadle in a House of Study in Yanovo, near Pinsk. Little is known of his childhood except that he was—he must have been—a good student and that, at a certain time in his life, he appreciated the pleasures of wealth—until, according to legend, one day, as he rode in his beautiful carriage, he suddenly understood the futility of an existence devoid of eternal values. And he realized that he had reached a turning point.

A strange legend, and one that leaves us wondering: Where did he get such a carriage? How could he afford such luxury? His father was poor—was his father-in-law richer? We do not know. We don't even know how he discovered Hasidism. As in the case of most Masters, his adolescence is shrouded in mystery. Judging from his posthumous work, *Bet Aharon*, his studies covered both Talmud and Kabbala, which is not surprising: in Lithuania, every self-respecting young Jew devoted himself to study.

His first exposure to Hasidism probably came through a chance encounter with one of the movement's itinerant messengers and preachers whom the Maggid had, since 1760, been dispatching to the most distant provinces, thus extending his sphere of influence.

The philosopher Solomon Maimon writes in his autobiography that after listening to one of these emissaries, his imagination had been so fired that he had felt himself irresistibly drawn to the great Maggid. He went to seek out the Master in Mezeritch. The same must have happened to Rebbe Aharon. He left Pinsk and went to find the Maggid. The encounter changed his life. He returned to Lithuania only to fulfill a mission: to draw the recalcitrant communities into the Beshtian kingdom.

The Besht himself had made two such attempts. We know that he visited Slutsk and other cities, and that he left, having failed. Worse, that he left under duress, barraged with insults. Such is the claim of the Mitnagdim.

Another version is that local Rabbis decided to put him through an examination to determine whether or not he knew Talmud. They asked him a simple, almost simplistic, question: If one has forgotten to include the *Ya'aleh ve-yavo*, the special prayer for the first of the month, in the Silent *Amida*, must one start all over again, from the very beginning? The Besht refused to answer. The Mitnagdim say, Because he didn't know the answer. The Hasidim say, Because he found the procedure undignified. It seems that the Besht got around the questions with a keen sense of humor: Why do you want me to tell you? he asked. *I* will not forget to include the special prayer the first time—and *you* will forget it the second time as well as the first.

The fact remains that, of all the provinces in Eastern Europe, Lithuania was the most stubborn in its refusal to join the new movement, which aspired to offer a spiritual renaissance to countless dispersed and despairing Jewish communities. One easily understands why.

In contrast to the Jews of Galicia and Podolia, Lithuanian Jewry could proudly point to its scholars and students. Even the average Jew had some measure of learning, for Jews lived mostly in large cities, not in isolated hamlets. Everyone had to study Torah and belong to the community. Under the reign of the Gaon of Vilna, everyone was taught how to live and fulfill himself as a Jew. Hasidism had no great attraction for Lithuanian Jews because it answered no great need.

And yet, in spite of that—or was it because of that?—the movement's leaders were strangely fascinated by Lithuania. Rather than give up in the face of difficulty and concentrate on other areas, they kept seeking confrontation. They kept on coming back to Lithuania. Levi-Yitzhak of Berditchev was, for a while, Rebbe in Pinsk. After the Besht died, even his own son—Reb Tzvi-Hersh—left another Hasidic stronghold and settled in Pinsk, remaining there, living with his father-in-law, Reb Shmuel Hasid, until his death in 1810. The Besht's son—in Pinsk! How did he manage to survive in the midst of the endless polemics and holy wars that the Hasidim and their opponents waged with blind fanaticism? Reb Tzvi-Hersh would have been welcomed anywhere and treated with respect and affection. Yet he chose Pinsk. Why? Was it an act of defiance? To show his opponents that he was not afraid of them? Or to show the Maggid's followers that *he* would succeed where they had failed? Or else to show his fellow Hasidim that their concept of Hasidism had become too simplistic, too comfortable? That, unlike them, he continued to see in Hasidism an act of total devotion, of *Mesirat-nefesh?* And that to be a Hasid in Lithuania required more courage and faith than to be one in Podolia or Galicia? If that was the reason, then he was right: it was anything but easy to be a Hasid in Lithuania. And Rebbe Aharon and his followers knew something about it; their lot was not an enviable one.

The first campaign, the first slander, the first measures against the new movement were conceived and implemented in Lithuania. People there still remembered the sad fate of Sabatean and Frankist followers who had also pledged to redeem the Jewish people by relaxing its laws and turning its need for joy into a sacred duty. Hence every new attempt, every new experiment not in strict accordance with Halakha, was considered suspect, if not heretic.

The Gaon of Vilna, who since his Bar Mitzvah had lived in seclusion surrounded by books and manuscripts, reaffirmed the ancient belief that a Jew is Jewish only if and when he obeys all Jewish commandments. He respected Maimonides as a codifier but resented his philosophical research. The Gaon believed that laws had to be obeyed and preferably, but not necessarily, understood. And here came a movement which demanded to be allowed to change the Jewish code of behavior; here was a movement whose leaders dared change the prayer book, abolish fixed times for services, and discredit the Talmud by claiming that to recite psalms is as important as to study Torah.

From anti-Hasidic sources and various documents we get the impression that, in some instances, the Lithuanian rationalists were surprised and distressed by the Karliner's public behavior.

Another area of disagreement—the Mitnagdim did not particularly appreciate the fervor, the exhibitionism of the Hasidim at services. The Hasidim shouted, sang, jumped up and down, danced and often even rolled on the ground to attain ecstasy. Moreover, they organized reunions in private homes—*shtiblech* —where, from the Mitnagdim's point of view, they wasted precious hours telling stories or singing popular tunes instead of studying Torah and its commentaries. Worse: they liked to drink a little bit—or much—or a little bit too much. For the Lithuanian Jews, scholars and others, that was blasphemy. Worse: there soon appeared cracks in their unity; to their amazement and chagrin there were, among their own people, some so weak as to be taken in by the new sect—that meant the threat was becoming more and more serious. Something had to be done—the wave had to be stopped—by any means!

It must be stressed also that the Maggid of Mezeritch, a brilliant organizer, understood that the emissaries he sent to Lithuania had to be the very best, if he hoped to achieve any measure of success.

Rebbe Shneur-Zalman of Lyady, the founder of Habad, was such a man, as was his friend Rebbe Mendel of Vitebsk: between them they covered White Russia but their impact was felt in Lithuania as well. Unequaled as a Talmudist, an astonishingly perceptive Kabbalist, Rebbe Shneur-Zalman had a great deal to offer to the proud young scholars in Lithuania: Hasidism's worst enemies could not accuse *him* of ignorance.

Another factor exacerbated the tensions. During that particular period, an epidemic of diphtheria ravaged the city of Vilna and hundreds of children perished. As is usual, certain people saw in the calamity a celestial punishment. And punishment implies sin. So sinners had to be found. Easy. The Hasidim. Once the culprits were named, all other sins were attributed to them as well. They were accused of lacking respect for the Gaon. Hence for his knowledge. Hence for the Torah itself. Obviously, they had to be reprimanded, chastised; and so they were. Some were publicly beaten, others merely thrown out of the city. The Hasidic *shtiblech* were emptied, their congregants humiliated. Finally, a decision came down to excommunicate them—all of them. Letters to that effect were drawn up and circulated and even dispatched to other cities, other countries. One letter was cosigned by the Rabbis of Amsterdam, The Hague, Metz and Prague. Ceremonies of excommunication, with the ancient ritual of the blowing of the Shofar and the lighting of black candles, took place. Jews were forbidden to marry Hasidim, to eat their meat or share their meals, or even to do business with them. Copies of the edicts were posted at public fairs. Hasidic books and writings were burned. It was open war. And Rebbe Aharon Karliner was among the first targets; he was on the front line.

Let us come back to Rebbe Aharon. The Maggid of Mezeritch loved him—and so do I. The Maggid called him "our best offensive weapon." And rightly so. Rebbe Aharon had the special talent of being able to recognize the best young students, the most sensitive ones, and draw them closer to Hasidism. But he did not keep the newcomers with him; he immediately sent them to Mezeritch, to the great Maggid.

Hasidic legend tells us how he went about convincing Reb Chaim-Haykel of Amdur, known for his saintliness and piety, to hurry to Mezeritch.

Reb Chaim-Haykel lived in the forest as a hermit, in total seclusion, seeking perfection through mortification and fasting.

When Rebbe Aharon came to Amdur, he did not go to visit the solitary saint in the forest, but preached in the synagogue. He was an impressive speaker and the entire town talked only of his sermons. Rumors finally reached even Reb Chaim-Haykel.

He became intrigued and chose not to resist his curiosity, since, after all, it involved study. Next day he arrived in town and went to the synagogue, which was packed. The audience expected another display of oratory, another session of rhetorical fireworks; everyone was convinced that, like the day before and the one before that, the preacher would again use his powers to sear the soul and elevate it to the heights of Torah where man's word and God's word fuse and become one. But the speaker was aware of Reb Chaim-Haykel's presence—the man for whom he had come. And so he surprised his audience by delivering the shortest sermon, the briefest lecture of his career —one sentence, only one. He said: "He who does not improve, gets worse." Having uttered these few words, he left the podium. The people couldn't believe their ears: What had happened to him? Was that his sermon, his lecture? Was he making fun of them? They were on the verge of shouting their protest, their anger, when suddenly they froze, for they saw the revered and saintly Reb Chaim-Haykel get up and push his way toward the preacher. He seemed shaken. "Help me, please," he said. "Your words are now inside me, they tear me apart." And the two men left together. "I would like to follow you," said Reb Chaim-Haykel of Amdur. "So be it," said Rebbe Aharon. "Go to Mezeritch."

Rebbe Aharon gave Reb Chaim-Haykel a letter of recommendation which the great Maggid read aloud, in his presence: "The bearer of this letter has lived a life of falsehood; he sought saintliness but removed himself from it; there is no sacred spark in him to be found." Hearing this, Reb Chaim-Haykel burst into tears. The Maggid let him weep and then said, "Stay, I shall guide you."

And he did. The Maggid took care of him for a whole year and made him into one of his most illustrious disciples. And Reb Chaim-Haykel became one of Rebbe Aharon's closest friends—his companion and ally against the Mitnagdim of Lithuania.

. . .

As were all his companions, Rebbe Aharon was totally attached to his Master, the Maggid of Mezeritch, and craved to spend as much time as possible in his presence.

On Friday afternoons, as is the custom, he would recite the Song of Songs in honor of the Queen of Shabbat. He had a beautiful voice, and when he sang, he never failed to attain ecstasy. Once he was interrupted by the Maggid's servant: "Please, Reb Aharon, the Master wants you to not sing so loudly. You disturb him, and that is serious enough; but what is more serious is that when you sing, the angels in heaven fall silent; they listen to you—and this you must not allow to happen. You are not to interfere with their praise of the Almighty."

One morning, as he began the service with the prayer *Adon Olam*, affirming God's rule over creation, he began to cry. "There are only two possibilities," he whispered. "Either it is true or it isn't—and in both cases I am at fault: Either God is the King of the Universe and I am not doing enough to serve Him, or He isn't. And whose fault is it? His? No. Mine, mine alone."

In the early days, when the two sides were still on speaking terms in Lithuania, certain Mitnagdim tried to pin him down:

"You preach Mezeritch, you dream Mezeritch, you wish to send the entire world to Mezeritch—but, for heaven's sake, what have you learned in Mezeritch, you yourself?"

"Me? Nothing," said Rebbe Aharon.

"Nothing? Then why have you been going there so often? Why have you returned so often? What's the use of going to Mezeritch if it's to learn nothing?"

"I told you. I have learned nothing in Mezeritch. Or to be more precise: I have learned the meaning of the word 'nothing' —the mystery which envelops all words. For instance, when I went to Mezeritch, I learned that I—Aharon, son of Jacob—am nothing. And yet—I exist, I am alive, I wait, I pray, I question and pray again, isn't it strange? I am nothing and yet I am *in* this world created by God, a man among men—isn't it strange to be nothing and at the same time to listen to you, talk to you, and—talk to God? . . . Well, that's what I learned in Mezeritch. As I told you: 'Nothing.' "

One of his friends, also a disciple of the great Maggid, once passed through Karlin on his way home. It was night and he knew nobody in the town. All the houses were dark. All the inns were silent. The stranger grew worried. Where was he going to spend the night? Why not go to Rebbe Aharon, whom he intended to visit the next day? Why not go right away? It was late—but Rebbe Aharon slept little. The question was, How to find his home? Just then he saw a solitary walker in the street. He stopped him: Would he be kind enough to point out the Rebbe's home? "Nothing could be simpler," said the passer-by. "Keep on walking, and when you see a house with light in it, you'll know that is it. Anticipating a happy reunion, the man hurried on to find the house. He found it. He knocked on the window: "Reb Aharon, Reb Aharon, open!" "Who is it?" Reb Aharon asked. "It is me," said the stranger. "Who is it?" asked Rebbe Aharon the second time. "It's *me*," said the stranger. "Don't you recognize me? Have you forgotten the days we spent together in Mezeritch?" "Only God and God alone may say 'I' or 'Me,' " answered Rebbe Aharon. "And if you have not as yet learned that, then you were wrong in leaving our Master. Better that you return to Mezeritch."

Rebbe Shneur-Zalman of Lyady frequently referred to Rebbe Aharon's virtue of *Yirat-Shamayim*, of his fear of God: "Rebbe Aharon of Karlin," he said, "lived in constant fear of God, yet he loved Him with his whole being. His fear was comparable to the one that seizes a man who, sentenced to death, looks at the guns aimed at his heart, ready to be fired at any moment. He is afraid to look and yet he looks—so as to increase his fear. Sometimes Rebbe Aharon's fear was such that neither images nor words could describe it."

And yet, this terrible fear, this total awe he experienced did not stifle or diminish his love of God. He was a Hasid after all, and Hasidism was meant to combat fear—and solitude. Hasidism defined itself, and its relationship to its members, in terms of love—exclusively.

We must also remember that the Besht, the Maggid, and other early Masters were not interested in bringing forth a new religion but wished to create a new humanity, to humanize ancient words and offer them to those Jews who had forgotten their meaning. What was the new element? To teach man the secret power of love in his relationship to God and His people. The Besht maintained that true love can envelop one's *entire* being: he who loves God loves His creation, loves His law, loves His people. And conversely: he who loves His people —meaning he who loves people—loves God; or, he who loves, loves God.

Until the Besht came along, the approved ways leading to God were few. One had to choose—between asceticism and a normal life, between esoteric knowledge and oral tradition, between love of God and fear of God. One had to side with God against man, or with man against God. The Besht and his disciples attempted to reach a synthesis: It is given to man to live on more than one level, to nourish more than one dream, to attain truth and fulfillment by following more than one path— for God is present to all people—or more precisely, God is presence. Forever. *To* all His creatures—*in* all His creatures.

When a simple shepherd is overwhelmed by a feeling of wonder at the sight of a sunset, when a child wants to say something but cannot, and so repeats one word over and over again until he is understood—well, that is a sign that God's gaze is upon them. And that is the secret of all secrets: the Master of the Universe, who has created three hundred and ten worlds and reigns over the infinite, has chosen to dwell in man's heart. "And you shall build for Me a sanctuary so that I may dwell among you" had a very personal, direct interpretation in Karlin: Every one of you will build inside himself a sanctuary for Me to live in. Why should the evil spirit be punished at the end of time? Didn't he accomplish the will of heaven by testing and tempting man? He will be punished, the school of Karlin answers, but for something else: for having tried to convince man that he is not a prince. God is the king and man is His prince, His priest and servant. Every man is a sanctuary and it is up to him to invite God inside. As Rebbe Mendel of Kotzk formulated it: God is where He is allowed to come in. God's favorite dwelling is neither a palace of gold nor an edifice of marble but man's heart—the weakest, most vulnerable organ of the body, this heart that aches because it loves—or doesn't—that is capable of shouting and being silent at the same time, of hoping and losing hope, of recognizing in God the source of both justice *and* compassion. To fear God without loving Him would mean staying aloof; to love Him without fear would lead to familiarity: thus one must do both. One must not live with fear *of* God but with fear *in* God.

It all depends on where you place the accent. In the school of Pshishke, for instance, the accent was on *Ahavat-Torah*, the love of Torah; in Medzibozh, and Rizhin, and Wizshnitz, on *Ahavat-Israel*, the love for the people; in Karlin—on *Ahavat-Hashem*, the love for God which was expressed by *Yirat-Hashem*, the fear of God, or rather, the fear *for* God—the fear not to offend, not to hurt Him. And the one did not exclude or deny the other: on the contrary, the one completed and enriched the other.

And so it appears that between a Hasid of Karlin and Hasidim of other Masters, there was no substantial difference: a Karliner did everything other Hasidim did, but he did it with more enthusiasm. With greater fervor.

That is what characterized Karlin: *hitlahavut*—fervor, enthusiasm. In Karlin one lived on the summits of mountains all the time. In Karlin the Hasid was constantly singed by sacred fire; and as he burned he shouted for more—such was his yearning to become flame and thus reach the divine source. And to forget who he was on this earth, to forget everything on this earth; to become an offering.

Rebbe Uri of Strelisk, the Seraphin of Hasidism, was an offspring of this school. Legend has it that, through his prayers, he had acquired such powers that he could obtain for his people anything they desired; therefore, each morning before services, he would make mental notes of the requests he was to present in heaven. However, as soon as he began to pray, his soul caught fire, and in his ecstasy he forgot what it was he had planned to ask.

In Karlin one tried to attain inner fulfillment by negation of the self. One hoped to create silence through words and a melody, a *Niggun*, inside silence. And prayer inside the *Niggun*. In Karlin, the *Niggun* dominated everything else.

Naturally, the opponents—the Mitnagdim—were annoyed. They found all this singing and dancing undignified, if not outright vulgar. To them, a Jew had to control his emotions and impulses; a Jew had but to follow in the footsteps of his ancestors—what was good enough for them should be good enough for him—and his ancestors certainly did not take part in spectacles.

And yet, it would be misleading to state that the dispute within Eastern European Jewry turned solely upon questions of incompatibility of customs or personalities. For, in truth, the differences between the Mitnagdim and the Hasidim are as old and as genuine as the ones that opposed the school of Shammai to that of Hillel.

The main difference rests on a basic question: What is man's aim in life? For the traditional Talmudist it was, and is, to obey God's commandments as given to Moses at Sinai; for the Kabbalist, it was to redeem the "holy sparks" from their exile, reuniting them with the original flame. For the emancipated Jew, it was, and is, to free himself from others and himself; for the Hasid, it was, and is, to insert, to integrate his life and thoughts into God's, to seek refuge in God and offer Him love and joy—so that He, in turn, could give them back infinitely multiplied.

The Hasid insists so much on the importance of gaiety, joy and celebration, not only to surmount his sadness and despair, but also to influence God and move Him to compassion and grace. Remember the saying of the Maggid of Mezeritch: *Veda ma lemala mimkha, veda,* and know that—*ma lemala*—whatever happens up above, is—*mimkha,* conditioned by you: if you are charitable, God will be, too; if you sing, God will sing, too; your joy is bound to reflect God's.

What is the difference between the Mitnagged and the Hasid? The Mitnagged loves the Torah, whereas the Hasid loves the person who loves the Torah. The Hasid puts the accent on man, who is bound to change, while the Mitnagged places it on the Torah, which is above change. The Mitnagged finds his happiness in books, the Hasid in people; the Mitnagged seeks knowledge, the Hasid experience.

It is characteristic that though he was revered by multitudes the same way the Besht was by his followers, the Gaon of Vilna lived alone and isolated, while the Besht was forever with people, among people.

And yet they had a common enemy: emancipation. Remember: this was the era of Moses Mendelssohn, Kant and Voltaire. Religion everywhere was on the retreat; the French Revolution had even proclaimed its death and had replaced it with the new cult of reason. The effects were felt among Jews too. Young students left their families and traditional milieus and went to Berlin, Vienna or Heidelberg. New laws would soon force Jews to give up traditional dress and customs and send their children to secular schools.

Logically, Hasidim and Mitnagdim should have joined forces against what was to become the assimilationist movement. The opposite occurred. Hasidism had to fight on both fronts. And the harder battle was waged against the Mitnagdim, particularly in Lithuania. The Gaon was merciless; his orders were precise: he wanted the Hasidim uprooted—and they nearly were.

The persecutions which had begun during Rebbe Aharon's lifetime grew more intense afterward. When he died, his son, Rebbe Asher, was still very young, and so Rebbe Aharon's place was taken by his disciple and friend Rebbe Shlomo—a great leader in his own right.

He would say, "I wish I could love the best of the just as deeply as God loves the worst of the wicked."

Rebbe Shlomo was humble; he felt unworthy of leadership. He said, "Once upon a time, it was easier; people had a sense of decency—not any more." Another time he remarked, "Nowadays people come up to me to tell me of their good deeds while they hide the others; once upon a time, it was just the opposite." So humble was he that he was convinced he would go straight to hell. Legend has it that when his soul ascended into heaven and was welcomed by exulting angels, he began to shout, "No, no, it's a mockery—my place is in hell, not in paradise"; and the Shekhina itself had to escort him to his rightful place.

But he did endure hell—in his lifetime. The Mitnagdim banned him from society, chased him from Karlin. He came to Ludomir, where he died a martyr's death one Shavuot eve when the town was invaded by Cossacks who had been given two hours to pilfer and murder. One of them burst into the House of Study where Rebbe Shlomo was praying. Legend has it that the Cossack spoke to him. But Rebbe Shlomo, in the true Karliner tradition, was totally absorbed in prayer and did not hear him; when one addresses God, one does not listen to killers. He died praying.

At Rebbe Shlomo's death, Rebbe Asher, Rabbi Aharon's son, was crowned Rebbe. He wanted to return to Karlin but could not: the Mitnagdim were still too strong. So he went to Stolin instead and there laid the foundation for another branch of the Karlin school. His son, the second Rebbe Aharon, eventually returned to Karlin.

With him, the Hasidic center in Karlin developed and became more dynamic. Gifted scholars and students came from all over to stay at the Master's court. As charismatic a figure as his grandfather, Rebbe Aharon knew how to attract good disciples, how to play on their fantasy, how to strengthen the structure of his movement.

Like his grandfather, Rebbe Aharon stressed the virtues of love of God, fear of God, of friendship and fervor. But he also aspired to be an innovator, and he was. Conceptually he drew closer to Rizhin. Now one could also find in Karlin symbols meant to evoke dreams of past grandeur and royalty. Like Israel Rizhiner,* he placed considerable value on external symbols; they too are reminders of God's greatness. And also like Israel Rizhiner, he fought melancholy and sadness with all the means at his disposal. There were two orchestras at his court, and they would play during the after-Shabbat meal and also on Khol-Hamoed. Of course the Mitnagdim used such "excesses," as they called them, to persecute him even more. In fact, by then the Hasidic movement everywhere was under attack.

By then the anti-Hasidic campaign had spread throughout Eastern Europe, from the Dnieper to the Carpathian Mountains. Fom Brody to Vilna, from Minsk to Metz, Mitnagdim publicly urged Jewish communities to expel "the new sect." In Lithuania, they stressed the heresy of the Hasidim in matters of Torah, in Galicia they denounced their outrageous customs. In Minsk the following measures were adopted: the Hasidic community was to be dissolved, its House of Study closed; its members were forbidden to use the Lurianic prayer book; their freedom of movement was limited so as to prevent them from leaving town to go to visit the Rebbe. Whoever wished to travel had to get a special permit. That wasn't all. Informers were hired to spy on them. In Brody, the Hasidim were warned that whoever would dress in white on Shabbat—as was the Hasidic custom—would be undressed in the street.

But don't think for a moment that the Hasidim were solely on the receiving end. No. They fought back. They hired their own spies. They issued their own excommunications. And their language was neither less brutal nor less direct. In some instances they were even craftier than the Mitnagdim. For example, they hired a man to travel through Galicia and Podolia, posing as the

* See *Souls on Fire.*

son of the Gaon of Vilna. And wherever he went, he told audiences that his father had ordered him to leave and be a wanderer so as to expiate the sins committed against the Hasidim. One can imagine the reaction of the Mitnagdim to that particular caper.

Today all these disputes seem senseless. Why should any Jew fight or hate another Jew, when the enemy does it so much better? But—don't look for logic where religious passions are involved. Both sides fought out of conviction, out of deep commitment, out of an irresistible desire to affirm the validity of their ideas and beliefs. Compared to them, today's Jew is weak, lukewarm, pallid—and nothing is worse than indifference and lack of involvement.

The great Rebbe Aharon could have left the battlefield and gone to Mezeritch or elsewhere; he could have worked among people who admired him. But he refused to choose the easy path. Obstacles did not deter him. God alone inspired fear in him—God, whom he loved. Men did not frighten him: he confronted them bravely. In Karlin, one learned that man must not fear others; in Karlin, one lived in fear only of God, meaning, in fear of giving God a love not sufficiently pure and not sufficiently whole. In Karlin, more than anywhere else, the synthesis between *Ahavat-Hashem* and *Yirat-Shamayim* was attained.

Now—let us return to the question which has been with us from the beginning: Of what did the great Rebbe Aharon die—and why so young?

Hasidic legend offers many answers, one more mysterious than the next.

Let us listen: It happened during the month of Nissan 1772. In Mezeritch everybody was busy preparing for Passover. Homes were thoroughly cleaned, books dusted. The matzo bakery was full of people. Pesach was in the air—the festival of freedom, the celebration of history.

The Maggid's closest disciples did not go home to their families; who would forgo an occasion to hear the great Maggid tell the eternal story of Exodus? Only Rebbe Aharon planned to go home to his wife, to his family, friends, disciples. He came to the Maggid to receive his blessings for the journey—and did. But no sooner had he left his Master's study than the Maggid called in his disciples and told them, "Don't let him leave—under any circumstances!" They ran after him and when they found him in his lodgings they told him, "Our Master wants you to stay." Puzzled, Rebbe Aharon returned to the Maggid and tried to explain why he had to go home—he was needed there. The Maggid looked at him silently, disapprovingly, for a long moment; then he said, "If you insist, so be it. I cannot hold you back." Rebbe Aharon was reassured. But—no sooner had he returned to his lodgings than the door opened again and his friends rushed in with the disconcerting news: "Our Master has asked us, for the second time, to tell you not to go." "But I have seen him," said Rebbe Aharon. "Twice. And he gave me his blessings. Twice." And he could not be persuaded to postpone his journey. He returned to Karlin, celebrated the Seder with his family and friends. And died two days later.

When the Maggid heard the news, he wept. "With him gone, what are we going to do in this world?" he asked.

His disciples wanted to know: "Since you knew, why didn't you use your authority to keep him here?" And his answer was: "There are times when we are given certain powers but are forbidden to use them."

Does this mean that had he stayed in Mezeritch he would have lived longer? Is there an implication that his death could have been postponed? That it was not yet irrevocable, not yet necessary, and thus perhaps, not natural?

I confess I don't know. I love Rebbe Aharon of Karlin, and his premature death not only saddens but troubles me. Especially since there is something mysterious about it, something that has never been explained satisfactorily.

Said Rebbe Pinhas of Koretz: It was foolish of Rebbe Aharon to die; he should have lived longer.

In Mezeritch people commented: It was his fear of God that

burned him. Or: He was too powerful for his generation; he would meet men and so influence them that he deprived them of their inner freedom. That was why the angels became jealous and prevailed upon God to recall him before his time.

Rebbe Shlomo Karliner said, "Like Hanoch, he ascended into heaven in a state of grace, in the midst of prayer; he ascended into heaven *like* a prayer."

All this is very beautiful, very touching, but I would still like to know of what he died. Had he been sick? No mention is to be found of any illness. There is a legend that tells us he was tired in Mezeritch, so tired that he once slept through one day and one night; and the Maggid forbade his disciples to wake him. Why was he so tired? What was the nature of his fatigue?

His followers tell of an evening when he arrived in the House of Study and found his disciples in tears. There were those who prayed without fervor, others who did not pray at all. There were those who studied without concentration, others who did not study at all. He looked at them silently, and then began to talk, emphasizing every word, every syllable: "My children, my children, I want you to know that joy will lift you up to dizzying heights; I also want you to know that sadness will pull you down into the abyss."

In his writings we find frequent allusions to his search for ways of fighting melancholy, to his determination to celebrate joy and give it wings. Are we to understand that like so many of his friends and companions he too was prone to melancholy, to depressions? Had the constant tensions created by anti-Hasidic persecutions ultimately affected his health, had they played a role in his sudden illness—and death?

He thought about death often. He wanted to be prepared for it. In his *Hanhagot Yesharot*, a kind of guide to moral precepts, he often speaks about solitude: he urges every Hasid to isolate himself one hour every day so as to rethink his actions and thoughts. Also, he would like every Hasid to spend one hour a day with a friend—and confide in him.

And then there is his testament: he wanted no eulogies—and

no immediate neighbors in the cemetery. His testament was written in the year of his death.

What is left of Karlin today? Most descendants of the great Rebbe Aharon perished in the Holocaust. Only those survived who managed to reach America and Palestine before the war. Reb Arele perished in Warsaw, Reb Moshe in Stolin, Reb Elimelekh in Karlin.

In the memorial book for Stolin, quoted by Zeev Rabinowits —the best authority on Karlin—we read about the death of Reb Moshe, on the 29th of Ellul 1942:

> The last time I saw the Rebbe and his family was before the great deportation. The ghetto was dark; we all felt that the end was approaching. We went to the Rebbe's house. It was after midnight. There too all was dark. The Rebbetzin and her daughter-in-law were crying. In his room, the Rebbe and some of his Hasidim sat at a table, wrapped in their prayer shawls. The Rebbe had his eldest son, Nahum-Shlomo, next to him. Suddenly he rose and went to the Holy Ark, opened it, began reciting the *Viddui* . . . and broke down in the middle: Our father, our king, have mercy upon us and upon our children. . . . The next day marked the end of Stolin. All the Jews were deported, but the Rebbe and his family were not among them. They remained in their room. Together. Then a fire broke out. And all were burnt alive.

Another descendant, Reb Shlomo, lived in Baranovitch. Just before Passover, 1941, he wrote a letter to his followers in Palestine:

"My dearly beloved friends—with God's help . . . though there is nothing for us to say, and the wise man will keep silent—I tell you that those who call upon the Almighty ought not be silent. Be not silent and let *Him* not be silent."

Most Karliner and Stoliner Rebbes and their followers were

swallowed up in the kingdom of night and fire, as were other Hasidim and other Rebbes. Most of the victims who ascended the burning altar were Hasidim: the killers and they could not coexist under the same sky.

And yet, and yet. There are still Karliner in Jerusalem and in New York. And they represent living proof that the killers were denied their final victory. Go to Jerusalem, go to Brooklyn, and you will see for yourself. You will hear the Karliner sing in ecstasy; on Shabbat you will hear them sing the song composed by the great Rebbe Aharon in praise of Shabbat—a song of longing and tenderness. What was he longing for? Shabbat. God . . . love . . . redemption. . . . Is it possible that he died of love? Of longing? I wish I knew. I wish even more that I were possessed by his intense longing, for the same things—whatever they may have been.

WOLFE
OF ZBARAZH

WHY DID HE decide to leave Europe and go settle in the Holy Land? What made him break with his familiar surroundings? The call of Jerusalem? Have not other Masters felt the same attraction for the eternal city? Why did he alone choose to make Aliyah?

Did he ever exist at all? Was he really a human being, a man made of flesh and blood? A man among other men, exposed, as they were, to both wonder and danger? Did he live among people? Did he truly see them? Did they actually see him?

If being a hero means having one's virtues exaggerated and one's powers idolized, then this Master was just the opposite. Rebbe Wolfe of Zbarazh was so unassuming, so hidden in his own shadow that he went unnoticed more often than not. As one seeks clues to him, to his life, one becomes utterly frustrated, so elusive is he—as a person, as a Hasidic Rebbe.

Not that he was the only one who was modest, austere and humble; others were too. But they were *famous* for their humility, whereas Rebbe Wolfe was not famous at all.

Other Masters sought solitude—not he. He did not consider himself important enough to disdain honors and avoid followers; he quite simply failed to notice them. When he did notice, he thought they were someone else's.

Could such a person have lived? Could the stories about him be true? Do the many legends really reflect his life?

. . .

A story: One day, Rebbe Wolfe of Zbarazh was invited to a circumcision. Naturally he accepted. One does not refuse such an invitation because, according to tradition, it is always issued in the name of Abraham himself. It was cold outside. An icy wind struck his face. As the sleigh moved slowly forward, he felt sorry for the coachman and his horse. If only he could walk . . . But it was far, too far to walk. Rebbe Wolfe began to feel more and more guilty. When he finally arrived at his destination, the inn was crowded with guests. Now that he was there, the ceremony could start. The father recited the solemn blessing, the *mohel* performed the ancient rite, and then parents and guests sat down to celebrate with food and wine the immortal people of Israel, which had just gained a new son. They sang and they danced with exuberance, and they did not notice their special guest, Rebbe Wolfe of Zbarazh, leaving the room. He had gone to look for his coachman in the courtyard. When he found him he asked him to go inside: "You are cold and hungry; you need food and a drink." "But the horse?" asked the coachman. "Rebbe, who will keep an eye on the horse?" "I will," said Rebbe Wolfe of Zbarazh. "You?" exclaimed the coachman. "I cannot allow you to do that. It would be unworthy of you." "Why?" said Rebbe Wolfe. "Why unworthy? If the Master of the Universe keeps an eye on the horse, why shouldn't I? Do you think I am more distinguished than He?"

Unable to counter such a forceful argument, the coachman joined the crowd, gulped down a drink, and then another one. No one missed the Rebbe. When the meal was over and grace had been recited, the guests left the inn, and in the courtyard, near the stable, they saw a man, half frozen, who was making strange movements with his arms and legs to keep warm. When they recognized him they began shouting, "Rebbe, is that you? *You* took care of our horses?" They were shocked, and he didn't understand why: "What is so wrong in taking care of poor people's tired horses?"

. . .

This anecdote is significant for three reasons. One: Rebbe Wolfe of Zbarazh was convinced that, as Jew and human being, he could, and indeed should, change places with the coachman. Two: the coachman must have thought so too, for, in spite of his initial protests, he did accept the exchange. Three: once the exchange occurred, neither the host nor the guests noticed it.

Let us hasten to say that the last fact is more significant than the first: one easily understands that a great Master should be humble, but not that he be so humbled by his so-called admirers! Didn't they invite him? Didn't he come from far away? Wasn't he considered—after Abraham and Elijah, who go to *all* such ceremonies—the guest of honor? And yet, after he had had one drink, nobody even bothered to look for him. Nobody paid any attention to him, and so allowed him to go outside and freeze among the horses. Thus they demonstrated to him and themselves that he wasn't really needed. They found it natural for him *not* to be at the center of their celebration, *not* to follow him, *not* to listen to his words, *not* to sing with him and for him. . . .

Rebbe Wolfe of Zbarazh: a Master unlike any other. Granted, we have said the same thing about all the others, and justifiably so—but he is not only special: he is unique. Others are modest—or want to be but cannot; their function and their followers compel them to discard modesty in the name of and for the sake of heaven. Many Masters shunned honors in order to combat their vanity—but Rebbe Wolfe did not even feel he deserved honors. In his case, the struggle against vanity is meaningless, a waste of time. Rebbe Wolfe could not even conceive of being vain.

Rather than guide and Master, Rebbe Wolfe was a brother, an older brother for his followers. A brother who never demanded anything, never asked for anything, never promised anything—who gave by giving of himself, who listened more than he spoke, who withdrew discreetly when you no longer needed him—or before.

Let us not yet touch upon his studies, his knowledge, his

53

hidden powers. For the moment let us simply stress his candor, his innocence. He was immune to falsehood: whatever he did, he remained authentic.

Zbarazh: a Jewish town like many others—somewhere in eastern Galicia. Which means that it endured the occupations, the harassments of various armies. Jews had lived there since the early sixteenth century and some had survived the siege of Khmelnicky, the invasion of the Turks, the raids of the Haidamacks. By 1941 there were some five thousand Jews left, and most of those were massacred that year by the Einsatz Kommandos. A town like many others, a story like many others. . . .

Where and when was Rebbe Wolfe born? Somewhere in the Ukraine, in the middle of the eighteenth century. That is all we know. Why such imprecision, so many omissions? Was there an effort by the Hasidic chroniclers to stress the aura of legend in his life? Even the most common data are oddly obscured. We know, for instance, that he had children, but most historians fail to mention their names or how many they were.

His birth itself is linked to a legend:

On that night, during the High Holidays, his father, the fierce and feared Maggid of Zlotchov, had a dream: the *hazzan*, the cantor, who had died shortly before, returned from heaven. "What are you doing down here?" the Maggid wondered. "Tonight souls are being reborn and sent back to earth," said the *hazzan*. "Mine too. Why? I'll tell you why. After I left your world, and as I prepared myself to appear before the celestial tribunal, I searched my memory: What had I done right and what had I done wrong? I conducted a thorough examination of my life and came to the conclusion that I had not done too badly: almost no serious sins, no major mistakes; in fact, it seemed to me that I was ready to enter paradise and take my rightful seat in its garden. Then I was led before the heavenly tribunal and the Judge scrutinized my record. Shaking his head, he said: You forgot one point. You forgot vanity. But because it was my only sin, my most recent one, it was decided to send me back into your world so as to enable me to remedy the situation. . . ." Legend has it that his soul entered the body of the Maggid's son, who later became known as Rebbe Wolfe of Zbarazh, a symbol of humility.

It seems that in his youth Rebbe Wolfe was anything but a Tzaddik. His behavior left much to be desired. He wasted days and nights with unsuitable friends doing unsuitable things. Lazy, unwilling to study, he enjoyed the more earthly pleasures. Was he aware of the anguish he inflicted on his poor father? The Maggid tried to discipline him—to no avail. By the time Wolfe turned twelve, his father was desperate. According to custom, the father had the scribe write phylacteries for his son's Bar Mitzvah. Came the day of Wolfe's Bar Mitzvah. Before handing the phylacteries to his son, he inspected them with great care. He read the two parchments and replaced them in their square boxes. And suddenly he began to weep. Tears began rolling down his cheeks into the boxes with the *tefillin*. That was the turning point for Wolfe. From that moment on, the young Wolfe changed his ways. His father's tears had succeeded where his sermons had failed.

The father—Rebbe Yehiel-Mikhel of Zlotchov—deserves closer study. An intimate of both the Besht and the great Maggid of Mezeritch, the Rebbe of Zlotchov was a fascinating personality. Intensely involved with the entire community of Israel, he aspired to be lifted up by those who were above him, and to lift up those who were below him. In other words: No person is the first nor is he—or she—the last. No one is absolutely just nor entirely unjust. An individual may be both sinner and saint—at different times or even at the same time. Whoever goes too far in one direction may easily find himself or herself going in the other. Excessive humility easily becomes false humility, which is dangerously close to vanity, excessive humility may numb both mind and soul. Too much modesty can prevent you from speaking up when necessary, from offering help when needed. From shouting the truth.

One morning, Rebbe Yehiel-Mikhel arrived late for services.

The congregation waited and waited for him to begin, but he took his time. No one dared utter a sound—with the exception of one man, a leader of the community, who stepped forward and addressed the Rebbe: "Excuse me," he said, "but . . ." "But what?" "You came late," said the man. "All right, you must have been busy. But now that you are here, why do you make us wait longer?" The Rebbe lifted his head and looked at him: "There are many congregants here," he said. "Yet you alone chose to speak up. Why? Why you? Is it because you are more learned than the others?" "No, Rebbe." "More pious perhaps?" "No, Rebbe." "But you are richer than they, aren't you? You are worth fifty thousand rubles, right? And that is why you have the audacity to question my behavior. Do you really expect me to be answerable to fifty thousand rubles?"

The Maggid of Zlotchov dared to speak that way because he knew his own value—not only as a leader but as a human being. He knew that to possess means little; what matters is substance. A person deserves respect for what he or she is, and not for any fortune they might have accumulated or inherited.

Of Rebbe Yehiel-Mikhel it was said that in his entire life he had never gone close to a stove for warmth, not even on the coldest winter nights. Also, that he never lowered his head toward the food on his plate, not even after days of fasting. And finally, that he never met with a man without telling him the truth.

Man is nothing but dust? True—but he can look at the sky. He is but ashes? True—but he can feel the fire. He is stronger than fire, stronger than hunger—even stronger than the forces that consume him. Contradictory? No: ambivalent. Ambivalence is characteristic of Hasidism in general, and Rebbe Wolfe's family in particular.

Let us explore this theme as it inevitably leads to dramatic dialectical situations.

Let us listen to some more tales.

One day Rebbe Wolfe heard unpleasant sounds coming from the kitchen. Putting aside the book he was studying, he went to find out what was happening there. He should have guessed it: his wife was having another fight with the maid. "She broke an expensive dish," the indignant Rebbetzin explained to him. "It was an accident," cried the maid. "It was an accident." "No, she did it on purpose," said the Rebbetzin. "She did it to annoy me and I am going to deduct its price from her wages." "Then I shall go to the rabbinic court," said the maid. "Go ahead. Sue me. Go right now; what are you waiting for?" The maid interrupted her work and said, "All right, I am going to the rabbinic court." "Me, too," said the Rebbetzin. "And me too," said her husband. "You? Why are you coming? I don't need you there." "*She* does," said Rebbe Wolfe of Zbarazh. "You are the wife of a Rebbe; she is only a poor maid. She needs me to defend her."

The tale is typical of the man: always ready and eager to defend the poor, the victim. Even when it meant opposing his own wife; even when it meant interrupting study and prayer. A person in distress came before meditation and concentration. Rebbe Wolfe was fully aware of the fact that the world was far from being just and charitable, that the oppressed were even more miserable than they appeared to be, and that many judges tended to favor the rich and the powerful. A Rebbe's wife had a better chance to be heard than her maid. He knew the facts of life, did Rebbe Wolfe of Zbarazh; he knew man's nature and he had no illusions about society's justice and mercy.

Still, how can one be simultaneously Rebbe and child, leader and follower? How can one reconcile giving and receiving, need and comfort, the duties of the Master and an awareness of not being one? Again, I can only tell you that Rebbe Wolfe of Zbarazh could. He was a Master who did not look like one. In fact, he looked like a big child lost in creation, a child who, without knowing it, illuminated the Hasidic universe. I told you before—he was different from other Masters. They performed miracles? He *was* a miracle.

One day Rebbe Wolfe was traveling from, or to, Zbarazh, to pay a sick call or perhaps to try to arrange some orphan's wedding. When he returned home he fell into a deep meditation. What about? His followers knew that his powers of concentration were total and unique. When he meditated, nothing disturbed him. And everyone respected his privacy, his occasional need for isolation. Only this time someone broke the rules. A student approached him and asked for help. He was destitute, hungry, desperate. Rebbe Wolfe listened to his woes, put his hand in his pocket, pulled out a silver coin and was about to give it to the student . . . but changed his mind. He put the silver coin back into his pocket and handed the young man a copper coin instead. Understandably, the student was not too happy. "What's the matter?" Rebbe Wolfe wanted to know. "I do not understand," said the student. "What don't you understand?" "Why the Rebbe changed his mind," said the student. "I will tell you why," said Rebbe Wolfe. "I wanted to teach you a lesson. A boy your age must never be ashamed to ask: there is no shame in receiving. What others give you isn't theirs anyway. But that is not all. I also wanted to teach you that a boy your age must not rely too much on miracles." The student blushed, bowed his head and withdrew, but Rebbe Wolfe called him back: "What are you thinking now?" "I am thinking, Rebbe, that the Rebbe has just shown me a new way leading to the Almighty; man must neither feel shame nor rely too much on miracles." "Right," said Rebbe Wolfe. "That is the way that leads to God." The young student later became one of the Rebbe's closest disciples.

And what do *we* learn from this story? First—that, surprisingly, Rebbe Wolfe of Zbarazh did have money in his pockets—sometimes. Second—that he was practical—sometimes. And third—that he was a perceptive educator with methods all his own. His many disciples not only admired and believed in him; they saw in him a Tzaddik, an exceptional human being endowed with secret powers. And all this in spite of his genuine humility—or was it *because* of it?

The question is relevant: There is danger in regarding humility as a virtue, especially in oneself; if I tell you I am humble, it means that I am not. How are we to know where true humility begins? Furthermore, how are we to reconcile man's vulnerability and his power? The Tzaddik and the Hasid? The Tzaddik and himself? On one hand, the Master—by definition—is endowed with powers; he can dictate his will on creation; he can cancel evil decrees and defeat wicked enemies. It is given to him to alter the rhythm of existence and modify the laws of nature. All he has to do is to utter one word, invoke one name, say one prayer— and the sterile mother will bear children, the broken heart will open itself to joy. The Tzaddik knows it—and *that* is his problem. He knows that whatever he desires he can obtain. How can one live with such knowledge and remain a Tzaddik?

A Tzaddik, more than anyone, must attain the extreme limits of humility, which means he must extirpate from himself the last vestiges of pride or self-righteousness. He must think of himself as unworthy and powerless—only then is he worthy of assuming power. He must subordinate his wishes, his thoughts, his aspirations, his hopes, his very heartbeat to the will of heaven; he must bend his being, his life. Let him become overly conscious of his importance and he will lose his powers instantly. Nowhere is the abyss as close to heaven as in the soul of the Tzaddik.

The Tzaddik inevitably leads a double life, thus living in constant contradiction with himself. In order to be what he is, he must think that he is not. To be a hero, he must think of himself as anything but a hero.

In his relations with his followers, the Rebbe must be *aware* of, but undaunted by, his limitations. Thus we deal with nuances of perception. A saint who knows that he is a saint— isn't. Or more precisely, no longer is. A conscience that is too clear is suspect. To ever be clear, conscience must have overcome doubt. As Rebbe Nahman of Bratzlav put it: No heart is as whole as one that has been broken. The great Maggid of Mezeritch, before him, said it differently: What do you do when you lose the key to the lock? You break the lock. So—break your heart and God will be allowed to enter. But in order to earn the right to say this to his followers, the Rebbe must lead the way and serve as a personal example. That is why the Tzaddik is often sad, whereas the ordinary Hasid is not. The Rebbe preaches ecstasy yet he himself remains melancholy, proving that he is able to reconcile sadness with happiness. Though he himself must aspire to perfection, he must be tolerant with his followers, knowing that they can only try to follow as best they may.

This complexity—one might say, this taste for paradox—is apparent also on the level of ideas. The Rebbe is expected to evolve in a mysterious universe; the Hasid must cling to reality. The Rebbe may be obsessed with eternity; the Hasid must deal with the present. The Rebbe immerses himself in the Book of Splendor, the Zohar; the Hasid studies the Bible. The Rebbe comments on the Talmud; the Hasid is satisfied with a simple prayer, a melody, a smile.

Of course, there were exceptions. Rebbe Menahem-Mendel of Kotzk was monolithic: for him, there were no half-measures, no compromises, no concessions, no consoling forgiveness. For him, it was all or nothing. Truth or damnation. Knowledge or stupidity.

But the typical Rebbe was tolerant and compassionate, always ready to reassure his followers, to comfort and console them and, above all, to stay with them. The typical Rebbe did not judge his followers; on the contrary, he tried to understand and defend them, and to make them smile.

In that tormented and torn century when the Jews suffered more than their neighbors—Jews were victims not only of the aggressors but of their fellow victims as well—in that era of upheavals, what did the simple Jewish villager need most? Peace and hope—and a sense of belonging. And in those days, who was better qualified to fill those needs than the Rebbe? He never chastised—he consoled. He was never a preacher but a friend. The Jews, poor and persecuted, were waiting for someone to tell them that while creation needs its creator, the creator too needs his creation. You miss God? He misses you too—yes, you. You may not be learned, you may not be pious—God needs you nevertheless. For there is something in you that is yours alone; there is something in every human being that can be found in no one else. You too are unique. . . .

This is precisely what the Jew, at the brink of despair, wanted to hear to help him forget despair. He needed to know that he belonged to a people, a community; that he was part of history. He needed to know that someone—the Rebbe, for instance— loved him enough to take an interest in his problems and share his joys. And also that there were other men and women who needed *him* enough to invite him to participate in their sorrows and celebrations. Thus the individual was no longer alone or mute: suddenly he was swept away by the *Niggun*, the music, the poetry of the Hasidic movement; for what is Hasidism if not a powerful and irresistible appeal to poetry?

In those times—in the lifetime of the Besht, the Maggid of Mezeritch or Wolfe of Zbarazh—the Hasid could not live in silence; he needed human words, brotherly voices that would help him, against all odds, to discover the world and its beauty, nature and its promise, man and his awesome fate. In those times of great misery, the Hasid needed someone to help him see, feel, hope and remember.

It was that quality of human warmth, of genuine generosity that attracted to the Hasidic movement, for a while at least, men such as Solomon Maimon and Bernard Lazare. Listen to Lazare's narration of his discovery of Hasidism:

"People spend time in their *shtibl* at any hour of the day, any day of the week, especially on Fridays and Saturdays. They pray, they sing, they sleep there when they have nowhere to go. . . . On Saturday evening, after studying the Law, they live it and teach it. The *shtibl* is the Hasid's universe: there he forgets his misery. And it is there that, through mystical sensuality, he escapes reality. . . . Strange people, the Hasidim: they sing joyous songs—and tomorrow they will have nothing to eat."

Tomorrow the Hasidim will lose every reason to hope, or even to go on living, but today, rooted in the present, they are carried by a powerful song of solidarity, by an overwhelming yearning: with their Master, surrounding him, they lift themselves up higher and higher in order to gather up there, in seventh heaven, where they will be given a taste of the ecstasy of eternity.

That is what the Rebbe offers his followers: something that he himself does not possess—a refuge, a haven, a source of joy and serenity.

But then the Rebbe, by virtue of the strength he incarnates and the majesty he evokes, cannot but represent to his followers the father figure par excellence, meaning someone good yet strict, charitable yet severe, tolerant with others but inflexible with himself; in other words, a singular human being in whom all attributes converge and in whom all contradictions are resolved. Let the Master show weakness and hesitation, and his followers will turn away from him.

Does that mean that Rebbe Wolfe of Zbarazh was not a Master at all? Is it possible that we were all taken in by his legend? No: there can be no doubt that Rebbe Wolfe occupies an illustrious place in Hasidic literature—a place comparable to that of Reb Nahum of Chernobyl or Reb Zusia of Onipol, whose contemporary he was. Important witnesses left us testimonies of his influence. Thus we are told that he was kind, docile, generous, humble—infinitely humble—and ready and willing to suffer and die for the sake of another human being; we know that he was straightforward, open-minded, warm and sensitive. What was the secret of so much kindness in a man who lived surrounded by cruelty. Who remained human in an inhuman society? Who responded with generosity and serenity in an era that lacked both? What was it in Rebbe Wolfe's personality that seemingly made him immune to anger, hate and self-pity? Had he always been that way? Had he changed, and if so, when? And why? Not enough of his life has been recorded in Hasidic annals to venture an answer. Not enough to trace the evolution of his personality. By the time we meet him, he is a mature man, a leader, a Master at peace with himself and the world.

His father, the Maggid Rebbe Yehiel-Mikhel of Zlotchov, was as known for his severity as his son was famous for his lack of severity. The father's sermons made his listeners tremble; his son's words appeased them. Whenever the father spoke, the town took on the atmosphere of Yom Kippur, the entire community turning to penitence. His rigor was so great that, according to Hasidic tradition, the Besht found it necessary to reprimand him: God and God alone may judge His creation with harshness; and even then, it is up to man to try to mollify Him. So unbending was the father that, if one is to believe Hasidic legend, he continued to fulfill the same duties after his death, chastising men and women for their sins in the world of eternity and truth. . . . In the afterlife, we are told, he presides over a tribunal which judges souls without any clemency. Was this why his son chose to rebel and take on his people's defense?

Rebbe Wolfe could not bear the sight of tears. He knew that when he saw his father weep the day of his Bar Mitzvah, an occasion that should be watershed and awakening for every Jewish boy. He then went on to deepen his sense of compassion. Did he acquire secret powers? Perhaps. If so, he used them only to mitigate man's suffering. Throughout his life, he opted to suffer rather than cause suffering. To weep rather than make others weep. To yield to others rather than use force to make them yield. Such was the substance of his teaching, the essence of his existence.

A story: a peasant came to spend Shabbat under the Rebbe's roof. As was the custom in Zbarazh, he was invited to partake of all meals at Rebbe Wolfe's table, together with the Rebbe's disciples and honored guests. The First Meal was a celebration; so was the Second. During the Third Meal a regrettable incident occurred: the peasant became too hungry to wait for the meal to be served. Didn't he know that the Third Meal was the most solemn and mysterious of all? He didn't care. He was hungry and there was no food on the table. Luckily there was food in his pockets. In fact, he always carried some tidbit in his pockets

—just in case. . . . And so he pulled out a piece of challah and some radishes and began to eat. And since he was eating, he wanted everybody to know what he was eating. So he made so much noise that the Master and his disciples found it hard to concentrate. But they tried. They sang the traditional melodies imploring the Queen of Shabbat not to leave them—not yet, not yet. . . . The disciples were humming nostalgic tunes and the peasant went on eating. The Rebbe spoke of his dreams of Safed and Jerusalem, and the peasant went on eating. Finally, one of the young disciples could remain silent no longer. He turned to the disrespectful peasant and whispered, "Hey, brother, how dare you?" Others chimed in. "What arrogance . . . what ignorance . . . get him out of here. . . ."

But then, just as the whispers of protest and indignation ran to a climax, the Rebbe raised his voice: "Do you know what I would like right now?" His disciples held their breath. What would the Master like? Every one of them would have given his life to please Rebbe Wolfe—but what would please him right now? What would give him pleasure? They leaned forward tensely, eager to hear better. "I would like a radish," said Rebbe Wolfe. "Yes, friends. What I really want now is a radish. That is all I want. Does anyone have a piece of radish for me?" And suddenly the mood shifted. The peasant was no longer the object of anger. Only of envy.

Another story: Rebbe Wolfe was journeying to a ceremony. He was late. The coachman knew it and began using his whip on his horse. The Rebbe stopped him: "Why do you hit the poor animal? Horses are living creatures. Why do you inflict pain on living creatures?" "But we are late, Rebbe, we are late." "So what? Is it the horse's fault? If we are late, why do you blame the horse?" The coachman knew the Rebbe well enough not to argue. He put the whip back in its place and began shouting instead. "Why are you shouting at the poor horse? Horses are living creatures. Why are you shouting at living creatures?" "But, Rebbe, what do you want me to do?" "Speak," said the Rebbe. "Speak to the horse."

To speak and not punish. To speak and not condemn. To speak in order to educate and enrich, not to repudiate and humiliate. To speak to cure, not to hurt and wound: Rebbe Wolfe of Zbarazh believed in using language exclusively on behalf of man, never as a weapon against him.

One day a number of Rebbes gathered in Lvov with the purpose of devising fierce measures against assimilation. Most of them considered the situation close to an emergency. Jewish youth was falling victim to alienation. Jewish boys and girls were imitating Gentile boys and girls. They dressed the same way, spoke the same way, visited the same places. Boys were shaving their earlocks, girls went to secular schools. Parents sent their children not to Yeshivot but to workshops. There was too much ignorance and laxity. If things were allowed to continue like that, the end of European Jewry was at hand. That is why the Rabbis had gathered in Lvov. To sound the alarm. To erect walls. To adopt new laws. To proclaim that emancipation meant treason; that modernization would inevitably lead to excommunication. The consensus was that there could be no leniency. But before the measures were put to a vote, they were submitted to Rebbe Wolfe of Zbarazh, who evidently had the power to veto them. And he did. "What are you up to?" he exclaimed. "You wish to excommunicate Jews? Why? Just because they misbehave I am to love them less than I love you?" The measures were discarded.

How did the Besht put it? A small Tzaddik loves small sinners; it takes a great Tzaddik to love great sinners. That is the basic principle of Hasidic teaching: our love for our fellow man must resemble God's; it must aspire to be infinite.

One day Rebbe Wolfe received complaints that certain Jews in Zbarazh spent their nights—may God forgive them—playing cards. The Master was urged to punish them or at least chastise them in public. He refused. "They play cards?" he said. "Let them. They won't play to the end of their lives, will they? One day they will stop. By then, they will have learned to overcome sleep and fatigue, and one day they will use their knowledge for study and prayer in the service of God. So why should I try to stop them, why should I condemn them?"

Was that his way of jesting? Did he have a sense of humor? Perhaps.

A poor Hasid came to see him, to talk to him about his poverty, hoping to obtain a blessing which would make him rich, or at least richer. He had hardly begun to speak when he was interrupted by Rebbe Wolfe, who indicated to him that another Hasid was waiting outside.

"But, Rebbe," protested the poor Hasid, "I just came . . . one minute ago. The man before me stayed a whole hour. Why do you discriminate? Is it because he is rich and I am not?" "No, no, my friend," said Rebbe Wolfe. "Let me explain it to you: the rich man who preceded you had to talk for a whole hour until I understood that he was poor, whereas with you, one minute was enough. . . ."

Still, I do not think it was meant as humor. He believed in what he said. He was convinced that the rich were also poor, that the wicked were also good, and that everybody was better than he. In this respect he went even further than the Besht. The Besht yearned to bring back sinners; Rebbe Wolfe did not look at them as sinners to begin with. Who was he to judge them—or anyone else for that matter? The Besht believed that every man was *capable* of goodness. Rebbe Wolfe believed that every person *was* good.

But then, how could he be so blind? Didn't he see evil around him? Didn't he realize that creation had been diminished by man? What did he think? That the Messiah had arrived, that Satan had been vanquished for good? How are we to explain such a degree of naïveté in a man who, after all, was duty-bound to act as leader, thus as guide, as teacher in things both spiritual and practical? How could he lead others in their everyday activities while remaining so totally out of touch with reality? How could he be both hero and antihero?

In truth, Hasidism in its early stages placed greater emphasis on the Hasid's role than on the Rebbe's. The Hasid was more

important than the Rebbe. The Rebbe's function and *raison
d'être* were to serve the Hasid, and not the other way around.
Created by the Rebbe, the movement existed for the Hasid—the
anonymous Jew who, as he encountered the Rebbe, ceased to
be anonymous.

In those times, the Hasid came from the lowest ranks of
Jewish society. And so did the Rebbe. The Besht recruited his
followers among the poor, the neglected, the wretched, the forgotten, the oppressed—and was opposed by the rich, the dig-
nitaries, the establishment's financial and intellectual elite. Who
clung to the Besht? Those men and women who, prisoners of
their solitude and misery, had cried and endured and despaired
in silence. The nameless, faceless human beings whose entire
existence seemed one endless, hopeless search for meaning and
destiny came to the Besht for help.

On a different level, that was true also of the other Rebbes,
the other Masters: they were far from being heroic figures. The
cult of the Tzaddik as a forceful leader of men on earth and as
intermediary and intercessor in heaven developed much later,
three generations after the Besht. Until then the Rebbe was
neither powerful nor glorious. The Besht was not a prince of
Jewish thought, nor was he the son of illustrious parents; he
wasn't even a Rabbi. He had appeared seemingly out of nowhere and had plunged into history and set it aflame. His origins were obscure, though it is known that they were humble.
Innkeeper, lime-digger, beadle, tutor: those had been his occupations. The Besht, a hero? Until he revealed himself, people
had hardly noticed him.

Most of his disciples were from modest backgrounds. Rebbe
Aharon of Karlin's father was a beadle, Rebbe Moshe Kobrin-
er's a baker, the Kozhenitzer Maggid's a bookbinder. . . . Both
Reb Uri of Strelisk and Reb Mendel of Riminov were sons of
tailors.

Many Hasidic Masters tried to relive the Besht's experiences.
In other words, before serving as teachers, they wanted to work
to improve themselves. Before they accepted the crown, they

endured anonymity, changing homes and disguises, living nomadic lives, wandering from town to town, from house to house: where they ate, they did not sleep; where they slept, they did not eat. They dressed as beggars and lived as beggars. They slept on the ground and endured insults and injuries without a tear or a protest. Everybody had rights over them, while they had none. To find themselves they first had to lose themselves. To deserve to be visible they first had to become invisible. Before revealing themselves they had to be totally unknown.

Countless legends describe the preparatory stages of a Tzaddik. We see him among wandering minstrels and fugitives from justice. We find him disguised as shoemaker, coachman, milkman; occasionally he does not even look like a Jew. In those legends the Tzaddik does everything imaginable—and unimaginable—to hide his shining face in darkness.

The most moving of legends concerning the Tzaddik's prerevelation exile tells of the two great Masters, Rebbe Elimelekh of Lizensk and his brother Reb Zusia of Onipol. It is said of them that wherever they spent the night, the Hasidic kingdom took root. They walked and walked and thus extended the boundaries of the Besht's movement. One day they arrived in a little town as dusk was falling. Noticing an inn, they went inside, hoping to spend the night there. Exhausted, they lay down behind the stove, which was the customary place for wandering beggars. Soon the place fell silent. And dark. All of a sudden, they woke in a panic, overcome by an inexplicable fear. So violent was their fear that they left the inn and the village in the middle of the night. The name of the place: Oushpitsin—better known to our generation as Oswiecim, or: Auschwitz.

As for Rebbe Wolfe of Zbarazh, his progression was different from that of his peers or predecessors. They began by being anonymous and ended up being celebrated; he remained withdrawn and unassuming all his life. When the time came to end his exile, he seems to have taken it with him. Throughout his entire adult life he felt inadequate and unworthy of leadership, of influencing others, of helping others. He never believed that he possessed keys to hidden treasures nor did he ever claim to be closer to truth than his fellow men. How could people ask him to intercede on their behalf? he wondered. How could he do for them what he failed to do for himself? More than anyone he needed help.

True, he became Rebbe; he had no choice. Like the holy Seer of Lublin and the Rebbe of Kotzk, he refused to wear the rabbinic crown; and like them, he had to yield to Hasidic pressure and ascend the throne. Being the son of the famous Maggid of Zlotchov conferred certain duties. His four brothers became Rebbes: he had to say yes as they did, lest he be accused of desertion.

Like his brothers, like most other Masters, he attracted students and their parents. To spend Shabbat in his home was a precious event. People came from afar to celebrate holidays with him and his friends. Hasidim came to ask for his advice in all matters. They drank in his words, they respected and admired and loved him, as only they could: he was their Rebbe, after all. . . . He alone remained unaware of the impact he was having. He never did anything to broaden his little province; quite the contrary, he did everything to keep it small. He refused to be treated as sage or Wonder Rebbe. He performed no miracles. He did not transform dust into gold, or foretell the future or impose his will on heaven. In fact, he did nothing that seemed out of the ordinary or spectacular. In spite of his prestige, he chose to lead a life of simplicity and anonymity. A Jew among Jews, a man among men: that is what he wanted to be. He had no charismatic powers, he only fulfilled his duties toward his fellow men, speaking to and hearing the mute, holding out his hand to anyone who needed it. That is all he aspired to accomplish and that is all he did. Never pretending to be more intelligent than others or more pious, he managed to be more generous and more humble than most. What was said of Rebbe Zusia—that he was a "genius" in humility just as others were geniuses in the sciences or in Torah —was true of Rebbe Wolfe as well. Loath to attract attention, he chose to pay attention to those who lived unnoticed. Therein lay his singular greatness.

If the stories by him or about him are so profoundly moving, it is because they emphasize his concern for the underprivileged, the outcasts, the misfits; even thieves benefited from his compassion.

One night his wife woke him up in a panic. "Wolfe," she whispered, "Wolfe, I hear noises! I hear thieves downstairs. Do something!" "All right," he said. "I will." He went to the door and began shouting, "Whatever I own, I gladly let you have! Do not worry, my dear thieves. You shall not be violating the law."

His loyal disciples bought him a watch, and one of his less loyal visitors stole it. But he refused to admit the theft: "All Jews are Tzaddikim," he said. "And Tzaddikim do not steal. If this Jew took the watch, he must have had a good reason."

Another time, other thieves—or perhaps the same ones—entered his house at night. Again his wife woke him up. Again he went to the door. In the meantime, the thieves had fled. So Rebbe Wolfe opened the door and began shouting, "Listen, my good thieves, listen to me: by mistake you have taken some jars with dangerous medication. Do not touch them! Do not touch them, remember, they are dangerous."

So much self-sacrifice and kindness after a while becomes annoying. How can one live with someone who never thinks of his own welfare? How can one love someone who loves everyone? How can one empathize with a man who protects the thieves who steal from him?

Well, I find him extraordinary. To live the way he did in a world that denied everything he stood for was not easy—and yet, he behaved as though it was. He actually failed to perceive the discrepancy between the world and his outlook on the world. Like Rebbe Zusia, he suffered and didn't even know it.

So—between the world and Rebbe Wolfe, I choose Rebbe Wolfe. With cynicism all around us, I look upon Rebbe Wolfe as a teacher who can help us fight cynicism and falsehood.

Granted, unlike many great Masters, he had no messianic

projects and was not involved in eschatological conspiracies; but he did something else. He brought redemption, on a small scale, to the individuals around him. He brought redemption without speaking of redemption. He performed miracles without calling them miracles.

At this point, we ought to raise again the question that has been troubling us all along: Who was he? A Rebbe in the classical sense or an anti-Rebbe in the modern sense?

The more one studies the sources, the more one gets the impression that they are deliberately vague about him: like Rebbe Hanina ben Dosa, he "carried heavy stones in his heart." What we do know is that at the end of his life he stopped all activities, broke all ties with his surroundings, and made Aliyah: Why? To be alone at last? Why did he seek total solitude? What did he hope to achieve? I don't know. Did he know?

As one reads and rereads all the sources about his life and work, one senses a mystery. Something must have happened to him, and we do not know what. Something must have happened, for he pulled up his roots, left Zbarazh, and went to the Holy Land. True, the Master of Medzibozh, Rebbe Barukh, sent him there. But were the two Rebbes really that close? And why did Rebbe Barukh choose him? And why did Rebbe Wolfe obey? If Rebbe Barukh needed an emissary, could he not have found a more suitable representative? In fact, anyone would have been more suitable than Rebbe Wolfe. The Tzaddik of Medzibozh and Rebbe Wolfe were at opposite poles: Rebbe Barukh personified anger, whereas Rebbe Wolfe believed in serenity; Rebbe Barukh exemplified ancient royalty, whereas Rebbe Wolfe exemplified present poverty. The one was the living example of a hero, whereas the other evoked the image of a perfect antihero. What was their common link, if indeed there was one? What motivated Rebbe Barukh to choose him, and what motivated Rebbe Wolfe to accept? The episode of Rebbe Wolfe's move to Palestine remains shrouded in mystery.

The years he spent there are missing in his biography: we

know nothing of what he did there. Hasidic chronicles of that period record only one story—not about him but about his wife, who had to take in strangers' laundry for a living. One imagines Rebbe Wolfe's misery—even darker than in Zbarazh. One imagines him in Safed or in Jerusalem. After that, he somehow vanishes from the Hasidic landscape. Why did he go to the Holy Land? What did he do there? Whom or what did he wish to elude or confront? What happened to the disciples he left behind in Zbarazh? When did he die? Of what? In what circumstances? We have no answers. All we know is that he died sometime between 1800 and 1820. Nothing is mentioned of the events preceding his death. Something must have happened, but the chroniclers, usually so full of stories, say nothing. There is only silence—disquieting, perplexing silence—surrounding his stay in Palestine. What does it all mean?

One possible explanation: Rebbe Wolfe wanted to leave Zbarazh, and European Hasidism, and Europe itself, in order to attain a higher degree of anonymity; he wanted to flee his admirers, his disciples, and the temptations they represented to him. Perhaps in Palestine he finally managed to live off stage—without anyone considering him a hero, or watching him, or questioning him, or following him. Perhaps at last his greatest wish had been fulfilled: the Rebbe of Zbarazh had become just another citizen of Safed or Jerusalem; the Tzaddik had become a simple Jew whom no one knew or wished to know. Perhaps at last he was left to his nostalgic silence and solitude.

BARUKH
OF MEDZIBOZH

AND IT CAME to pass that one of the celebrated Rebbe Barukh's disciples was caught in Satan's net. The poor man was following a dangerous path leading to darkness: he read forbidden books, played with perilous thoughts, and looked into hidden areas which only the chosen may approach with their gaze. He dwelled on the edge of the abyss, tempted by damnation.

When his Master, Reb Barukh of Medzibozh, learned about this, he felt sad, but told himself, Well, the boy is young and gullible. Next time he comes, I will talk to him; I will reprimand him and bring him back to God. But the disciple kept him waiting. And in the meantime, other rumors, increasingly disquieting, reached the Master. The disciple, he was told, had stopped praying; he had stopped studying; he had stopped meeting members of the Hasidic community. In fact, he no longer lived among Jews.

Though more and more distressed, the Master told himself, He will come to see me, he'll have to; and I shall be more severe than ever, more rigorous than ever, and he will be compelled to return to the fold. But the disciple continued to stay away.

Finally the Rebbe felt he had no choice. He decided to go and see him. And one morning, without telling anyone, he left his house and journeyed to a faraway town, there to confront his disciple. And before the young man could collect his thoughts and utter a word, the Rebbe spoke to him:

"You are surprised to see me here, in your room? You shouldn't be. I can read your thoughts, I know your innermost secrets. You are alone and you are trying to go deeper into your loneliness. You have already passed through, one after the other, all but the last of the fifty gates of knowledge and doubt— and I know how you did it.

"You began with one question; you explored it in depth to discover the first answer, which then allowed you to open the first gate. You crossed that gate and found yourself confronted by a new question. You worked on its solution and found the second gate. And the third. And the fourth and the tenth—one leads to the other, one is a key to the other. And now you stand before the fiftieth gate.

"Look: it is open. And you are frightened, aren't you? The open gate fills you with fear, because if you pass through it you will face a question to which there is no answer—no human answer. And if you try, you will fall. Into the abyss. And you will be lost. Forever. You didn't know that. Only I did. But now you also know."

"What am I to do?" cried the disciple, terrified. "What can I do? Go back? To the beginning? Back to the first gate?"

"Impossible," said the Master. "Man can never go back; it is too late. What is done cannot be undone."

There was a long silence. Suddenly the young disciple began to tremble violently. "Please, Rebbe," he cried, "help me. Protect me. What is there left for me to do? Where can I go from here?"

"Look," said Rebbe Barukh. "Look in front of you. Look beyond that gate. What keeps man from running, dashing over its threshold? What keeps man from falling? Faith. Yes, son: beyond the fiftieth gate there is not only the abyss but also faith—and they are one next to the other. . . ."

And the Rebbe brought his disciple back to his people—and to himself.

This story is not characteristic of Rebbe Barukh; normally he would have found it undignified to pursue a recalcitrant pupil. He was used to people coming to visit him at his court to pay him homage. Why, then, did he make an exception? In matters of *pikku'ah nefesh*—when a soul is in danger and in need of rescue—all rules must be discarded. Still, the way Rebbe Barukh dealt with his disciple is perplexing: he discussed faith with someone whose problem was precisely that he had no faith. A strange man, Rebbe Barukh of Medzibozh—one of the angriest among the Hasidic Masters of his time.

Like his grandfather, the Besht, whom he was eager to resemble, Rebbe Barukh did not fare well with historians. Heinrich Graetz ridiculed the Besht and Simon Dubnow underestimated Rebbe Barukh. Both judgments are unsubstantiated and unfair.

Like the Besht, Rebbe Barukh aroused passion in friends and opponents alike. Simple people were totally loyal to him; as for the Masters, their admiration for him was qualified.

Rebbe Israel of Rizhin declared: "In his presence a pious man became more pious, a wise man grew wiser, and an imbecile more stupid."

Rebbe Zvi-Hersh of Zhidachov so yearned to hear Rebbe Barukh sing the Song of Songs that he hid in his study. Later he confided to friends, "The Master was in ecstasy, his entire being aflame, evolving in another world; and when he came to the verse *Ani ledodi*—'I belong to my beloved as my beloved belongs to me'—he repeated each word with such fervor that I, too, found myself thrust into another world."

Yet how is one to explain his taste for power, his thirst for authority? The Besht did not wish to impress anyone and impressed everyone; his grandson also impressed his followers—but he *wished* to impress them. Their personalities were different and so were their life styles. The Besht was constantly traveling; his grandson held court in his palace. The Besht was poor; his grandson was not. The Besht spent himself in efforts to spread joy; his grandson struggled with melancholy. The Besht spoke softly; his grandson shouted.

No wonder Rebbe Barukh was criticized, not only by opponents of the movement but also by some of its leaders. Some disagreed with his precepts, others with his methods. Too sensitive and self-centered, he resented the slightest sign of deviation or dissension. He considered himself the only ruler—the keeper of the Hasidic flame.

There were those who objected, but rarely in public. Celebrated Masters such as Rebbe Levi-Yitzhak of Berditchev, Yaakov-Yitzhak, the Seer of Lublin, Israel of Rizhin, Rebbe Shneur-Zalman of Lyady often came to spend Shabbat under his roof. Thanks to him, Medzibozh became a capital once again, attracting Hasidim from all the provinces. Medzibozh, the small village in Podolia, became a center for pilgrimage, a glorious symbol of a glorious kingdom.

Appropriately, Rebbe Barukh's story is linked to a legend—a legend about his mother, who has a special place in Hasidic literature.

The Besht had two children: Reb Tzvi-Hersh and his sister Udil. They were totally different in character and temperament. Reb Tzvi-Hersh was shy, unassuming, withdrawn—unable and unwilling to assure his father's succession at the head of the rapidly expanding movement.

His sister, on the other hand, was an extrovert. No woman was as romanticized, as admired in Hasidism, as she was. She brought to the movement an added dimension of youth and charm.

Udil—the name probably derives from Adele, Adella—was honored by Hasidim as though she were a Rebbe herself. And, in a way, she was. People were used to seeing her at her father's side. Full of life, ideas, projects, she was frequently involved in important events. She generated excitement, enthusiasm; she seemed to be forever in the middle of a story. Her advice was often sought. Hasidim believed that the Shekhina rested on her face.

Married to Reb Yehiel Ashkenazy, she managed to take care of him, of their grocery store, of their two sons, and of her father. When the Besht was sick, she was at his bedside. There existed a special friendship, a singular complicity between the two. One has the feeling that he was closer to her than to his own wife—her mother.

She often accompanied the Besht in his travels, something her brother and her mother rarely did. Udil seemed to be everywhere—never disturbing, never embarrassing; on the contrary, she made herself welcome, she made people feel good. She participated in the extraordinary adventure which her father had begun; and her father lovingly encouraged her to participate more and more, taking her along even when he and his disciples went on their frequent retreats. When they prayed, when they conducted their mystical gatherings, when they celebrated, she was nearby. Udil: the feminine example of the grace, wit and beauty of the Hasidic movement.

One evening she was present at a celebration. Her father's disciples sang and danced for hours and hours on end, seeking to achieve communion with God, aspiring to let their souls enter His. They chanted with fervor, they danced with exuberance, until they left behind all links with things earthly. Eyes closed, shoulder against shoulder, hand in hand, they danced in a circle around their Master, around God and His people. Udil found the spectacle so beautiful that it took her breath away. Suddenly she noticed that one young student was losing his balance. His shoes had so many holes they had fallen off his feet. He had to break the circle and leave his friends. He looked sad and lonely.

"Poor young man," Udil said to her father.

The Besht smiled. "Promise him a pair of new shoes, if he promises you to intercede in heaven to let you have another son."

Both promised. And thus, in return for a pair of shoes, Udil was blessed with another son, Barukh. Tradition has it that she wanted him—and only him. She had given birth to one son already, the future Rebbe Ephraim, author and scholar—but Udil wanted a real Rebbe, not a writer. And she had Barukh.

. . .

What do we know about him? Much—but not enough. As we consult Hasidic sources, we detect a certain reticence toward him. Few books are devoted to him; and his place in other Masters' legends is surprisingly modest. One could say that in those he is known mostly by the hostility he aroused. The Masters found him quarrelsome, arrogant, moody, and would have preferred not to deal with him. But how could they avoid it? He was the Besht's grandson, and his impact on Hasidism could not be denied.

A few essential facts: born in 1757, he was three or four when his grandfather died. He grew up in the house of the Maggid of Mezeritch, studied with Rebbe Pinhas of Koretz and married into a wealthy family. At first, he lived in Tulchin. Later he moved to Medzibozh, where he died at the age of sixty-eight.

He was a precocious child, and the Besht loved him. From an early age, he displayed a remarkable self-confidence and even a certain arrogance.

A legend: A disciple presented the Besht the following problem: Scripture tells us that "Abraham lifted his eyes and saw three men before him." The comment on this in the Zohar is that the three men were our patriarchs: Abraham, Isaac and Jacob. How was it possible? wondered the disciple. How could Abraham have seen . . . Abraham?

The question was pertinent, and the Besht was about to answer it when his grandson, little Barukh, boldly intervened: "What a foolish question! The Zohar does not speak about people but about symbols—and our three patriarchs symbolize God's attributes: grace, power and magnificence."

True or not, we don't know—but the story does reflect Reb Barukh's personality. Frank, almost brutally so, he continued in the footsteps of the child who spoke his mind, who treated someone else's disciple as though he were his own, and who, undaunted by the presence of the Besht, dared speak of the Zohar at the age of three.

. . .

Little Barukh loved his grandfather, and spoke of him more than of his own father or mother. Tradition has it that when Rebbe Pinhas of Koretz saw the small boy weeping over the death of the Besht, that moved him more than the tragic event itself.

Barukh studied with Rebbe Pinhas, but failed to learn that Rebbe's concept of wealth. Rebbe Pinhas used to say, "What shall I leave my children when I die? All the monies that my Hasidim *wanted* to give me—and that I refused to accept." As for Rebbe Barukh, he accepted. Unlike Rebbe Pinhas, unlike his own elder brother, Reb Ephraim, he seems to have had some attachment to earthly possessions.

Once he felt the need to explain why he accepted money from his followers: "Imagine you must go to see the king. But the king is in one place and you are in another. The king is in his palace, inaccessible, surrounded by walls and fences, with guards standing at the gates. What do you do? You bribe the guards. You begin with those standing watch outside, then you make your way inside. Naturally, the closer you come to the king, the more important the guards—and the higher the bribes. Well," he said, with a smile, "Tzaddikim are but keepers of the gate; they too can be bribed."

Having married a rich woman, he could afford to study—but did not. His two brothers-in-law, both pious and learned men, were irritated by his behavior: whenever they studied, he slept; whenever they slept, he played games. So annoyed were they that they complained to his father-in-law, who decided to take all three to Mezeritch. In the coach, Reb Barukh was humiliated by his companions: they made him sit next to the coachman. However, on the way back he had the best seat. For the Maggid of Mezeritch had told his angry visitors, "Leave Barukh alone; he knows what he is doing, and so do I. His games are serious—*if* you know how to read them. I know and so does he. And so does God."

. . .

With the Maggid as protector and the Besht as grandfather, Reb Barukh could not fail. He was treated as a prince by Hasidic Masters and followers alike. They were taken with his youth, his exuberance—and his memories of the Besht.

When he became Rebbe, he went to Tulchin. Why Tulchin? Perhaps because of the memories connected with that hamlet. Tulchin had been the scene of unspeakable massacres during the Khmelnicky uprisings (1648–1649). Reb Barukh chose to live there for a while, but not too long. Did he leave for the very same reasons that had made him come? *Because* of the memories? Or was it because of the Mitnagdim, the opponents of Hasidism, who made his life miserable with their constant attacks and slanders?

The fact is he returned home to Medzibozh, his grandfather's capital. There the Hasidim were masters, there they had nothing to fear from the Mitnagdim. From that point on, Medzibozh was linked not only with the Besht's name but with his own as well.

From visitors, disciples and chroniclers we know much about his life there. His home was not really what we would consider a palace, but for the Hasidim it was. He had *gaboim* and *shamoshim*, secretaries and servants, and displayed his riches especially on Shabbat and during holidays.

He had children, whom he loved—among them an ailing daughter, whom he loved the most. When medications were needed for her, he would personally journey to the big city.

In his home, as in that of his grandfather, women were not relegated to the kitchen or to secluded chambers. Was it Udil's influence? In Medzibozh women participated in festive meals and sat together with distinguished guests—something the holy Seer of Lublin objected to violently. One of their early disputes was on that subject. When the holy Seer was invited to Reb Barukh's Shabbat table, he was shocked to find the Master's wife and daughters there. Worse: they took part in the conversation.

An episode: One day, as Rebbe Barukh was saying grace, repeating three times the verse *Vena al tatzrikheni adoshem elokenu lo lidey matnat basar vedam*—"May I not be dependent on other people's gifts"—his daughter Reisele interrupted him: "But, Father," she said, "how can you say such a thing, do you not live from people's gifts? Do you really wish God to stop people from offering you money?" "Only God gives," answered Rebbe Barukh. "But sometimes He uses messengers."

He was hospitable and enjoyed entertaining his guests with stories, parables and songs. Before a fast he would offer them candy. A symbolic gesture: Yes, there are reasons for us to mortify ourselves, but sweetness too is part of life and willed by God.

Once he was surprised by Reb Moshe of Ludomir while he was quarreling with his wife. "Do not worry," he told the visitor. "It is just like the Almighty disagreeing with the Shekhina, His Divine Presence—it is all for the sake of *Tikkun*, it is all meant to correct creation and shorten exile."

It was in Medzibozh that Rebbe Barukh was seized by melancholy. We do not know what provoked it or when it was first noticed. Nor is it possible to describe accurately the attacks of morose languor. We only know that one day he was beset by them. They remain unexplained, inexplicable. Yet, how could anyone teach the Hasidic idea and not receive its message of joy? How could he claim to continue the Besht's mission and yield to sadness? How could Rebbe Barukh be a Hasidic Master and look at creation with anger?

Is this why he aroused such hostility among his peers— because he did not conform to the traditional Beshtian concept of the Tzaddik, whose task it is to guide and console, and to serve as an example? Rebbe Barukh differed from the others in many ways, and perhaps in all ways.

To begin with, he claimed to be their superior—no, more than that: their overseer. "Rebbe Barukh is climbing to heaven . . . on our heads," said Reb Sholem, the Maggid of Mezeritch's grandson.

True, Rebbe Barukh belittled other Hasidic Masters. The Besht's heritage was his alone, he maintained; he alone could spread it to Jewish communities in Podolia and beyond. He wished to be recognized as the one and only spokesman of the movement's Founder.

Modesty was surely not his major virtue. "My soul," he remarked, "knows its way in Torah, all gates are open to me." Once he told of a dream he had had: "A number of Masters and scholars were sitting around a table presided over by Rebbe Shimon bar Yohai, who planted the fear of heaven in our hearts for not serving God as we should. We all began shivering. Then Rebbe Shimon bar Yohai noticed me. He rose and came over to me and placed his hand on my shoulder. 'Barukh,' he said gently, 'you need not worry, I do not mean you—you are perfect.'" Another time Rebbe Barukh was seen pressing the Zohar to his heart, saying, "Rebbe Shimon bar Yohai, I know you, and you know me."

At the same time, he liked to boast about his humility. Said he: "If there are a thousand humble men in this world, I am one of them; if there are only two, I am one of them."

Small wonder that many of his peers disliked him. He often quarreled with them—he even had a dispute with the great Rebbe Shneur-Zalman of Lyady, who dared collect funds for ransoming prisoners in Reb Barukh's domain, in Tulchin. "But this is an emergency," Reb Shneur-Zalman argued. "We must save those Jews!" "If you are a Tzaddik," Reb Barukh replied, "save them with prayers, not with money."

There was another reason, too, for their dislike. In those years disciples of the great Maggid of Mezeritch were already at work in hundreds of dispersed communities between the Dnieper and the Carpathian Mountains, revolutionizing Jewish life everywhere. They spoke to the forlorn and forsaken villagers in their own language, they shared their burdens and misery, they tried to turn imagination into a magic vehicle to spirit them away from misfortune. A small barrack was now formed into a sanctuary, simple words became litanies. These new Masters were successful because they lived *with* their followers, helping them cope with poverty through faith and faith alone. But this Rebbe insisted on being different. And he was.

Like the Rizhiner somewhat later, Reb Barukh dressed like a prince, behaved like a prince, spoke like a prince. He was the first Rebbe to introduce the external trappings of power and privilege into Hasidic lore. He was the first to stress the element of *malkhut*, of royalty, in the Tzaddik's role. His meals had to be royal feasts, his home a royal court.

A story: One day as Reb Barukh visited his brother, Reb Ephraim, he was struck by the poverty of his home—his candlesticks were made of clay and not of silver. "Do not be sad," said Reb Ephraim. "The light is the same." Shortly afterward, Reb Barukh gave his brother a pair of silver candlesticks. But when he came to visit him next, they were not to be seen.

"Where are they?" he wanted to know.

"At the pawnbroker's," said Reb Ephraim. "I needed money."

"And you don't mind?" asked Reb Barukh.

"No," said his brother. "I'll tell you how I look at it: I would rather be at home and have my silverware at a stranger's than the other way around."

A hint of criticism? Maybe, though it would seem out of character; Reb Ephraim, the elder brother, was a gentle, sweet, unassuming man who never offended anyone—and would not have sought to hurt his brother. So humble was Reb Ephraim that in his important book, *Degel machnei ephraim*, he contents himself with quoting the Besht and his immediate disciples and almost never speaks on his own behalf. Still, Reb Barukh must have envied him, for he once remarked, "I have not written a book—thank God for that."

He was suspicious of both the written word and the oral word. He was suspicious—period.

As he grew older, he became restless, moody; he felt a stranger everywhere—even in his own home. Uprooted, alienated, the king in him felt threatened. His obsession was that all men are strangers in the world. And that God Himself, in exile, dwells as a stranger in His own creation. One day he told his disciples, "Imagine someone who has been expelled from his country. He arrives at a place where he has no friends, no relatives. The customs and the tongue of the land are unfamiliar to him. Naturally, he feels lonely, terribly lonely. Suddenly he sees another stranger who, like him, has no one to turn to—no place to go. The two strangers meet and become acquainted. They talk, and for a while stroll through the streets together. With a measure of luck, they may even become good friends. This is true of God and man; they are two strangers who try to become friends."

What a depressing concept of man and his relation to God. No wonder that many Masters rejected it—and him. They could have fought him publicly on these grounds alone. Why didn't they? Out of respect for his grandfather? Yes, that too. But they respected the grandson as well. He had great charisma. They may not have agreed with his methods, but they could not fail to recognize his genuine qualities of leadership. Also, they were afraid—afraid of his somber gaze, afraid of his dark outbursts of anger.

Anger became his particular sign, his distinction: the ability to be harsh, just as his peers were gentle. They blessed their followers; he insulted his. They sought to appease; he to annoy. However, his followers were not to be discouraged; they clung to him even more. They believed that the angrier he was, the kinder he was. They took his curses for benedictions—which only made him angrier.

Forever misunderstood, he tormented others—and himself. Why? Because of what was happening in the world, to the world? International politics left him indifferent. He did not mix into the affairs of Napoleon and the Czar, and he expected them to stay out of his. Because of what was then taking place inside the Jewish world? Possibly. The war between the Hasidim and their opponents surely affected him. But what interested him most was what was going on inside the Hasidic universe.

Like his grandfather, Rebbe Barukh understood that in order to improve the world, one has to improve oneself first. If God does not dwell in me, whose fault is it? Have I prepared for Him a dwelling place worthy of His glory?

Often Reb Barukh was beset by doubts. The Besht was so great, so intense, unique—and he, Reb Barukh, was the Besht's successor. Worse: The Besht was so majestic—and others pretended to take his place. How could Reb Barukh keep calm? Strange: the grandson's way differed so much from his grandfather's. Is this how the Besht would have expected his grandson to lead his community? With anger? In sadness?

We do not understand. No one seems to have tried to delve into the mystery. No attempt seems to have been made to explain his bizarre outbursts, his depressions. People chose to move away from him, rather than criticize him or judge him. Perhaps they did not dare antagonize the grandson of the Besht, the son of Udil, a Master who every morning wore the Besht's very own *tefillin*.

And yet, we must insist, he was a man of greatness. He had an intense inner life; he was endowed with a burning vision. Though he could have led a peaceful life filled with honors, he chose to reject the safe course of merely preserving a glorious heritage. Instead, he walked the perilous new path of self-interrogation. As the Besht's grandson, he could have kept what was given to him; he chose instead to risk everything and antagonize everybody. He despised the serene existence of the Tzaddik. He was constantly rebelling, not always knowing against whom or what. And even there we find him poignantly human.

Listen:

Rebbe Moshe of Savran came to spend Shabbat in Medzibozh. After services, Reb Barukh paced up and down the room singing *Shalom alekhem*, welcoming the angels of peace who come carrying the light of Shabbat and its serenity on their wings; then he recited with his customary fervor the prayer *Ribon kol haolamim*—"Thank You, Master of the Universe, for Your generous gifts—those I have received and those yet to come. . . ." Suddenly he stopped and said in a loud voice, "Why am I thanking You now for gifts to come?" He repeated the question several times and, after a long silence, began to weep.

"Why is the Rebbe crying?" wondered Rebbe Moshe of Savran. "Because of the question?"

"Yes," said Rebbe Barukh.

"And . . . the answer? What is the answer?" asked the disciple.

"Here it is," said Rebbe Barukh. "We thank Him now for gifts to come—in case we will not be able to do so when we receive them." And again he began to weep.

"Why is the Rebbe crying?" asked the disciple once more. "Because of the answer?"

"Yes," said Rebbe Barukh, "because of the answer. I think of the future, which, God willing, may prove to be good to me—but what if I will be unable to give God my gratitude? How could I live without expressing my gratitude?"

Later he added, "You see, the question is good—and so is the answer. And both make me cry."

But on another Shabbat, when he had a guest from Jerusalem, he stared at him for a long while and then asked, "Are you sad?"

"Yes," said the guest, "I am; I cannot help it. I have traveled too much, I have seen too much, lived too much."

"But it's Shabbat, my friend. You are not traveling now, nor are you witnessing any suffering."

"I am sad nevertheless," said the guest.

"Then I order you to shake your sadness away!" And after a silence, he added, "Come, I'll teach you."

One of his sayings: God and man's love of God are alike—for they are boundless.

Another one: People are careful not to swallow live ants but are ready to eat up their fellow men.

Also: Every person is a vessel taking into itself whatever its owner pours into it: wine or vinegar.

The world looks brightly illuminated, he said, for those who don't want it—and gloomy and dark to those who seek to possess it.

He also said: I am afraid of Cossacks—one is enough to frighten me. Ten would frighten me even more—and a thousand, a thousand times more. And yet, they frighten me less than the tiniest of sins that I could commit.

"Say something," pleaded the holy Seer of Lublin in the course of a famous encounter. "I am told everywhere that you talk so well. Please, Rebbe, talk. Say something, anything. I would so like to take your words with me—even one. You talk so well—won't you talk to me?"

"No," said Rebbe Barukh. "I would rather be mute than talk well."

Rebbe Levi-Yitzhak of Berditchev, who loved peace—and to make peace—managed nevertheless to appear on Reb Barukh's blacklist.

Perhaps it had to do with the fact that Reb Levi-Yitzhak had sent two emissaries to report on Reb Barukh's way of life. Did he study Talmud? Did he observe all the laws of Torah? Was it true that he read other people's thoughts?

The emissaries brought back their report, and the answer was yes, to all three questions, even the last. Yes, Reb Barukh could read other people's secret thoughts—and he had proved it. The message he sent back with the emissaries was as follows: "Go and tell the Rebbe of Berditchev that God sees and forgives. Not I—I see and don't forgive."

Actually, this was not true: Reb Barukh forgave Reb Levi-Yitzhak. The two Masters had great affection and esteem for one another. And there was a beadle in Berditchev who could corroborate this.

Reb Barukh was told of a certain Mitnagged in Berditchev who, unfortunately, happened to be a good scholar; so he used his scholarship, naturally, to make Reb Levi-Yitzhak's life miserable. He would interrupt his lectures, ridicule his sermons; in short, he was unbearable, as only erudite Mitnagdim can be.

"Let him come to see me, and thereafter he will keep quiet," said Reb Barukh.

Somebody informed the Mitnagged, who repeated Reb Barukh's remark in public. "Good," he said insolently. "I shall go and see him. Who is he? What is he? What is his strong point?" "The Zohar," he was told. "Good," he said. And he began studying the Zohar—page after page, chapter after chapter, with commentaries and commentaries on commentaries— until one day he felt he was ready. And he went to Medzibozh equipped with a difficult passage of the Zohar, expecting, with this passage, to trap Rebbe Barukh right away. To his surprise he found the Master poring over the Zohar, open to the very page he had meant to confound him with.

"You seem astonished," said the Rebbe. "What puzzles you: that I study Zohar? Or that I made *you* study Zohar?" And without allowing the Mitnagged to reply, he continued, "Usually you study Talmud, right?" "Right." "And you know the Talmud?" "Yes," said the visitor.

And the Rebbe told this story: "Do you know the legend about the light that shines above the child's head before he is born? This light enables him to study and absorb the entire Torah. But one second before he enters into the world, the child receives a slap from his personal angel; in his fright, he forgets all that he has learned. Well, there is something in this legend that one fails to understand. Why study if it is all to be forgotten? Do you know the answer?"

The visitor remained mute.

"No?" said the Rebbe. "Let me explain it to you. It is to teach man the importance of forgetfulness—for it, too, is given by God. If man were not to forget certain things, if he were to remember the time that passes and the approaching death, he would not be able to live as a man among men. He would no longer go to plow his field, he would no longer wish to build himself a house or have children. That is why the angel planted forgetfulness in him: to allow him to live. But tell me, what happens when the angel forgets . . . to make you forget?" Rebbe Barukh looked at his visitor and waited before continuing: "If he forgets—I can still do it for him."

And because the erudite Mitnagged had used knowledge against his fellow man, Rebbe Barukh punished him. The Mitnagged forgot all that he had ever known and became a simple beadle in the synagogue—where Reb Levi-Yitzhak could, from then on, speak and lecture without fear of being disturbed.

Another story:

Rebbe Barukh's grandson, Yehiel, came running into his study, in tears.

"Yehiel, Yehiel, why are you crying?"

"My friend cheats! It's unfair; he left me all by myself, that's why I am crying."

"Would you like to tell me about it?"

"Certainly, Grandfather. We played hide-and-seek, and it was my turn to hide and his turn to look for me. But I hid so well that he couldn't find me. So he gave up; he stopped looking. And that's unfair."

Rebbe Barukh began to caress Yehiel's face, and tears welled up in his eyes. "God too, Yehiel," he whispered softly. "God too is unhappy; He is hiding and man is not looking for Him. Do you understand, Yehiel? God is hiding and man is not even searching for Him. . . ."

Weeping over God and man alike, Rebbe Barukh could not help sinking into melancholy. Like other Hasidic Masters before and after him, he knew that the secret of redemption lies in the union between Creator and creation. But what if Creator and creation were to remain strangers forever? Reb Barukh's despair was of an existential nature. Divine severity was less threatening to him than divine separation. Let God be our king, our father, or even our judge—but let Him not be estranged from us!

Perhaps that was the secret of Reb Barukh's anguish and

anger: And what if he was wrong? And what if, due to man's foolishness, God were to hide His face forever? And what if the Besht and his allies were powerless to bring God and man closer together? And what if they were unable to protect the people of Israel from new and old dangers? And if the Besht was power-less—what could his grandson do? What was there left for him to do?

People came to him with pleas for heavenly intercession, with pleas for miracles—and he reacted with outbursts of rage: he was against miracles. When Prophet Elijah performed miracles on Mount Carmel, the people shouted, "*Adoshem hu haelohim* —Look! God is God.*" Said Rebbe Barukh, "The Prophet was admirable and so were the people, for they did not shout: 'Look! Miracles, miracles.' But . . . 'Look! God is God.' They disregarded the miracles."

But his followers wanted miracles. What could he do? Levi-Yitzhak of Berditchev chose to side *with* his people—against the Almighty. Not Reb Barukh. Hence his rage—at himself, at the situation in which he found himself. For his followers, who forced him to choose. For his peers—in order to provoke *their* anger. Yes, he wanted them to be angry, and to begin by being angry with him.

Then there was melancholy. Sadness. Despair. So great was his suffering that a famous jester, a *shokhet* named Hershele Ostropoler, had to be engaged to cheer him up. Poor, penniless Hershele had a biting sense of humor. Which was why he was forever being asked to leave his positions; he would invariably antagonize his employers. Hundreds of stories circulated about his sharp tongue and quick mind.

Once his wife complained, "The children have nothing to eat; go get them some bread." Hershele went to the marketplace with a whip in his hand, shouting, "Who wants to go to Zhitomir for half the price?" Many people, to save half the fare, flocked to him instead of taking the coach. He made them pay and then said, "Follow me." He led them out of town, and farther. Halfway to Zhitomir, the "passengers" asked him, "Hershele, where are the horses?"

"Who spoke of horses?" he said. "I spoke of half fare. . . ."

Later he told his wife, "See? The important thing is to have a whip—if you have that, horses will come to you anyway."

One night he was awakened by his wife: "Hershele, wake up, listen. Thieves! There are thieves in the house." "Really?" said Hershele. "If they find anything valuable, then *we* are lucky. . . ."

One evening Reb Barukh told Hershele to light the candles, for it was dark in the room. The jester lit one candle. "Hershele," scolded the Rebbe, "one candle is not enough. I cannot see." Next day Hershele lit more than one, more than ten, more than thirty—he wasn't going to stop lighting candles. "Hershele, Hershele," scolded the Rebbe again. "Are you going to blind me now?"

"I don't understand," said the jester. "Yesterday you were against darkness, now you are against light."

And Reb Barukh burst out laughing. "Hershele," he said, "you want to teach *me* when to be angry?"

With his stories and witty aphorisms, Hershele often made him laugh—and sometimes made him angry. For Hershele was irreverent in the classic manner of jesters. He told the Rebbe things the Rebbe did not wish to hear. So much so that at least one Hasidic source maintains that on one occasion Hershele went too far . . . and the Rebbe grew too angry . . . so angry that he ordered his followers to throw the jester out. And Hershele, brokenhearted and sick, never returned.

Hershele, too, was a tragic figure—as tragic and as secretive as his Master. Whatever it was the Rebbe wanted to achieve with anger, Hershele tried to achieve with laughter.

Again and again we come across this word, "anger." It dominated the Rebbe's last years. Once he explained his behavior by pointing to the Zohar, which speaks of a certain anger that is "blessed from above and from below," and that is named— Barukh. At his deathbed his followers found the Zohar open to that very page.

He had tried to find an explanation; his contemporaries had not. They did not really seem to resent his anger. Rather, they appear to have been puzzled. As for me, I try to understand him, and I love him. Others accepted his taste for luxury and power; I accept his anger. Surely, he wanted to teach us something about the Tzaddik, namely, that though the Tzaddik must be revered and feared, he must also be measured in human terms. The Tzaddik is human—and must be. No true greatness, no real holiness can be attained if it is at the expense of one's humanity. To deny one's weaknesses is but another weakness. The Tzaddik is no angel, no heavenly saint—the Tzaddik is simply more human than his followers, and that is why he is their leader.

Of course, that idea was introduced by the Besht; but Reb Barukh developed it. The Besht said: "Once upon a time we tried to come closer to God through study, prayer, fasting, mortification and contemplation—but I propose to open a new way, a way that leads through love: love of God, love of Torah and love of Israel."

Perhaps his grandson, Reb Barukh, wished to open up another, yet unknown way: one dominated by anger, by rage. He may suddenly have perceived that love alone—in a world without love, filled with violence and peopled with strangers—was not enough to assure the survival of his people. Perhaps he thought that a certain measure of anger, of rage, was necessary for the people of Israel. Hence his sadness, hence his despair: How can one not despair of a world in which rage is needed for redemption?

The key to his enigmatic behavior may possibly be found in his excessive passion for *Shir-hashirim*, the Song of Songs. What is the Song of Songs? A love song? Yes, it is without a doubt—a sublime chant of love. But what kind of love? Unhappy love, heavy with melancholy and nostalgia. It is a song of endless waiting and faithfulness, it is majestic and moving but marked by tragedy: the couple remains separated, torn apart. God waits for Israel while Israel is waiting for God, who is looking for His Shekhina, who is following Israel, who suffers with God, and at times for God, and always because of God.

And yet—beyond sadness, beyond despair, there *is* love, and there always will be. Without such love, which transcends all other love, man's life would not be less tragic but less lofty and therefore empty and meaningless.

A romantic idea? Never mind. This was, after all, the beginning of the nineteenth century, at the very beginning of the Romantic movement, with its agonies and dreams, its tears and outcries.

Rebbe Barukh died in 1811—leaving us his own Song of Songs, but not his rage. He took along his many masks but bequeathed to us a most precious gift: his passionate love for his people.

The more you study his sayings, his stories, his life, the more you discover beauty in the man himself. Suddenly you realize that more than his contemporaries—or ours—he grasped the awesome weight of certain questions. More than his peers—and ours—he understood that one must never avoid questions, as one must not turn one's gaze away from the abyss. Remember the story of the disciple and the fifty gates? One must go through the gates. And confront truth. And look into the eyes of despair—and never mind if you will remain prisoner of your own anguish. Alone . . . you probably will remain prisoner. So . . . don't be alone. A Hasid is never alone, even if the Tzaddik is.

There is beauty in the fact that Rebbe Barukh spoke of faith, not as opposed to anguish but as encompassing anguish. "Faith and the abyss are next to one another," he had told that young disciple. "I would even say, one within the other. True faith lies beyond questions; true faith comes after it has been challenged."

We have learned much from his tales but most importantly that love and anger are compatible, provided they are motivated by *Ahavat-Israel*, love for one's people and for mankind.

Granted, we are all strangers under the sun. Granted, God's ways are not always understandable—or bearable. Is that reason enough—ever—for us to abandon another human being, friend or not yet friend, to solitude, danger and death?

I find Rebbe Barukh beautiful. He left the splendor of his palace and the comfort of his faith to save a young man by helping him surmount his fear and doubt. I find Rebbe Barukh admirable. In order to help his disciple, he chose to open and close the gates *with* him, to confront the perils *with* him and finally, to approach the awesome abyss *with* him. . . .

He risked not only his soul for someone else's, but also his faith for someone else's: that was his concept—and the Besht's too—of *Ahavat-Israel*. He was angry? Naturally he was. He was angry because he cared, because he was concerned, because he was present to anyone in need of human presence.

To the desperate young student he had said: "I know there are questions that remain open; I know there is a suffering so scandalous that it cannot even have a name; I know that one can find injustice in God's creation—I know all that as well as you do. Yes, there are reasons enough for man to explode with rage. Yes, I know why you are angry. And what do I say to you? Fine. Let us be angry. Together."

MOSHE-LEIB
OF SASSOV

Ask the old Hasidim. Ask them to tell you what the great Tzaddik of Nemirov was known to do during the week preceding Rosh Hashana. They will tell you that in the early morning hours, when Jews everywhere rise to go and say their prayers of penitence—the *Selihot*—with special fervor, the Tzaddik of Nemirov had a way of disappearing. He would disappear and could be found nowhere. Neither in the synagogue nor in the houses of study nor at the *shtibl* nor—least of all—at home.

Where could the Rebbe be? Well, where *should* he be, except . . . in heaven? Is not a Rebbe inundated with requests and pleas on the eve of the solemn days of judgment?

Jews need a livelihood, they need peace, health, a few nice Jewish boys for their daughters. . . . Jews wish to be honest and pious, but their sins are many, and Satan, with his thousand eyes, surveys the world from one end to the other, prying into everyone's life and tempting young and old, worthy and unworthy. Who is there to redeem a sinner if not the Rebbe? Who is there to help, if not the Rebbe? Clearly, he personally had to go to heaven to take care of things—everybody understood that.

But one day a Lithuanian Jew—a stubborn enemy of Hasidism—came into town. And when he heard the story, he laughed. You know how those Lithuanian Jews are: they know the Talmud and nothing else—nothing else exists for them. And Talmud to them means logic. And logically the Tzaddik could not go up into heaven, since Moses himself had to stop ten levels *below* heaven. Now, tell me: what is the use of arguing with Lithuanian logic?!

Still, they did try. They asked the visitor, "And where do you think our Rebbe goes?"

"That is no concern of mine," he answered, shrugging his shoulders, but secretly, he made up his mind to solve the mystery.

When the evening prayers were over, the Litvak slipped into the Rebbe's bedroom and hid under the bed, ready to spend the entire night there to see where the Rebbe went when the others ran to recite the *Selihot* in the synagogue.

Anyone else would have dozed off. But not a Litvak—no! He kept awake by concentrating on a complicated Talmudic passage.

Just before daybreak he heard the beadle as he went from house to house, from door to door, calling out: "*Shtet oiff zu Sliches*—it's late! Get up for *Selihot* services!"

The Rebbe needed no one to wake him; he had been lying in bed moaning for hours. Anyone who ever heard the Rebbe moan knew that the moans expressed all the woes and sufferings of his people; they were enough to make you burst into tears. But a Litvak's heart is as cold as stone. He lay still under the bed listening, while the Rebbe tossed in his bed.

Soon the Litvak heard the house come to life. A few whispers, the splash of water, doors opening and banging shut. Then, with everyone gone, silence reigned again, and all was dark, except for a faint beam of moonlight creeping in through the crack of one of the shutters.

The Litvak admitted afterward that when he was left alone with the Rebbe in the dark and empty house, he was frightened. To be left alone with the Rebbe at dawn, just before *Selihot*— that's nothing to joke about. But a Litvak is a Litvak: obstinate beyond reason. So he lay there, trembling. Waiting.

At last the Rebbe got up. He washed his hands, his face. Then he went over to the closet, pulled out a bundle containing peasant's garments—and put them on.

And dressed like a peasant, the Rebbe left the room—with the Litvak trailing him like a shadow. The Rebbe stopped in the kitchen to pick up an ax, tucked it in his belt, and left the house. Now the Litvak was trembling even more, but he followed the old man nevertheless. His heart was pounding hard as he followed the Rebbe, who was making his way through the silent, unlit streets leading out of town. They came to a forest and the Rebbe kept on walking. After a few minutes, the Rebbe stopped at a young tree. The Litvak was astonished to see the Rebbe pull the ax out of his belt and start chopping away at the tree until he had felled it and split it into logs and kindling. Then he tied the wood into a bundle, threw the bundle over his shoulder, tucked the ax back into his belt and started back into town. At the end of a narrow road, there stood a wretched hut. He knocked at the window.

"Who is there?" a frightened woman's voice came from within.

"It's me," answered the Rebbe with a thick accent, sounding like a peasant.

"Who are you?" asked the woman.

"Vassili," the Rebbe replied.

"Vassili who? What do you want?"

"I've got some wood to sell—cheap, very cheap, almost for nothing. I saw no smoke rising from your chimney so I thought you could use some of my wood."

And, without waiting for an answer, he entered the shack, while the Litvak hovered near the door. And the Litvak saw the inside of the hovel. Under ragged bedclothes, a sick woman was lying helpless.

"Wood?" she said. "You sell wood? I have no money."

"It doesn't matter," said the Rebbe. "I trust you. How much is it anyway? Six coppers? I trust you for six coppers."

"But how will I ever manage to pay you? I'm sick, don't you see how sick I am?"

"Foolish woman," said the Rebbe. "I trust you—why don't you trust God in heaven? Isn't *he* worth six coppers?"

"And who will light the stove for me?" the sick woman groaned. "I am a widow, my son is away at work—do I look like one who has the strength to get up and light a fire?"

"Don't worry," said the Rebbe. "I'll do it."

And, stooping down to put the wood into the stove, he whispered the first *Selihot* prayer. And when the fire caught the kindling, he said the second prayer. And then the third. Then it was time to replace the lid on the stove.

And that's how a Litvak became the Rebbe's most devoted follower. And whenever a Hasid would tell how the Tzaddik of Nemirov would rise early on the solemn days of *Selihot* to ascend straight into heaven, the Litvak no longer sneered but said quietly, "To heaven? If not higher."

This classic Hasidic story, made famous by the great Yiddish writer and poet Y. L. Peretz, was inspired by a short and poignant tale told by the celebrated Master Reb Zvi-Hersh of Zhidachov.

But in *his* version the hero is not an anonymous Tzaddik of Nemirov but the legendary Reb Moshe-Leib of Sassov, protector of the poor and defender of the hungry, the woman is not Jewish but Christian, and the action takes place on a winter night, not before *Selihot*. Also, the man who surreptitiously follows the Rebbe is not a Litvak but another Rebbe—Reb Zvi-Hersh himself. As for the rest, the story is the same—as is the moral of the story: to help a poor old widow is more important than to ascend into heaven through prayer.

This is the very substance of Hasidism. The holy man must not necessarily look holy; he may appear as a peasant, a wanderer, a worker, a merchant. He must not necessarily stay within the covers of the Talmud, the Zohar, or the prayer book; he may—and indeed should—leave his house, leave his shelter, leave his study and his work, and go into the forest, and perhaps chop wood in order to come closer to God.

This concept of humanism—meaning, of absolute commitment to compassion and human warmth—nowhere attained a higher degree of realization than in Sassov. If Reb Moshe-Leib takes care of a sick woman, it is not to attract her to the Hasidic movement, but to give her faith in her fellow man; if the Master disguises himself as a peasant, it is to impress upon her that one need not be a Rebbe to be charitable. In Sassov, what matters is compassion.

Sassov—who doesn't know Sassov? The chroniclers of Hasidic geography have ranked Sassov among the foremost capitals of the Beshtian kingdom. And yet, like Medzibozh, like Kotzk, like Bratzlav, it was, and is, nothing but a village. Were it not for Reb Moshe-Leib, nobody would know its name.

Sassov is in the Ukraine—not far from Lvov. The first Jews settled there in the sixteenth century. In 1726, they obtained special privileges from Jacob Sobieski, son of King Sigismund III of Poland; their communal and religious institutions were all declared tax-exempt.

In 1939 the community numbered 1,500 souls. All perished in Belzec and Zlotchov. Today, Sassov looks like all Jewish small towns used to look. Only there are no more Jews. Except for Rebbe Moshe-Leib, whose memory remains linked to Sassov.

Who was he? Here, I must confess, my attitude toward him has undergone several radical changes. When I first discovered him, I was happy to have found a Rebbe who was . . . happy. I mean, really happy, totally happy with his lot. In him, I said to myself, I had found, at last, one great Master who was not involved in messianic conspiracies like the Seer of Lublin, who did not repress anguish like the Rebbe of Berditchev, who was not engaged in endless battles against despair, one who had not succumbed to melancholy like the Rebbe of Kotzk. Reb Moshe-Leib seemed to me full of true joy. His joy was neither subterfuge nor pretext nor vehicle—it was an end in itself. And I was grateful.

Later, I became . . . annoyed. The very serenity that had appealed to me earlier began to disturb me. How could he? I wondered. How could he—the Master and friend of his followers—be happy when they were not? Could he have been blind to their woes? Could he have been that insensitive, that self-centered?

Then came the third stage. As I went over the texts and testimonies again and again I recognized my error: Rebbe Moshe-Leib, who seems so carefree and at peace with himself, was neither. And I began to love him.

A tale:

When Rebbe Moshe-Leib decided to go and study with Rebbe Elimelekh, he walked all the way from Sassov to Lizensk. Penniless and hungry, he refused to beg. If God wants me to eat, he said to himself, let Him worry about food; and if He doesn't want me to eat—how can I go against His will? His logic was perfect but his stomach remained empty. A day passed, then another. On the third day he decided that something was wrong: If God doesn't want me to eat, that means that He doesn't love me—but . . . if He doesn't love me, how can I love Him?

Then he went one step further: How do I know that He doesn't love me? Only because He doesn't feed me? Is food *that* important? If it were, I would be no better than an animal. Animals are hungry and I am hungry. The difference? *I* can endure, they cannot. You see, Moshe-Leib, he said to himself, hunger is more important than food. Think of all the overfed, overnourished princes and leaders who can eat and eat, and eat until the end of their lives—are they happy? No, they are not. They are not happy because they are not hungry. But you are, Moshe-Leib. As hungry as a lion—so what are you complaining about? Thank God for your hunger! Louder, Moshe-Leib! You have a strong voice, shout! Tell God how *grateful* you are—and not only how hungry you are.

And he did. And with his powerful voice, he shook the forest . . . and the heavens.

·   ·   ·

This episode reveals much about him. We learn that he loved to walk and shout, and to be in love . . . with God. That he was physically strong, that he sought fervor and attained it. We also learn that more frequently than not he was hungry and destitute. And—lastly—that he knew much about gratitude.

All these are essential elements in Hasidism. Most Masters taught their followers the necessity and the art of turning sadness into joy, evil into good and despair into hope. Instead of fighting melancholy, you must transform it into joy, into ecstasy.

Thus sadness, as point of departure, may be stimulating—but it must never become an end unto itself. And hunger may, for a while, be stimulating—provided it is your own, not your fellow man's.

And never to be hungry at all is also a curse. Said Rebbe Pinhas of Koretz: Rather than possess what I desire, I prefer to desire what I possess. And Reb Mendel of Kotzk, echoing Reb Moshe-Leib's words, said: For having seduced Eve, the serpent was sentenced to forever crawl in, and eat, dust. What kind of punishment is that? asked the Master of Kotzk. Condemned to eat dust, the serpent would never be hungry—is that a punishment? Yes, answered the Kotzker. That is the worst punishment of all: never to be hungry, never to seek, never to desire anything.

Now—who was this peculiar Rebbe from Sassov? We know that he was born in 1744 in Brody—a city famous for its scholars and its fairs, and also for the connections the Baal Shem Tov had established there before his revelation. We know that he was learned in Talmud and Kabbala. That his parents were neither poor nor rich. That he married, probably twice, and had at least one daughter, Temerl, perhaps more—and at least two sons. And that he died in 1807 in Sassov.

He never met the Besht—and this is difficult to understand. When the Besht died, Reb Moshe-Leib was sixteen. Surely he must have heard about the great teacher and his new way of life. Why then did he not try to meet him? Or his successor, the great Maggid of Mezeritch? Instead, he became a follower of the Maggid's disciple, Reb Shmelke of Nikolsburg. By then he must have been in his early twenties. Why did he wait so long?

One reason—the most obvious one—has to do with his father's fanatic opposition to Hasidism. Martin Buber retells a curious legend: Young Moshe-Leib ran away from home to join Reb Shmelke, whereupon his father, Reb Yakov, became so enraged that he put aside a special whip for the day when his son would return. Misplaced—accidentally or by design—by a servant, the whip wasn't there when the day arrived. Reb Yakov became even more enraged: his son had returned and he could not even punish him! As for the son, he could not bear the sight of his father's frustration, so he went himself to look for the whip, found it and brought it to his father. At that moment, the father broke down, made up with his son *and* with Hasidism.

The story seems implausible, improbable. While that is true of many Hasidic stories, it is even more true of this one. It would make sense if the Master in the story were the Besht. But Reb Shmelke? Also, by then, Reb Moshe-Leib was no longer a child. Can you imagine his father punishing him with a whip? But what does it matter? As long as the story ends well, all is well. The father lost his anger and Hasidism gained a follower.

I think that Reb Moshe-Leib had a different reason for going to Nikolsburg. He was attracted to Reb Shmelke not as a Hasid but as a student. Reb Shmelke was considered one of the Talmudic giants of his time, and the best students flocked to his Yeshiva from all over the country.

That is why he went to him rather than to the Maggid of Mezeritch. Like Reb Shmelke, and the Maggid himself, he began as scholar and became Hasid only later.

He studied in Apta, Nikolsburg and Lizensk. At the court of Rebbe Elimelekh he was involved in an incident whose true nature has never been revealed. Some sources claim that the old Rebbe Elimelekh resented the young disciple's self-assurance. For example, Rebbe Elimelekh, in his discourse, would raise some scholarly question; and instead of waiting for the teacher to come forth with an appropriate answer, Moshe-Leib would rush in to offer his own. When this happened, Rebbe Elimelekh, Master of Masters and founder of a school, understandably would be miffed.

Moshe-Leib sought questions, he believed in them, but in his own way: first he had to find the answers. To his disciple, the holy Jew of Pshiskhe, he made the point that Maimonides, too, in his book *Guide for the Perplexed*, raises disturbing questions and offers reassuring answers; and that what people don't know is that he wrote the answers first; then and only then did he fill in the questions.

Another version of the incident in Lizensk: Reb Elimelekh became angry when the young disciple interrupted him in the middle of a sentence—but why was Reb Moshe-Leib so disrespectful? Because, says this more magnanimous commentator, Reb Elimelekh was saying something negative about someone —perhaps someone from the dissident school in Pshiskhe?— and Reb Moshe-Leib could not and would not listen to anything derogatory about *any* Jew.

His son once remarked: "My father was lucky that the Torah does not command us to say evil things about our fellow man— for if there existed such a law, my father surely would have transgressed it."

Another biographical anecdote:

In his youth, Reb Moshe-Leib associated with boys his own age, which was natural, except that they spent their energy not on Torah but on seeking pleasure. He would leave the House of Study in the evening and join them in taverns of ill-repute, and stay with them until the early morning hours. But, warns Hasidic legend, do not jump to conclusions: his sole purpose was to save them all.

In fact, continues the legend, many, many years later, when he was already a celebrated Master in the Hasidic kingdom, one of his former companions came to Sassov out of sheer curiosity; he was eager to see who this Rebbe was who could attract so many followers. He recognized Moshe-Leib immediately and remembered the good times they had had together. What an actor, he thought, he manages to fool all these people. They don't know what we used to do—and where—once upon a time. But then, something happened to him. Watching and listening to Reb Moshe-Leib, he realized his mistake: Moshe-Leib had indeed fooled him, and his former associates, not *now*, but *then*. When he and the others were young and foolish and sinners, Moshe-Leib had already been a Tzaddik, a Just Man, in disguise, a hidden Rebbe, who had wanted to help them, to keep them from further degradation.

Another strange story: While studying under Reb Shmelke in Nikolsburg, Reb Moshe-Leib overheard a poor man talking to his friend about his miseries. He had a daughter who was an old maid; not only was she not beautiful, she was also not intelligent—actually the man used simpler and harsher expressions: she was ugly and stupid. No wonder no one wanted to come near her. No wonder that he, her father, was heartbroken. Reb Moshe-Leib, deeply affected by the man's woes, felt he had to do something. He sent for the local matchmaker and said to him, "Go tell this man that I would like very much to marry his daughter." The matchmaker tried to discourage him—in vain. Then he went to see the girl's father, who at first thought Reb Moshe-Leib was making fun of him. No, Reb Moshe-Leib was serious. A marriage contract was arranged, duly signed—and the wedding took place soon after. Only then did Reb Yakov, Reb Moshe-Leib's father, hear about it. He came running to Nikolsburg, quarreled endlessly with his son and finally managed to persuade him to divorce his wife.

This anecdote rings true—or at least it does contain an element of authenticity. Reb Moshe-Leib was known for his quick impulses when someone else's suffering was involved. Even so —very little is known about that first marriage. Nor about his second one. He spent little time at home, wandering from Master to Master, from fair to fair, seeking opportunities to be helpful to any and all who needed help.

Remarried, he continued his studies. His father-in-law, a merchant and a practical man, was not pleased. He admonished Reb Moshe-Leib: "You cannot live from Torah alone—you must provide for yourself and your family." He gave him some money and sent him to a fair in the next town. Of course, Moshe-Leib chose to go to the local House of Study. That evening, when he returned home, his children greeted him, shouting: "Papa, Papa, what did you bring?" He fainted. Later, he explained: "Suddenly I told myself that one day, upon arrival in the other world, I would be asked the same question: 'Moshe-Leib, Moshe-Leib, what did you bring us?' " Never again did his father-in-law send him to the fair.

His philosophy? He had none. All he desired was to be able to bring joy to the wretched, the poor, the orphans, the widows, the oppressed—and some measure of hope to those who were deprived of hope. How did he go about it? Not through emissaries or go-betweens; he himself went everywhere. He kept informed of all the sick children, all the unfortunate creatures in his region; he visited them all, comforted them all, shared their sorrow and their pain if he could do nothing more. For instance: the Rebbe had a list of all the poor and lonely widows in Sassov, and would go every morning simply to say "Good morning" to every one of them. Often, he could be seen hugging and kissing Christian children because they were sick or sad, or simply because they needed comforting.

Do you wish to know, asked Reb Moshe-Leib of Sassov, whether whatever you are doing is right? Ask yourself whether it brings you closer to man. If it does not, then you are heading in the wrong direction—you are moving away from God. For even the love of God must be measured in human terms. One must love God *and* man and never act against man or without man—such was Hasidism as practiced in Sassov.

"In the beginning God created heaven and earth." What does that mean? In the beginning, said Reb Moshe-Leib of Sassov, man must know that all is God's creation, all men are His and all that they possess—or wish to possess—is His. How can He love them if they do not love one another?

Here is what happened one Yom Kippur eve:

The House of Study was packed with worshippers ready to intone the solemn and awe-inspiring prayer of Kol Nidre, but the Rebbe was late. Where, but where could he be? What could be more important than to lead the holy community of Sassov into prayer—the most magnificent prayer of all? Curiosity turned into worry and then into fear: what could have happened to their Tzaddik? And what if Satan, in his cruelty, had succeeded in hurting his powerful opponent? Minutes went by, long endless minutes. The sun had almost set. Soon the time for this prayer would be over; it would be too late.

There was a woman among the worshippers who was worried about her infant: she had left him home all alone, thinking she would be back in an hour, immediately after Kol Nidre—and now, more than an hour had gone by. So she decided not to wait but to go home to her child.

To her surprise she found that her infant was not alone. A man was cradling her child, singing to him softly. Said the Rebbe, "What could I do? As I walked past your house I heard a child crying—I had to stay with him."

He had an exquisite sense of humor.

He was once seen giving away his last coins to a drunkard, who, of course, headed straight toward the next inn for another drink.

"Why aren't you more discerning?" someone asked the Rebbe. "You give charity—that's understandable. But why waste your money on a drunkard?"

"God gave *me* money, didn't He?" answered Reb Moshe-Leib. "Why should I be choosier than He?"

He once remarked: "It is easier for a poor man to have faith than for a rich man. The poor man has nothing, so he must rely on faith; but the rich man does have other things—he doesn't need faith, or, at least that's what *he* thinks: so who is the poorer of the two?"

"When I present myself before the heavenly tribunal, he once said, I shall ask to go to hell. After all, who is in paradise? The learned, the saints, the pious—and they don't need me."

On another occasion he added, "Should I end up in hell, I swear that I shall not leave it unless I bring everyone else along with me. And I shall say, All my life I tried to free prisoners— why shouldn't I do it here too?"

Mingling with common people, involved in their day-to-day problems, Reb Moshe-Leib wanted to be their friend more than their teacher. And he was. He spoke to the people in Yiddish, Polish, Hungarian; he understood them all.

His favorite area of activity was not the synagogue but the various markets, where he was a familiar figure. He felt he was more needed there, he could accomplish more. He would speak to forlorn villagers who had come to sell or buy—or simply to look around and *be* among people. When they were too busy to listen to him, he took care of their horses. So humble was he that when some coachman mistook him for a servant, he obeyed his orders instead of protesting.

Like the Besht, but unlike the great Maggid of Mezeritch, he was forever on the move, going from village to village, from tavern to tavern, seeking out broken hearts and wounded souls, jailed innkeepers and faceless wanderers: he wanted to be their brother. And he was.

But how can you absorb so much pain? he was asked. How can you take in so much suffering from so many people? And he answered, If their pain is only *theirs*, then my work and my life are wasted. Their pain is also mine—so why shouldn't I try to alleviate it?

In the name of *Ahavat-Israel* he felt compelled to deal with the issue of human suffering in the most personal manner possible.

But what *is* Ahavat-Israel? What *is* love? Said Reb Moshe-

ELIE WIESEL

Leib of Sassov: "I feel I ought to tell the truth and confess that
I learned its meaning from two drunkards. Yes, drunkards. I
saw them sitting in an inn, drinking—and drinking silently. But
from time to time they would stop for a brief exchange. 'Are
you my friend, Alexei?' asked the younger one. 'Do you love
me?' 'Yes, Ivan, I do. I am your friend.' They emptied another
glass and dreamed their separate dreams in silence. Again the
younger peasant turned to his companion: 'Alexei, Alexei, are
you really my friend? Do you truly love me?' 'Yes, I am your
friend,' said the older peasant. They emptied another glass and
another hour went by in silence. Again the younger peasant
spoke up: 'Tell me, Alexei, tell me the truth; are we friends? Do
you love me as a friend?' Finally, Alexei got angry. 'How many
times must I tell you, Ivan, that I do?! Don't you believe me?
Are you drunk? You are my friend and I am yours; and my
heart is full of brotherly love for you. Must I go on repeating it
all night?' At that point, Ivan looked at Alexei and shook his
head sadly. 'Alexei, Alexei,' he said, 'if you *are* my friend, if
you *do* love me, then how come you don't know what is hurting
me?' "

The moral of the story? Truth can be found everywhere, even
on the lips of drunkards, in the noisiest of taverns. Only it is
preferable to have studied first. Had Reb Moshe-Leib spent all
his time in taverns, he would have become not a Master but a
drunkard. Simplicity is an art; to acquire it is not simple. You
must first learn many complex and obscure lessons; only then
can you master simplicity. The peasant and the poet utter the
same words; but their meaning is not the same, for their experience has not been the same; and their silence is not the same.

Another lesson: Learn to listen. Learn to care. Learn to be
concerned, to be involved. The opposite of love is not hate but
indifference; the opposite of life is not death but insensitivity.
Ivan was right: if Alexei did not know what was hurting him, he
could not really have been his friend.

Reb Moshe-Leib learned even from thieves. Here is a story
he told. "One day," he said, "I was desperate. I needed money

108

—I needed it badly to ransom a Jewish innkeeper from jail. I knocked at innumerable doors, I pleaded with countless merchants—in vain. So I decided to give up and go home.

"As I was ready to leave, I was informed that a Jewish thief had been arrested and jailed. I ran to see him. He had been beaten so badly, his ribs were broken. He was in terrible pain. I recognized him. 'Why did you do it?' I asked. 'I mean; why did you do it again? Last time, you were caught and beaten—why did you start all over again?' 'I'll tell you: I needed the money.' 'And now? Will you stop at last?' 'No,' said the thief. 'I'll try again, and again—until I succeed. . . .' Well," said Reb Moshe-Leib, "if a thief has the strength to go on trying—why shouldn't I?"

Listen to another of my favorite stories:

Rebbe Uri, the celebrated Seraphin of Strelisk, needed money to marry off an old maid, orphan to boot. Where could he go? To people who had money. The problem was, he didn't know any; he knew only people who needed money—for themselves or for others. One of them was his friend Reb Moshe-Leib of Sassov, who also was running around the country collecting funds for beggars. He went to see him. At first, the two remained quiet for several hours, reflecting. Then Reb Moshe-Leib turned to his friend and said, "Uri, my friend, I wish I could help you with money but I have none. Still, there is something I can do for you: I shall dance for you." And he danced for his friend all night. Next morning, after prayers, he told his friend: "I must go. Wait for me." He left and returned two days later, with a considerable sum of money. "Let me tell you what happened," he said. "Years ago, I came into a strange city and was lucky enough to find a young boy who consented to be my guide. In return I promised him that I would come and dance at his wedding. Passing through Zlotchov after I left you, I heard music and singing. There was a wedding going on. Though I was not invited, I went closer—and recognized the bridegroom. I remembered my promise and kept it: I danced for the young couple and did my best to give them joy. When they heard my story—your story, Uri—they felt sorry for the poor old maid and they and their guests opened their hearts and their pockets. Here is the money, Uri, go and tell the girl that now it is her turn to rejoice."

Concluded Reb Moshe-Leib, "When somebody asks something impossible of me, I know what I must do: I must dance."

From the encounter of the two Rebbes we thus learn that there is always *something* one can do for one's friends. What is Hasidism if not the belief that man must have faith in God *and* in people? You suffer? Pray to God but speak to your friend.

Remember the disciple who complained to the angry Master of Kotzk: "Look, Rebbe! God created the universe in six days —and it's ugly!" "Would you have done better?" snapped Reb Mendel. "Eh, I think so," stammered the forlorn disciple. "Yes?" shouted the Kotzker Rebbe. "Then what are you waiting for? Start working—right now!"

When it comes to helping someone in need, do not rely on prayer alone. Let the person in need pray, not you, your task is to help.

Said Rebbe Moshe-Leib of Sassov: We are told that the holy spark exists in all things—even in evil. Even in *apikorsut,* in atheism? What holiness can we ascribe to *apikorsut?* Imagine, explained Reb Moshe-Leib, a beggar meeting a wealthy man and asking for a contribution. "I wish I could meet all your expectations," says the wealthy man. "But I cannot—and I shall tell you why. You are, after all, entitled to an explanation. I cannot help you because I believe in God and in His justice. If He had wanted you to have my money, He would have given it to you, not to me. Why do you expect me to oppose God's will?" Well, said Reb Moshe-Leib, when it comes to charity, be an *apikores*, do not use God as an excuse; help those who need help. If nothing else, pray with them; dance for them. There is always a way. And if there is none, invent one. If you accept the challenge, you will succeed.

When the legendary Reb Levi-Yitzhak of Berditchev fell ill, he wrote an urgent plea to his friend Reb Moshe-Leib of

Sassov, asking that he keep him in his thoughts as he danced in honor of Shabbat. And because this was a special case, Reb Moshe-Leib wore special shoes that particular Shabbat. Witnesses later said that they had never seen him dance with such concentration—with such fervor.

Isn't all this rather simplistic? Is *this* the message of Hasidism? One dances, one sings, one tells a story—and one collects charity?

And here, I admit that one could feel irritated with our hero Reb Moshe-Leib. What made him so great? So he was a good dancer and an occasional baby sitter. So he fraternized with Masters and coachmen alike, and was at ease with both. I am troubled. He was too good, too kind, too perfect. He never lost his temper, never became annoyed or upset. Forever loving, forever caring, forever giving—is such behavior . . . human?

Other Masters became involved in messianic conspiracies and mystical struggles—what about him? They were tempted by despair—what about him? They confronted melancholy—what about him? They had problems, conflicts, crises—what about *his* conflicts, his crises?

My problem with Reb Moshe-Leib was that most tales about him—or by him—stress his joy, his warmth, his ecstasy; he seemed threatened by nothing, hurt by no one. Forever serene, at peace with himself and the world, forever singing and dancing and consoling and rejoicing—how could one not be disturbed by him?

Then I found a clue which made me revise my perception of the man. Perhaps he was not really as monolithic as he appeared. He too may well have been haunted by shadows but just didn't show it.

I came across a saying of his which startled me. *Ashre hagever asher teyasrenu ka,* says the Psalmist. "Happy is the man who is chastised by God." Reb Moshe-Leib translated it differently: Happy is the man who is chastising God, who is questioning him, and taking him to task for not fulfilling His obligations toward His people.

What? He too had quarrels with God—the God of love, the

God of mercy? He too thought that the Creator was too severe with His creation? He too, like the Berditchever, turned his prayer into an argument with the Almighty?

Strange—it was out of character. But . . .

Then I found another clue:

Said the Tzaddik of Lentzne: "Reb Moshe-Leib is a true miracle-maker for he *is* a miracle; his heart is at the same time entirely broken—and entirely whole."

He was sad but few people knew it. He was so busy creating joy around him that nobody noticed the sadness within him.

Like most great Masters, he too carried a secret within himself. He would often meditate for hours—in total silence. Tears would flow from his eyes, his lips would move soundlessly, and he would be transported into another world.

His son Rebbe Shmelke tells of a childhood memory. He was five and went with his father to the Rosh Hashana services. "I hid under his *tallit*," said Reb Shmelke. "And I heard him speak to the Almighty in Yiddish: 'Master of the Universe—we have been praying and praying, waiting and waiting, and redemption has not come. Why not? We can bear it no more, Master of the Universe. Do you hear me? We have reached the end.' "

A neighbor of his endured one tragic loss after another. All his children died in the year of their birth. Their mother one day asked Reb Moshe-Leib's wife, "Rebbetzin, what kind of God is our God? He is not merciful but cruel; He takes back what He has given." "Don't say that," answered the Rebbetzin, trying to console her. "One must submit to His laws, one must say, His ways are inscrutable but just." At that point Reb Moshe-Leib, who had heard the conversation from his study, appeared at the door and told the grief-stricken mother: "And I am telling you *not* to accept His ways. My advice to you is to shout, to scream, to protest—do you understand me, woman? I want you to protest. . . ."

. . .

Yes—there seems to have been another dimension to his personality. He too had obstacles to overcome, memories to cope with. His submission was not uninterrupted; his exuberance covered multiple layers of melancholy.

He too wanted to be alone. "A man who does not keep an hour a day for himself is not human," he once remarked. To be involved with other people's lives can become too absorbing: in order to give, man must *be*; and man's being is rooted in solitude. Yes—he too needed to be alone when he addressed God as defender of his people, and when he had to reveal his anguish to God, to God alone.

One of his remarks shows insights that later were to characterize the school of Pshiskhe. "What is life?" he once asked. "It is like walking on the razor's edge. On the one side there is the abyss—and on the other side as well. Yet you continue walking."

And what happened to other great Masters also happened to Reb Moshe-Leib. He too saw the abyss—and he too transcended his own fear, his own pain, and put them in the service of others. He too continued to walk.

Toward the end of his life, he had two friends who never left his side; they were jesters. And when his sadness became unbearable, they would tell him funny stories to make him laugh —and then his laughter became unbearable.

At fifty-nine he fell ill. His physicians gave up all hope, and he knew it. His pain became more and more violent, excruciating. But he never complained. All he kept on saying was "I do not wish to stop the suffering—that is impossible—I only wish to suffer *for* the people of Israel." Not instead of, but for.

A strange yet characteristic incident took place at his funeral. A band of musicians in a carriage appeared out of nowhere at the cemetery; they sat there looking bewildered. The coachman explained, "We don't know what happened. We were on our way to a wedding in Brody; suddenly the horses became wild and began running, running—and here we are. Whose funeral is this?" Among the musicians there was an old man who then cried out, "What? Reb Moshe-Leib of Sassov? He died? Now I understand . . . years ago, we were at the wedding of two orphans whom he had brought together. He danced and we played—and he loved our melodies. He loved them so much that he said, 'I would like this *Niggun* to be played at my funeral.' So what are we waiting for, friends? Let us accompany the great Tzaddik with his *Niggun*—let us play, with more fervor, and more and more. . . ."

Before we leave Sassov, let us take a minute to ask ourselves these last questions: Was Reb Moshe-Leib the forerunner of all those helpless men and women who, generations later, eternities later, continued to sing and rejoice even in the ghettos? Even in the kingdom of night? Even as they went into darkness? Was their *Ani Maamin*, their faith in the coming of the Messiah, a reverberation of his? Is joy possible—is faith possible—is hope permissible—when death is sovereign? Is joy the answer? Is memory the answer? Is there an answer?

How did Reb Moshe-Leib of Sassov, the symbol of compassion and love in Hasidism, put it? "You who wish to find the fire, look for it in the ashes."

THE HOLY SEER
OF LUBLIN

THIS IS ONE of the most mysterious and troubling episodes in Hasidic literature—an episode that chroniclers and storytellers are still reluctant to explain, or even explore.

The year: 1814.

The place: Lublin. Inside the House of Study, Hasidim—old and young, students and peasants, innkeepers and travelers—participate in the traditional ceremony of rejoicing with the Torah.

They have come in the hundreds, and more, from beyond mountains and rivers; they have crossed many borders and overcome many obstacles to be here tonight.

Never have there been such crowds or such fervor. With their old Master, the holy Seer of Lublin in their midst, the weak forget their weakness, the old make light of their age. Tonight the poor are less poor, the sick forget their illnesses. Tonight all worries are forbidden.

Surrounding their Master, people sing and dance with frenzy. Like him, with him, they lift the Holy Scrolls higher and higher, as if to follow them—and follow *him*—and they do. He carries them away, far away. They trust him. No matter that they do not know the outcome or even the purpose of his secret plan. *He* does, and that should be enough, and it is. What matters is to be present. Hasn't he taught them that passion succeeds where reason fails? Tonight they are consumed by passion.

They all feel it now: this celebration is unlike any other. Every word reverberates in higher spheres, every impulse is echoed in invisible palaces up there in heaven, where Israel's fate is being determined—and mankind's too.

Just before the holiday the Seer had dispatched emissaries to friends and disciples, urging them to mark this Simhat Torah with particular emphasis. "I have one favor to ask of you," he told his old friend Reb Israel, the Maggid of Kozhenitz. "Rejoice on this festive event, let yourself go, let your soul soar."

And to his own community, gathered from all over his kingdom, he repeated over and over again, "Drink and celebrate—it's an order. And if your ecstasy is pure enough, contagious enough, it will last forever—I promise you that."

In spite of his age and his fatigue, he himself leads the assembly with astonishing vigor. It's as though his intention is to move the entire creation from darkness to redemption.

Yes, now it's clear to everyone: this holiday is destined to be special; man's future hinges upon it. Let Israel attain perfection through joy—and man will know no more anguish.

"*Sissou vesimkhou besimkhat Torah,*" orders the Master. And the Hasidim obey. They let go of their senses until they see nothing and nobody. And they fail to notice when the Master suddenly breaks away from the crowd and moves slowly, quietly, toward the door. Still unnoticed, he opens it, and retires into his private study. He stays there all alone, while down below, on *his* orders, the happy, exuberant Hasidim continue to celebrate.

No one knows what he did there—no one knows what really happened to him then. All we know is that at one point the Rebbetzin heard strange noises coming from the Seer's study—sounds like those of a child weeping. She rushed into the room and shrieked with fear. The room was empty.

Down below, they heard the scream. And for a second they remained frozen in silence. Then they heard the Rebbetzin crying, "He told me to keep an eye on him—now he is gone, gone. He has been taken away."

Taken away? By whom? Why? Where? The Rebbetzin didn't know. She claimed to have seen monstrously large hands pulling the Rebbe out the window—that was all.

Those who were there will never forget that night. Everyone ran into the street. The night was dark, opaque. Minutes went by. Nothing. The Rebbe? Swallowed by darkness.

Hours went by. Still nothing.

Suddenly, fifty feet away from the House of Study, a certain Reb Eliezer of Khmelnik heard a weak moaning in the shadows. Approaching, he saw a man lying on the ground, twisting with pain. "Who are you?" asked Reb Eliezer.

"Yaakov-Yitzhak, son of Meitil," whispered the man.

Reb Eliezer called out for help. The older Hasidim quickly conferred about who should carry their stricken Master—and how. Reb Shmuel of Karov held his head and heard him softly intone ancient poignant lamentations, repeating the words "And the abyss calls for another abyss."

Thus ended, prematurely, tragically, a memorable celebration which was meant to last beyond the night. Having put their Master to bed, the Hasidim, silent and distraught, returned to the House of Study. Defeated.

What had happened? Who had done what to the old Seer of Lublin? And what had *he* done . . . to whom? To himself? No one knows—no one will ever know.

Hasidic literature has shrouded this disturbing episode in secrecy. It is considered almost taboo. A strange conspiracy of silence has surrounded it ever since it took place.

Some sources refer to it cryptically as the Great Fall—*Hane-fila Hagdola*—without entering into details. Usually they add the expression *kayadoua*—"as everybody knows." And, as usual, it means the opposite. Whenever Hasidic texts say *kaya-doua*, it means that nobody knows. Or that nobody is supposed to know.

Most sources indicate that the Great Fall had important

metaphysical or mystical implications. Why the Fall? Had the old Master *fallen* from his second-floor window? The window, according to testimony, was too narrow for a man his size to pass through. And also, empty bottles were left standing intact on the sill.

So the feeling persisted that the accident had some connection with the supernatural. Perhaps the work—or the vengeance—of Satan, who surely resented the holy Seer's messianic experiments, which no one may conduct with impunity.

At this time, as we shall see, the Rebbe of Lublin had been involved in perilous activities, trying to use Napoleon's wars to precipitate events—and he was punished. That was the general belief. Seeking and failing to achieve cosmic salvation, the Rebbe's quest had ended in personal catastrophe. The fact is that he never recovered. He stayed in bed for forty-four weeks. When he died, the entire Hasidic world went into mourning.

For he was one of its most dazzling and most secretive figures. His impact was felt throughout its communities from Galicia to the Ukraine. Some of the greatest Masters had been his disciples. How many? Some say sixty. Others, one hundred and twenty; and still others, four hundred. What does it matter? Hasidism is better known for its boundless fantasy than for its accuracy. All agree that Lublin was one of the most dynamic centers of the Hasidic movement.

Said Rebbe Naphtali of Ropshitz: "The holy Seer is dead—and the world goes on? I don't understand."

Said Rebbe Moshe of Ujhely: "Our Master possessed all the qualities and virtues of the Prophet Isaiah—except that he did not dwell in the Holy Land."

Uri, the Seraphin of Strelisk, remarked, "Lublin *was* the Holy Land: our Master's court was Jerusalem; his House of Study, the Temple; his private study, the sanctuary; and in his voice, the heavenly voice could be heard."

And Rebbe Zvi-Hersh of Zhidachov said: "As long as our holy Master was alive, we would gather around him and place our arms on each other's shoulders, and thus we were able to reach heaven. Now, with him gone, we have no longer the strength to look up. Even our dreams have changed."

In order to understand Lublin and its messianic currents and undercurrents, we must look at the setting. Before we investigate the accident, we must get acquainted with the victim—and his times.

We are at the beginning of the nineteenth century. Nations wage wars and man is their eternal victim. Europe is upside down, churning in blood and fury. The era of Enlightenment has brought forth its own myths, its own prisons, its own darkness. Wars, wars, more wars. Frontiers, systems, loyalties come and go. The earth trembles. Priests change their style, kings lose their thrones, and sometimes even their heads, paving the way for other kings, other kinds of kings.

Napoleon has reached the Holy Land, has invaded Russia, and he dreams of world domination. Military conquest does not satisfy him; wherever his armies appear, they bring emancipation. But is this good for Jews? Or not?

In Eastern Europe, opinions are divided. Persecuted by fanatic Russian and Polish Jew-haters, the Jews feel just as threatened by Austrian liberals. They must opt for either spiritual or physical safety—the two seem to be incompatible.

Rebbe Shneur-Zalman of Lyady, the eminent Hasidic thinker and teacher, says: "I prefer Czar Alexander; under his rule, we suffer—but we remain united and unblemished as Jews. Under Napoleon, it will be the opposite."

Reb Mendel of Riminov, on the other hand, favors Napoleon, in whom he sees the incarnation of the legendary Gog and Magog, who will be defeated by the Messiah. But first he must be victorious. So some opponents and skeptics say that Napoleon's *second* military headquarters, headed by Reb Mendel, are in Riminov.

In the Hasidic universe, everyone's mind is set on the messianic dimension of the apocalyptic events. All these defeats and victories succeeding one another . . . all this blood being shed.

Clearly, the end of the world is near. So why not take the initiative and hasten it? It could save Jewish lives; in fact, nothing else could save them. The Jews need the Messiah as never before. Since he is so near, why wait for him? Why not run *to* him?

Moreover, the times seemed ripe. The wars. The total upheavals. The *Chevlei Mashiah*: the pangs of messianic birth. All the symptoms, all the signs were there. That is why the three conspirators—Reb Mendel of Riminov, the Maggid of Kozhenitz, and the Seer of Lublin—worked on their plan so feverishly. They met secretly to compare notes and coordinate their activities. Often the Seer disappeared from Lublin, and no one would know where he had gone. In fact, he regularly went to Kozhenitz or to Riminov—for strategy sessions. They really believed that with their *kavanot* and *yikhudim*, with their words and deeds, they could influence events and developments on the battlefield.

Said Reb Mendel of Riminov: "Let the blood flow from Pristik to Riminov—as long as it means that redemption is imminent."

One Kol Nidre evening the Maggid of Kozhenitz opened the Holy Ark and exclaimed: "*Ribono shel olam*, Master of the Universe, please say *salakhti kidvarekha*—say that you have forgiven our sins. And send us the Redeemer. If you need a Tzaddik, Reb Mendel of Riminov is one. If you need a Prophet, the Seer of Lublin is one. If you need a penitent, I, Israel, son of Sarah of Kozhenitz, proclaim here and now that I am ready for sacrifice in the name of the living community of Israel."

What, then, went wrong? Why hadn't the Messiah come? The three Masters, and their friends and allies, could not agree on tactics. That's why. Had they all supported Napoleon, he would have conquered the world, only to hand it over to the Messiah. The trouble was that except for Reb Mendel of Riminov, no one gave the French Emperor unqualified support. Legend has it that Napoleon knew this and came clandestinely to plead with the Maggid of Kozhenitz to win him over completely. He failed —and lost the war.

Another legend claims that one of the Seer's sons served in the Austrian army. Somehow—who knows how?—he was introduced to Napoleon at a military parade. And the Emperor told him, "Tell your father that I am not afraid of him." Such insolence could only lead to—Waterloo.

After Waterloo, following the Seer's plea, the three conspirators decided on Simhat Torah to make one last attempt to bring the Messiah. Again, had they rejoiced on that holiday, as only they could rejoice, the event might have occurred. But —*lo ikhshar dara*—the generation wasn't ready. The Maggid of Kozhenitz died a week before Simhat Torah, on the eve of Succoth, and the Seer had his famous Great Fall.

The accident caused great joy among his opponents, the Mitnagdim. But the Seer remarked, "They are silly to overdo it. I can assure them that when I die, they will not be able to drink to the occasion—not even a glass of water." Sure enough, he died on the ninth day of Av, which is a day of mourning and fasting. Even for Mitnagdim.

Who *was* the Seer?

From personal testimonies and recollections of disciples and followers, we possess enough material to piece together his biography and his portrait.

We know that Rebbe Yaakov-Yitzhak Horowitz was born in 1745 in a village near Tarnigrod in Poland. He grew up in the home of his grandfather, Reb Kopel, in Yusepov.

Three times married, he was the father of four sons and a daughter—and the author of three important books of commentaries.

Having had a solitary childhood, he was attracted to the young and vibrant Hasidic movement, first as disciple and then as Master. He settled in Lublin around 1800. Active in Jewish politics of the times, he fought unsuccessfully for the emancipation of the Jews, but successfully against their induction into military service.

Though founder of a school, he established no dynasty of his own. His disciples became leaders in their own right.

Tall, robust, tense, extremely perceptive, eloquent, he was unquestionably charismatic; he seemed always to be the center of any gathering. He radiated wisdom, beauty and authority. He rarely said "I"—rather, he said "We." He rarely ate in public. There was an aura of royalty surrounding him.

In his presence, one felt shaken, purified . . . transformed. What struck people most were his eyes—one larger than the other—which often took on a disquieting fixity when looking at someone. Hasidim were convinced that he was searching their inner depths. Nothing resisted his gaze, neither time nor space. He would go to the window and observe what was happening continents away, centuries before. It is said of him that he was able to trace one's soul back to Cain or Abel, and determine precisely how many times it had migrated since—and where.

His surname—the Seer—has remained his exclusively. Other Masters were endowed with powers, but none with his vision. In his early youth he prayed to God to take that vision away; he found it a burden. He saw too much, too far. But his plea was not answered.

Some legends maintain that for a period of three—or seven— years he chose not to lift his eyes from the ground, so as not to see the world. Others claim that for seven years he chose silence, in order not to use and abuse language.

Though he was accessible, generous and compassionate, there existed between him and his followers a barrier which prevented them from coming too close, from lifting the veil.

Serious, at times melancholy, he would nevertheless sit with his close disciples once a week and try to make them feel gay and happy. That was on Saturday nights, at the meal called *melave-malka*, during which Hasidim accompany the Queen Shabbat on her way to exile for another week. At that meal the Master would encourage his followers to speak up and entertain the audience.

The rest of the week he was often withdrawn, and even forbidding.

Listen to an anecdote: a Hasid who had just been received by the holy Seer was so enraptured that he told a friend of his,

"You know? The Rebbe of Lublin looks . . . looks like an angry lion." "Have you ever seen an angry lion?" asked the friend. "As a matter of fact, no." "No? Then how do you know what an angry lion looks like?" "Well—I didn't know. *Now* I do," said the Hasid.

At the age of three, Yaakov-Yitzhak often ran away from *heder*—for which he was regularly punished by his teacher, until one day the *melamed* surreptitiously followed him into the forest—and heard him shout, "*Sh'ma Israel:* Listen, Israel— God is our God." Only then did his teacher stop punishing him.

But his father wanted to know: "Why are you wasting your time in the forest? Why do you go there!" "I am looking for God," said the three-year-old boy. "Isn't God everywhere?" asked the father. "And isn't He everywhere the same?" "He is—but I am not," replied the child.

At fourteen he went to Yeshiva, first at Zhulkova, where he studied under the renowned Talmudist Reb Moshe-Hersh Meisels, and then under the celebrated Reb Shmelke of Nikolsburg, in Shineve. There the regime was extremely rigorous. An average day meant fourteen hours for study, four hours for prayer, four for sleep, one hour for communal activity, a half-hour for meals and another half-hour for rest. Only the young Yaakov-Yitzhak was exempt from these rules.

For a while he led a marginal existence. Legend has it that he concealed his erudition. Only Reb Shmelke knew his true value and permitted him to go his own way. To fast, to seek solitude. To purify his mind and soul through *dvekut*—concentration, attachment—and prayer. When Yaakov-Yitzhak prays, remarked Reb Shmelke, the heavenly host of angels say Amen.

It was there, in Shineve, that he decided to close his eyes to the visible world and live the life of the blind: no solitude equals theirs. But later he had to open his eyes, for his solitude was threatened: he was getting married. And once again we stumble on a dramatic incident.

The marriage was arranged by Reb Shmelke and Yaakov-

Yitzhak's grandfather, Reb Kopel. The girl? From a good family, naturally. Her father was a wealthy merchant from Krasnograd. The groom, when informed of the decision, agreed. How could he say no to his teacher and to his beloved grandfather? A date was set. Preparations began amid the usual excitement.

Many people came to attend the ceremony. Let us look in on them as they partake of the customary "groom's meal" on the eve of the wedding. They sing, they play music, they laugh. The groom delivers a speech. Suddenly, he turns to his grandfather with a strange request: He would like to see the bride. General amazement. What? Now? Before the ceremony? Doesn't he trust his grandfather? But Yaakov-Yitzhak, nicknamed Reb Itzikl, quotes the Talmud: A man ought not to take a woman as his wife unless he has seen her first. Well, since the Talmud is on his side, the grandfather has no choice but to satisfy his whim. The bride is fetched from her chambers to meet her fiancé. Reb Itzikl lifts the veil—and begins to shiver. The bride leaves, and he is still shivering.

It's all right, people think; he has never seen a woman before, let alone his own. Only natural that he reacts this way.

When the meal is over and the guests have left, the groom turns to his parents and declares flatly, "I am not going to marry her. Let us go away, far away, far from here—far from her. We are not suited to each other."

You can imagine their reaction. "What happened, Itzikl? All the time you said yes, now all of a sudden you say no. What has come over you?"

"Nothing," says the groom. "Only that I have seen her. That's enough. I don't like her; she is not for me."

"How do you know?"

And Itzikl replies, "I have seen her face, the face of a stranger."

They implore him, they plead with him: to offend and shame a nice Jewish girl publicly is a sin, an outrage. Reb Itzikl is obstinate. Finally his father has an idea: marry her—and divorce her. And that is what he did. He married her and left as soon as the ceremony was over. He didn't even bother to wait until the next day. Or to change his clothes. He ran away. Where? Two versions: to Mezeritch or to Lizensk. From there he sent her a divorce.

To justify his behavior, Hasidic legend tells us that he was lucky to have run away: she was not right for him. The proof? *Kayadoua*—as everybody knows—the girl later left her family and her people and married a Polish nobleman. And that was what he had seen at their first meeting.

The escape itself inspired many a Hasidic storyteller. Several versions offer variations on the same theme. One version: He ran away not knowing where he was going. He was tired, hungry and cold. He was picked up by coachmen who were on their way to Lizensk—or Mezeritch. Somehow, during a stopover at an inn, a beautiful woman tried to seduce him. He ran away— which made Rebbe Elimelekh call him Joseph Hatzaddik, the Just, after the Biblical Joseph.

Another version: On his way to Mezeritch—not Lizensk— Reb Itzikl loses his way as he crosses an immense, thick forest. Strong winds begin to blow. A snowstorm begins to rage. Frozen, tired, blind with fatigue and fear, Reb Itzikl feels close to death. He leans against a tree and recites the *Viddui*, the last confession before death.

Suddenly he stops in the middle, for the storm has subsided abruptly. The forest has become hospitable, and there does seem to be a way out after all. Reb Itzikl begins to walk. After a while, he comes upon a light. A house. No, a castle. A palace. He knocks at the door. No answer. He pushes the door open. It is warm inside. The castle seems empty, but it isn't. A woman appears. A beautiful woman—probably the most beautiful woman alive. She invites him to come and sit next to her; her voice is soft and caressing—never before has he heard anything like it.

"I am so alone," she whispers. "Come closer; I have been waiting for you, for you alone."

Reb Itzikl is seized by a violent temptation but it is fleeting.

For he immediately remembers: It is forbidden to remain alone with a woman other than one's own. And then, God, too, is waiting. And so he runs from the castle, away from the woman, away from temptation. And then he realizes that it has all been an illusion. There is no castle, no woman—only the forest.

When he arrived in Mezeritch, the great Maggid received him with unusual affection: "The other side—the evil impulse—tried to get you. I am glad you won."

Reb Itzikl stayed a while in Mezeritch. So poor was he that he couldn't even afford challah for Shabbat. But to be close to the undisputed leader of the movement was his reward. He learned the principles of the Baal Shem Tov's new way of life, based on love of man and love of God and lived in a constant state of exultation. Ancient words came to life; human encounters offered new meaning. He observed the singular relations between Master and followers as they existed in Mezeritch: the disciple *chose* his Rebbe, to whom he then owed absolute allegiance. He also learned the vital importance of friendship in Hasidism. And of beauty. And sincerity. Mezeritch was a laboratory of the soul: those who came as disciples left as teachers.

The Maggid loved Reb Itzikl. Of him he said, "A soul like his has not been sent to us since the times of the Prophets."

But like most of his friends who gathered in Mezeritch, the Seer didn't stay there. In due time he moved to Lizensk, where he became the protégé of Rebbe Elimelekh. There, too, he began by leading an isolated life—far from his fellow students, bent on silence and truth. And there an incident occurred which one must remember as one explores the mystery of his Great Fall.

One day Reb Itzikl left Rebbe Elimelekh's House of Study and went for a walk in the woods. He climbed a hill, then a mountain, and sat down on a rock projecting over a precipice. There he meditated on the meaning of life and the futility of man's endeavors. God is God and man is small—so small; Reb Itzikl felt grateful to God for noticing man at all. I wish I could give Him something, he thought. But I have nothing, I possess nothing. All I can ever offer Him is myself. So he stood up, ready to throw himself over the edge. Fortunately, it so happened that a certain Reb Salke was standing not too far behind him. He caught him in time and brought him back to Lizensk. Years later the Seer would often remind Reb Salke of the incident, and would add cryptically, "Yes, Salke, we remember what you have done for us in Lizensk—that is why our love for you is not whole."

How many years did he stay in Lizensk? This is not clear, though he did stay long enough to become Reb Elimelekh's favorite disciple. It was his task to take care of young, scholarly followers. To teach them, guide them—open them to Hasidic fervor. Thus the disciple became Rebbe and began attracting followers of his own—whereupon the old Rebbe Elimelekh felt hurt and betrayed. He asked Reb Itzikl to wait before establishing his own community. Too late. The first break in the life of the young movement could not be avoided. The Seer moved to Lanzhut, then to Rozvadov and finally to Lublin—the new center, the youngest, the most dynamic in Hasidism.

As had happened in Mezeritch and Lizensk, an attempt was made in Lublin to intensify Jewish life—to reconstruct the Jewish world through simple prayers, simple stories. And human contact. People mattered more than doctrines.

Here the Seer's followers lived together, sharing possessions as well as dreams. They came here for the same reasons their forefathers had gathered in Jerusalem long ago: to be together, to participate in new experiences. Here one could forget one's misery, one's hunger; one's earthly problems mattered less or not at all. Close to the holy Seer, one found meaning in what seemed to have none. In Lublin one was again allowed to see Jewishness as a magnificent adventure.

In Lublin one learned that God is present everywhere and

that man can talk to Him about all his problems—and not only about theology. And one also learned that the Rebbe must be available to every one of his followers and listen to their pleas on any level, and be their ally on any terms.

What was Hasidism if not an attempt to tear down everything that separated one man from another—and from himself? Hasidism tore down the walls that exist between God and man, creation and creature, thought and deed, past and present, reality and soul: the secret lay in oneness.

In Lublin the Hasid could dream again—without feeling guilty—of his own possibilities. To the lonely Jew, the Seer said, "God, too, is alone—alone because of you." To the melancholy Jew, he said, "God too is sad—sad because of you." To the poverty-stricken Jew, he said, "It is up to you to alter your condition. You can defeat misfortune; invoke joy or create it, and things will change for you and others as well." For this is basic to the Hasidic message: there is total interdependence between man and heaven; one affects the other.

Like other Masters, the Seer advocated passion and compassion, and enthusiasm, fervor—*hitlahavut*—fervor, above all. "I prefer a passionate Mitnagged to a lukewarm Hasid," he said. For absence of fire, absence of passion, leads to indifference and resignation—in other words, to death. What is worse than suffering? Indifference. What is worse than despair? Resignation—the inability to be moved, to let oneself go, to let one's imagination catch fire.

At that moment in Eastern Europe, when hundreds of Jewish communities felt abandoned by mankind and noticed by the enemy alone, this was a powerful, irresistible message.

Thus, by putting the emphasis on *Ahavat-Israel*, on its repercussions in higher spheres, on its redemptive quality, Hasidism kept alive many Jews who came close to giving in to shame and hopelessness. And it restored to the Jew the idea of joy.

This is why in less than fifty years the Beshtian movement swept through Eastern Europe's Jewish communities. The spark kindled between Kossov and Kitev now illuminated them all.

Which was good—and not so good. There were many Hasidim, and that was good. But there were many Tzaddikim, and that was less good. Soon they would begin quarreling, and the movement would lose something of its original purity.

From Mezeritch and Lizensk came numerous Tzaddikim. They were active in the Ukraine, in White Russia, in Lithuania, in Hungary and, naturally, in Galicia. Suddenly it was so easy to be a Jew—a Hasidic Jew: all you had to do was to choose a Rebbe for yourself. He knew all the answers; his was the supreme authority.

The Seer, conscious of the perils inherent in success, referred to them occasionally: "I prefer a rascal who knows that he is a rascal to a Tzaddik who knows that he is a Tzaddik." He also said: "Tzaddikim are sinners too, except that they don't know it. In the other world, they are led into hell—and they believe they're on a visit, or on a mission to help those who are there permanently, but then the gates are shut and they stay inside." And repeating the last sentence, the Seer would laugh and say, "Oh, yes, they stay inside."

Except for Reb Barukh of Medzibozh, the Besht's grandson, the Seer maintained cordial and even friendly relations with most of his illustrious contemporaries. He would visit them and they would visit him. His quarrels with Reb Barukh? The most notorious had to do with his attitude toward women. At the Shabbat meal the Seer would sit with his followers, while Reb Barukh would have his wife and daughters at the table. The Seer found this offensive. And yet, in other ways, he deferred to women, allowing them to dress elegantly and taking them to the door as they left his study.

Many Gentiles were attracted to him. One of them, the famous Prince Adam Czartoryski, was received with special warmth in Lublin. A Hasid wondered aloud, "Why him and not me? I, at least, am a little bit of a Jew, while the Prince is not." Answered the Seer, "I prefer a Gentile who is a Gentile to a Jew who is only partly or halfheartedly Jewish."

Like the Besht, he knew and loved nature, and brought it back into Jewish life. Everything in creation testifies on behalf of God's work, he said. All things are examples. Take a raven, for instance. He has three distinctive marks. One: he accepts no strangers into his circle; if he croaks so hoarsely and loudly, it is so as not to hear outsiders. Two: he is convinced that in the world of birds he alone exists—that other birds are nothing but ravens in disguise. Three: a raven does not tolerate loneliness; the moment he loses his way and breaks away from his companions, he goes from dark anguish to death.

In the spirit of Hasidism, the Seer urged his followers to encourage belief in two cardinal principles: *emunat-Tzaddikim* and *dibuk-haverim*—faith in the Master and fidelity to friends.

And he did love his followers, both collectively and individually. He would call each and every one of them *Yidele*—the affectionate diminutive for *Yid,* Jew. He listened to their sorrows and shared in their pain. More than in Mezeritch, more even than in Lizensk, the Rebbe in Lublin was an integral part of the individual Hasid's life.

Teacher, guide, friend—the Seer was also miracle-maker. In Lublin, miracles occupied the forefront. People came for miracles and found them. Innumerable legends speak of the Seer's powers. It was sometimes enough for the poor, desperate men and women to implore him to intercede on their behalf, and heaven would submit to his will. Lublin was the needy, the sick Jew's last recourse. When everything else failed, he went to the Rebbe. Financial disasters. Health problems. Doubts, crises, threats. The Seer had cures for every ailment.

I know all this may seem shocking, even revolting to the rationalists among us. But one must look at the overall situation of that time. Before judging, one must take into consideration the immense suffering Jews were subjected to. What they needed most was a reason to believe. The very possibility of believing was a miracle in itself. That was why Tzaddikim performed miracles. To spark the imagination. To inspire awe. To help souls open themselves to faith and hope. *Vayar Israel et hayad hagdola asher assa adoshem bemitzrayim*—and the Jews saw the miracles in Egypt; thanks to them, they could believe. What does the Tzaddik do? asked the the Seer of Lublin. Through his prayer he reveals God's greatness. Miracles were meant to encourage man's faith in God—to make him feel that whenever man speaks, God listens. And that the laws of the soul are more important than those of nature.

Did the Seer have *ruakh-hakodesh*? Was he endowed with prophetic powers? His followers were convinced of it, and he himself never denied it. Indeed, he made a point of periodically issuing legal decisions based on his clairvoyance. An example: A woman was accused of adultery. Said he: "Did anyone see her commit the sin?" "No, but she was seen as she entered a room alone with a man." "Is that all?" said the Rebbe. "Then I tell you she is innocent." And he explained: "I know that in your hearts there is a doubt; still, to protect a person, I am entitled to invoke my inner sight against your doubts."

Such was the nature of all his miracles. He used them *for* the community; they were but means to an end—namely, to comfort and console, to encourage and uplift those lonely human beings who felt unworthy of God's attention.

He himself, incidentally, would sometimes utter remarks that led observers to assume that he did not take his miracle-making too seriously. That people believed in them was all right, but he was too intelligent, too lucid not to laugh at himself.

A story: Rebbe Levi-Yitzhak of Berditchev, his older friend and companion, admonished him one day for making a public display of his mystical powers: "Is this what I taught you?" he asked. "I am sorry you feel that way," said the Seer. "Just give me the order and I shall stop immediately." "No, no," said the Berditchever, "you may continue, you may."

One of the Seer's younger sons, who had been present at the meeting, asked him later, "Did you really mean it, Father? Were you ready to give up your *ruakh-hakodesh*, your prophetic gift?" "Oh, no," said the Seer, laughing. "Thanks to my second sight, I knew in advance that he would *not* ask me to stop."

. . .

"I dislike fools," he said. "Even if I should see, in the next world, a fool being invited into paradise and given every possible honor, I would run from street to street and shout, 'Fools remain fools, no matter where they go, and I don't ever envy them.'"

He also said: "People go to Riminov to get sustenance and to Kozhenitz to get cures. But they come to Lublin to get the Hasidic fire."

To a Hasid who complained that he suffered from impure, alien thoughts, he said: "Alien? They are not alien—they are *yours*."

A Hasid came to ask for permission to spend Shabbat with the Maggid of Kozhenitz. "What kind of Hasid are you?" said the Seer. "When I was a Hasid, I went to see all the Masters— and I didn't ask anyone's permission."

A great scholar—and opponent of Hasidism—in Lublin, Reb Azriel Hurwitz, nicknamed *Der Eizerner Kop*—mind of iron— once had a friendly conversation with the Seer. "I don't understand," said he. "I am more erudite than you, more learned and a better scholar than you, and yet people come to you and not to me. Why is that?"

"I don't know," answered the holy Seer. "Perhaps we ought to turn the question into an answer. You don't understand why people don't come to you, that's why they don't come. I don't understand why they *do* come, that's why they come."

Another time, the same Reb Azriel said to him, "Reb Itzikl, people call you Tzaddik, whereas both you and I know that you are not. Why not admit it publicly? If you do, people will go away." "Perfect," said the Seer. "Good idea."

The following Shabbat, before the reading of the Torah, he ascended the *bimah* and declared: "I want you all to know that I am not a Tzaddik; on the contrary, I am a sinner. I do not study enough, nor do I pray enough. I do not serve God the way I should. So—go and find yourself another Rebbe, one worthier of your trust."

Naturally the reaction was unanimous: Our Master is even greater than we thought. He is the greatest of all—look at his humility.

Next, Reb Azriel suggested that the Seer do the opposite: that he state publicly that he was a true Tzaddik, so the people would resent his vanity and leave him alone. But the Seer refused, saying: "I agree with you that I am *not* a Tzaddik—but I am not a liar either."

In spite of their friendly arguments and Reb Azriel's open, relentless hostility to Hasidism and Hasidim, the Seer deeply respected his scholarship; he would even send the best of his disciples to study under him.

What he himself had to give was not learning, though he was learned, but the art of human relations, which, of course, goes beyond learning. He taught his followers not how to study but how to listen, how to share, how to feel, how to pray, how to laugh, how to hope—how to live. What the Besht had done for his followers, the Seer did for his: he gave them a sense of dignity. Simple innkeepers, city coachmen, villagers from afar came to Lublin once a year, and that was enough to make them feel part of the Jewish people. What Kant said of himself—that because of his books, people would no longer think as before—was, in a larger sense, true of the Seer. Once he entered the lives of his followers, they no longer lived as before. It is said that even his opponents fell under his spell: those who attended his Third Meals of Shabbat would sit down as opponents and get up as admirers.

And yet, he who gave so much to others was himself longing for change. He gave joy to others but rarely to himself. Often he would remark: "Strange—people come to me sad and leave happy; whereas I . . . I stay with my sadness, which is like a black fire." In moments of doubt he would groan, "Woe to the generation whose leader I am."

He sought joy with such intensity that he ignored other considerations. Said he: "I prefer a simple Jew who prays with joy to a sage who studies with sadness."

A notorious sinner in Lublin had free access to him, for the Rebbe enjoyed his company. To his Hasidim who cautiously voiced surprise, he explained, "I like him because he is cheerful. When *you* commit a sin you immediately regret it; you repent for the pleasure you have felt. Not he. His joy continues."

Once he asked, "Do you know the real sin of our forefathers in the desert? It was not their rebellious behavior, but their ensuing melancholy."

To fight melancholy, he had, like Reb Barukh, a kind of clown, a court jester—Reb Mordechai Rakover—who would tell him jokes to make him laugh.

With the exception of Rebbe Nahman of Bratzlav, no other Hasidic Master placed such emphasis on the concept of exuberance and celebration. In Lublin, Hasidim were urged to live not only in fear of God but also in fear for God and, above all, in joy with God.

Legend has it that Reb Mendel of Riminov, who wanted his followers to aspire to silence through quiet meditation, was shocked when he discovered the cheerful mood of Lublin. He looked at the Hasidim at services and uttered a simple *Na*—and all were struck with awe and fear. Whereupon the Seer uttered a simple *Ho*—and they happily resumed their singing and handclapping.

Exuberance, joy, celebration, enthusiasm, fervor, ecstasy: this is what the Seer of Lublin gave his disciples and followers —weapons against melancholy, sadness and despair.

Why was he himself haunted by sadness? Because of his tragic break with his teacher, Rebbe Elimelekh? No. He was melancholic before their first meeting. Because of his opponents *outside* the movement, the early Maskilim who preached emancipation? Or the militant Mitnagdim, who once, just before Rosh Hashana, drove him out of Lublin? Well—other Masters had similar and worse experiences.

But they, too, seem to have been subject to spells of depression. From the Besht to the Maggid, to Reb Levi-Yitzhak, to Reb Barukh, to Reb Elimelekh, to the Kotzker—all endured pain and anguish. The reasons were manifold. Mystically inclined, they constantly thought of the Shekhina suffering in exile, and if the Shekhina suffered, how could *they* not suffer with her? The Seer of Lublin said, "A Hasid, like a child, should cry and laugh at the same time." And he explained how he managed to combine the two when lamenting over the Shekhina's suffering every night at midnight: "Imagine an exiled king who visits his friend; the friend is sad that the king is in exile, but still he is happy to be seeing him."

There were other reasons for the Masters' melancholy. Most Hasidim came to the Rebbe to unburden themselves of their misery and anxieties. And the Rebbe listened—listened well. And empathized. And identified. Well, how long can one go on absorbing tales of woe and tears? Of hungry children and persecuted fathers? Week after week, day after day, hour after hour, the Rebbe would listen to the misfortunes of his people in the various small communities ruled by mostly merciless landowners. How could he stay immune? One morning he had to wake up with a broken heart.

But in the case of the Seer of Lublin, there were other elements, of a more personal nature, that affected his mood.

He survived both his Master, Rebbe Elimelekh, and his successor, Yaakov-Yitzhak, the "Jew of Pshiskhe." He had hurt the former and was hurt by the latter.

In truth, one fails to understand. Why had he been in such a hurry? Why hadn't he heeded Rebbe Elimelekh's pathetic pleas to wait and inherit his kingdom . . . later? Why had he inflicted such suffering on the old teacher? And why did he complain when the same thing happened to him? What the Seer had done to his Master, the Jew of Pshiskhe did to *his*. The Seer, too, felt rejected, betrayed. Rebbe Elimelekh had foreseen it. He had warned the Seer: "You have no pity for my old age—or for yours."

The break between Lublin and Pshiskhe was tragic for both leaders. There were no major differences between Lizensk and Lublin, but there were between Lublin and Pshiskhe. The young rebels claimed that Hasidism in Lublin had become too popular, too popularized; they rejected its emphasis on miracles and advocated instead a return to study, devotion, self-fulfillment—a return to the true source of their inspiration. Relations between the two groups grew bitter, angry. Intrigues, gossip, clannishness turned brother against brother, father against son. Several times the Jew of Pshiskhe came personally to plead with his Master not to reject him, not to condemn him. The wounds eventually healed, but the scars remained.

Before the Jew of Pshiskhe passed away, he said, "I had the choice; it was to be either him or me. Since my prayers could save only one life, I preferred it to be his."

When the Seer learned of his death, he wept and said, "He will be our emissary in heaven to hasten the coming of the Messiah." His disciples wept too, so much so that he had to console them. "True," he said, "a great teacher died—but remember: God is alive; don't cry."

His was the tragedy of the survivor. He felt alone, rejected by both his Master and his favorite disciple. He still had friends, followers, companions, particularly the Maggid of Kozhenitz and Reb Mendel of Riminov, his two co-conspirators. Together, the three Rebbes attempted to shake the laws of time and bring redemption. The story of that mystical conspiracy is among the most beautiful in Hasidic or messianic literature. It ended in failure. All three died in the same year. And the Seer—who could see so far and so deep—must have known from the beginning that the Messiah would not come, not yet, not before a long time. How could he help being sad?

On his deathbed, he wanted his wife—she was his third—to promise him not to remarry. She refused. He did not insist. He remained quiet, at peace. Then he began reciting *Sh'ma Israel* with increasing passion, his face aflame as never before.

And now, let us go back to that Simhat Torah evening in Lublin? What really happened? What caused the accident? Was it an accident? What kind of accident?

Why did the Seer leave the festivities? Why did he stop dancing? Why did he tell the Rebbetzin to keep an eye on him? Was he afraid? And if so—of what, of whom?

Was it a sudden attack of sadness, of depression? Was it his way of telling God, Either You save Your people or erase me from Your book? I no longer wish to go on living—unless You put an end to Jewish suffering?

Could it be that, having failed to bring the Messiah through joy, he thought of trying . . . despair?

Perhaps he realized suddenly that it was too early for real redemption. That the ruins of Jerusalem would not disappear so soon. His old Master was gone. His young disciple and successor was gone. His trusted companion, the Maggid of Kozhenitz, was gone. His allies and accomplices were disarmed. He must have felt lonelier than ever—more despondent than ever.

Perhaps he remembered the first time, in his youth, in Lizensk, when he had felt the irresistible urge to jump into the abyss and become an offering to God. To God—who had refused his gift of joy.

Could it also be that in a sudden flash of fear the Seer had a glimpse of the distant future when night would descend upon the Jewish people, and particularly upon its most compassionate and generous children—those of the Hasidic community? Was that why he strayed outside? To wait under the somber sky, abandoned and shattered, to wait and wait through several generations, if necessary, for other victims of other catastrophes?

Lublin: the sanctuary, the center for messianic dreamers. Lublin then, Lublin now.

Somewhere a group of Hasidim join a nocturnal procession. They sing and they dance as they come closer to gigantic flames that reach into the sky. After all, it's Simhat Torah and they must celebrate the eternity of Israel and wait for the Messiah, whose idea of eternity—but not of Israel—must be different from theirs.

Lublin, during the darkest hours, became a center for torment and death. Lublin, an ingathering place for condemned Jews, led to the nearby concentration camps at Belzec and Majdanek. Lublin meant the great fall, not of one man, nor of one people, but of mankind.

And yet, and yet . . .

What do we learn from all this? We learn that the tale of Lublin survived Lublin, that the beauty of Lublin was mightier than Lublin. We learn that what the Tzaddik may do, the Hasid may not. The Master may come close to despair, his followers may not. Hasidism is a movement out of despair, away from despair—a movement against despair. Only Hasidism? Judaism too. Who is a Jew? A Jew is he—or she—whose song cannot be muted, whose joy cannot be killed by the enemy . . . ever.

MEIR
OF PREMISHLAN

O N   T H A T particular night, Rebbe Meir was
alone with his helper, Reb Arye, in his study. The Master was
meditating. Reb Arye was saying psalms. It was snowing outside. The streets were empty. The town was asleep. At midnight, Rebbe Meir sighed and, as was his custom, sat down on
the floor and quietly began to recite the lamentations over the
destruction of Jerusalem and God's exile from one eternity into
another.

It was cold in the room but the Rebbe did not feel it. He did
not feel the cold because he was far away, wandering with sages
and poets of long ago, with fallen princes and their children. He
did not feel the cold because he was dreaming about redemption.

Hurry, God of Abraham, Isaac and Jacob. Your patience is
no longer a virtue. Your children can bear it no longer. Look at
us: we are tired, poor, helpless; do something—and if not for
our sake, then for the sake of Your name!

For centuries and centuries Masters and disciples have repeated these litanies at the same hour, shedding the same tears
—and with the same results, or rather, with the same lack of
results. Would Rebbe Meir of Premishlan be more successful
than they? Was he worthier than they? He knew the answer—he
was humble enough to know it—and yet, like those before him
and those after him, he said his prayers, wept and finally stood

up, ready to retire. Tomorrow would be another day; more Jews would come and plead with him to intercede on their behalf, more Jews would place their faith in his powers.

Suddenly there was a knock at the door. Both Master and helper stopped reading, stopped breathing. Who could that be? Foe or friend? An evil emissary or his victim? "Open," said the Master to his helper. "But Rebbe, we don't know who it is!" "Open! It may be someone who needs help. A sick woman perhaps. A prisoner on the run. Do not waste time." Reb Arye opened the door. A soldier stood outside, asking to be allowed in. He spoke Yiddish. "I am hungry," he said. "Hungry?" asked Rebbe Meir. "You said you are hungry?" He ran into the kitchen and returned with bread and milk. The soldier sat at the table and ate. "Tell me," said the Master, "don't they feed you in the army?" "Oh, yes, they do," said the soldier. "But their food is not for me. That is why I came here tonight. You see, Rebbe, I was taken into military service by the Czar years and years ago and I have forgotten everything I learned in my parents' home; everything, except that I am Jewish and that Jews eat kosher. So wherever I go with my unit, I seek out Jewish homes to get a proper meal."

Visibly moved, Rebbe Meir went to the window and looked out at the snow covering the town. For a while he said nothing. Then he sighed and said, "That the Messiah will come one day is certain; we all know that, don't we? But thanks to whom will he come? Thanks to Meir? No. Thanks to you, Reb Arye? No. He will come thanks to this soldier who goes around knocking on doors, reminding us of who we are."

The longing for the Messiah, the poverty and loneliness of the Jew in exile, the compassion of the Master, the unknown visitor—many of the ingredients of the classic Hasidic story can be found in this one. Except that in most stories the unknown guest turns out to be the Prophet Elijah, or one of the thirty-six Just Men, whereas in this one it is simply a soldier who refuses to relinquish the only tie that binds him to his past, to his people.

Perhaps the reason for this difference lies in the Master

himself: Rebbe Meir of Premishlan rarely indulged in messianic pursuits and mystical meditation; his constant preoccupation was to feed those who were hungry and reassure those who were afraid. He never claimed that he entertained relations with lofty personalities such as Rabbi Shimon bar Yohai or the Ari Hakadosh; he preferred to be with villagers and peasants and talk to them not about the secrets of creation but about everyday concerns and worries affecting them.

Thus, he was renowned and revered by followers of Beshtian Hasidism everywhere.

For Hasidism was—and remains—a universe in itself. Its Masters have opened many ways to the human heart and within the human soul. Some have advocated joy, others discipline. Some have expressed themselves through anger, others through friendship. Rebbe Barukh of Medzibozh and Rebbe Pinhas of Koretz, the Seer of Lublin and Rebbe Naphtali, the Jester of Ropshitz—each one had his trademark, his distinct seal, his specific color. What about Rebbe Meir of Premishlan?

A warning: do not expect too much of him. Rebbe Meir of Premishlan was the poor man's Rebbe; he made no startling discoveries, provoked no tumultuous upheavals in the world of the mind or the soul, and conquered no important fortresses for the Hasidic kingdom.

No revolutionary doctrine is attached to his name; no original system bears his imprint. He seems just another Rebbe, another Tzaddik—one of many. Simpler than some, wiser than others.

At first you love him but you do not admire him. You love him for his human qualities; only later, imperceptibly, does your love take on a measure of admiration as well.

For many years his main preoccupation was to ransom prisoners: *Pidyon shevuyim* was his obsession. If one allows one's fellow men to be in jail, one's own freedom is compromised: that is the substance of our tradition, a tradition that compels us to act, always, and with every means, on behalf of prisoners everywhere.

Rebbe Meir: obsessed with freedom, he wandered from prison to prison, a living link between prisoners and their families—between prisoners and the outside world. His simplicity was deceptive. Wait until you hear about the way he made preparations for his death; wait until you hear about his strange relationships with other Masters; wait until you get acquainted with him. It will not be easy—though it may seem so. No walls separate him from his followers; no secret zone darkens his being. Just tell him that you need him and he will receive you. Tell him that you are suffering and he will be your companion. Tell him you need a presence and he will share your solitude without invading it. This may seem unusual today, but in those days many Hasidic Masters treated their followers in that way, with similar compassion.

Not much is known about his childhood. What is known—and stressed—in various sources is that his grandfather was the "Great Rebbe Meir of Premishlan," the Besht's companion and friend. We know that he was born around 1780 and that he died around 1850.

As we scan the decades and the events that filled them, we find him with the Seer of Lublin as disciple, and with the Rizhiner as friend, and with Rebbe Uri of Strelisk as opponent and adversary. For a long time he refused to marry, until Rebbe Levi-Yitzhak of Berditchev prevailed upon him to have a family. Since Rebbe Levi-Yitzhak was the matchmaker, he could not refuse. And so he married the daughter of Reb Itamar Hakohen, a renowned Kabbalist. They had one son and five daughters. The son became a Rebbe and the daughters all married Rebbes.

His teacher was Rebbe Mordecai of Kremenets. His disciples were Rebbe Shlomo Kliger, Reb Yoseph-Saul Natanson, and Reb Hayim of Sanz. He was their Rebbe and they would travel to Premishlan to consult with him about their communities or simply to spend Shabbat with him.

Rebbe Meir is generally described as a man of the people who was as much at ease with coachmen as with scholars. He had a biting tongue, a keen sense of humor and, in the true tradition of the Besht, an immense hunger for love.

Passionate and compassionate, he expressed his feelings and

ideas with grace and simplicity: his sentences were short, to the point; and they somehow sounded aggressive to those in power, but soothing to those who were made to suffer by those in power.

Most of the legends about him deal with his ability to perform miracles. When words were sufficient, he found them; when they were not, he resorted to action; when action failed, he invoked miracles. When everything else fails, the Master must transform failure into victory, sadness into joy—and what is this metamorphosis if not a miracle?

He was no longer alone in doing this. Most Hasidic Masters had gained a reputation as Wonder Rebbes.

A story: One day he dispatched a special messenger with an urgent letter to be handed over personally to Rebbe Israel of Rizhin. So important and so secret was the message that the man was instructed to hide it in his shoe. When he arrived at the Rizhiner's court, he refused to discuss his assignment with anyone but the Tzaddik himself. After being admitted to the Rizhiner's private study, the emissary sat down on the floor, removed his shoe and took out the letter, which he respectfully handed over to the Master who symbolized the royalty of Hasidism. Rebbe Israel Rizhiner read the note and smiled. "Meir has a question for you to answer," Rebbe Meir had written. "Since we shall soon celebrate the holiday of Shavuot, when we are supposed to eat *kreplach,* Meir thought he would ask your advice: How many is one supposed to eat? One? Not enough. Two? That is an even number and even numbers are unholy. Three? Too many—after all, one must not be a glutton. So what should Meir do?"

"Tell Rebbe Meir of Premishlan," said the Rizhiner, "to prepare one—but let it be as large as two."

Another story:

In the town of Sutcheva there lived a man named Natan-Shimon who, woe unto him, refused to acknowledge the holiness of holy Masters. And yet, he needed them. He had no children. He was sick. "Why don't you go to Rebbe Meir of Premishlan?" his wife asked him. "So many people go—why don't you?" "I have no time to waste," he answered. "Well," said she, "*I* went to see him. And he has a message for you: You were in Galatz last week, weren't you? You were there on business; but you did something bad there—and he knows what you did." Natan-Shimon paled; he decided to go to Premishlan. Only he was ashamed to admit it publicly. Thus when friends asked him where he was going, he answered, to Lemberg. But when he arrived in Premishlan, Rebbe Meir sent him back angrily: Go home and tell all your friends that you are going not to Lemberg but to Premishlan to see Meir! The poor man had to obey.

Later, he become Rebbe Meir's fervent admirer. Since you live near the border, the Master told him, you may be able to help . . . one day.

And so it was to be. Natan-Shimon helped smuggle the Rizhiner from Russia into Austria. In fact, he carried him on his shoulders part of the way. They stopped at a checkpoint: "Do not worry," Reb Natan-Shimon told the Rizhiner Tzaddik. "I know what to do. You just stay here and wait for me." And he went inside the sentry house and invited the policemen to play a game of cards. Strange as it may sound, Reb Natan-Shimon, the Hasid, was an excellent player. Still, he managed to lose four hundred rubles and his partners were much too happy to bother going outside to look for illegal aliens. And so the Rizhiner reached Sadgora and there established his new court. All his life he remained grateful to the Tzaddik of Premishlan.

But who was Rebbe Meir? If you wish to know a Hasid, get to know his best friend and his worst enemy.

Rebbe Meir's closest friend was the Hasidic Master we just left in his palace in Sadgora, Rabbi Israel of Rizhin—who was all that Rebbe Meir was not: rich, famous and domineering. He behaved like a king, spoke like a king, and his symbols—both mystical and real—were those of a king. His court was luxurious, his costumes regal; he was surrounded by aides and servants, musicians and jesters. It is said that on his journeys he was escorted by a retinue that numbered a hundred. Eight white horses pulled his golden coach. He considered himself a descendant of King David and felt it proper and necessary to represent the concept of *malkhut Israel*—of Israel's immortal kingdom.

As for Rebbe Meir of Premishlan, he lived in a small house, at first with his parents, then with his wife, Malka, and their children. For a while he had to work as a tutor to support his family.

The Rizhiner ate from golden plates and used golden cutlery, whereas Rebbe Meir had hardly anything to eat. The Rizhiner had accumulated great wealth, whereas the Premishlaner distributed the little he had. How then is one to explain—or understand—the friendship between the two? What could have drawn them one to the other? Merely the fact that they were opposites?

One day they met on the road. The Rizhiner was traveling to attend a celebration and the Premishlaner to collect funds for charity. They stopped and looked at one another with some embarrassment and amazement. The Rizhiner felt he had to justify his expensive carriage and splendid horses: "I need them," he said. "Should I happen to drive into the mud, I would need six strong horses to pull me out." "Not Meir," answered the Premishlaner. "Meir has only one horse, and it is weak and small and old; it can hardly pull him on a flat road—it would surely not be able to pull him out of the mud; therefore, my friend, Meir must be careful, very careful not to fall into the mud. . . ."

He referred a man to the Rizhiner, saying, "You need intercession in heaven; his is more valuable than mine. But do what Meir tells you. When you arrive in Sadgora, go to the palace. Ask to be admitted into the Rebbe's study. And there you must start singing a particular Sabbath song; sing it even if it is not Sabbath. You'll see: heaven will help you."

So the man went to Sadgora, rushed to the palace and asked to see the Rizhiner, explaining that Rebbe Meir had sent him.

The Master's aides were glad. The Rizhiner was going through a deep depression; any message from his friend Reb Meir would improve his mood. And true enough, when the man entered the Tzaddik's study, he started right away to sing a long, a very long, Sabbath song, with passion and fervor—as though he were singing it on Sabbath and not on a simple Wednesday. The Rizhiner reacted with laughter; he shook with laughter; and seeing him laugh, all his aides began to laugh too. Never had they laughed so hard; they could not stop laughing. At the end, the Rizhiner remarked, "I don't know what Reb Meir wants from me and why he sent you to me; but you helped me and therefore you yourself have also been helped."

On another occasion Rebbe Meir sent one of his Hasidim to go and see the Rizhiner with another one of his messages: Tell him, he said, that he has taken the high road whereas Meir is following the low road; but we shall both arrive at the same place—together.

What brought these two Masters together? Actually, let us turn the question around: Were they together? We are told of their close relationship, of the esteem and warmth they felt for one another; we are told of their lasting friendship—but not of their spending much time together. In fact, we are told the opposite: their contact was maintained through emissaries.

Still, they *were* friends. True friends. On what basis? Perhaps both believed in Hasidic pluralism. Both believed that there was more than one way to implement the Besht's principles and programs. That study without prayer would be as sterile as prayer without study. That to emphasize meditation alone, compassion alone, miracles alone, nobility alone, would distort the image of both the Hasid and the Master. Nothing in creation is monolithic. Words contain silence, and silence exists only thanks to surrounding words. God needs man for His glory and man needs God for his memory. One can love the poor and be a Hasid, one can aspire to riches and be a Hasid; but one cannot be alone and be a Hasid. Both Premishlan and Rizhin constituted, each in its way, a protest against human solitude as opposed to, rather than integrated into, God's own solitude.

The despairing Jew, living marginally in his faraway village, had to ask himself some disturbing questions: Where is God in my life? Where am I in His? Does He hear me? Am I heard by Him? Is He my king, my father, my friend? Is He—could He be—my enemy? Worse: Is He—could He be—indifferent to the fate of His creation? Hasidism answers emphatically: No—God is not indifferent; God is an answer to indifference.

Yes, both Rebbe Meir and Rebbe Israel yearned to reach the same goal; and each needed the other to be able to follow his own road without ever losing sight of the road ahead.

In some places, men are one another's prisoners; in the Hasidic kingdom they were one another's companions. One man was not another man's boundary but, on the contrary, an opening unto other men. Thanks to Premishlan, Rebbe Israel felt freer to experience Rizhin; thanks to Rizhin, Rebbe Meir felt that Premishlan had its own merits. God dwelled in both places. For, according to the cardinal principle of the Besht and his disciples, *let atar panui minei*—no place in creation is devoid of God; God is everywhere.

At first, we are more attracted to Rebbe Meir than to the Rizhiner. The reasons are obvious. Eastern European Jewry was enduring such misery that the very thought of a Rebbe living in luxury is—understandably—shocking. We naturally prefer the modest, unassuming, poor Rebbe Meir who lived with his people, on their level, sharing their poverty, their anguish, their sorrow, their thirst and their hunger.

But—wait a moment. First impressions may be misleading; they certainly bear checking. Are we sure that of the two Masters it was the Rizhiner who was excessively preoccupied with earthly matters? And what if it were the opposite? The Rizhiner had everything, therefore he did not have to think of food or rent money; he could devote all his time, all his energy to spiritual pursuits, to truth and justice and inner peace. As for Rebbe Meir, he had no time to spare for lofty excursions of the soul: he had to think of jobs and meals and rent for his followers. . . . And so is it not possible that the Rizhiner may have been more idealistic than his destitute friend? The Premishlaner thought of bread, the Rizhiner of redemption!

And yet, as we reflect upon their friendship, we like Reb Meir more than ever. Without judging the Rizhiner—who are we to pass judgment on a Master, especially one whom we love with all our heart?—we must come to the inevitable conclusion that when there are people going hungry, they must come first; their well-being must take precedence over all ideals—no, their well-being must become our ideal. The Messiah can wait and he should: first priority goes to the sick child who needs medicine; or to the desperate mother who needs to be consoled; or surely to the father who loses his mind when he is unable to feed, to preserve, his family.

I think that the Rizhiner knew this and that is why he clung to his friendship with Rebbe Meir, who reminded him of the other road, the small one, the neglected one. As for Rebbe Meir Premishlaner, he was too busy with his poor Hasidim to think about such matters.

Now—let us look at the third point of the triangle and examine his relationship with his fierce and outspoken rival, Reb Uri, the so-called Seraphin of Strelisk.

Actually they should have gotten along well, for they had much in common, more in common than Rebbe Meir had with the Rizhiner. Reb Uri, too, was penniless. He too worshipped in ecstasy—unlike the Rizhiner, who insisted on self-control and proper decorum. He too was forever on the road trying to rescue persecuted villagers and to ransom jailed innkeepers. But then, why the hostility between the two *poor* Masters?

There were at least two reasons. The first: Reb Uri resented the Premishlaner's boasting about his powers. The Seraphin believed that whoever is initiated into secret knowledge must keep it to himself; one must take care not to reveal too much to outsiders. And because Reb Meir used to tell people what he saw in heaven—or in the human heart and mind—the Seraphin went so far as to try to deprive him of his powers. To this end, he sent two of his trusted Hasidim to Reb Naphtali of Ropshitz to enlist his support. The two men arrived in Ropshitz on a Thursday and the Tzaddik received them warmly—so warmly that they could not say anything about Reb Meir; Reb Naphtali was doing all the talking. They returned the next day. Again he told them stories about his Masters, invited them to stay for Shabbat, and again not a word was said about Reb Meir. During Shabbat, the Tzaddik naturally spoke of and listened only to words of Torah. On Sunday, Reb Uri's two Hasidim returned, this time determined to tell Reb Naphtali openly and firmly what their Rebbe expected him to do about the Premishlaner. But again, Reb Naphtali did not allow them to say a word. Having spoken on and on about many things, he accompanied them to the door; there he stopped and said, "Reb Meir's father, the late Reb Aaron-Leib, appeared to me last night and said, 'I have left behind me a small flame, please, do not let it be smothered. . . .' At that moment, a man announced: 'Reb Meir is here!' The Premishlaner appeared seemingly out of nowhere, and angrily commented, 'My father called me a small flame? No, Rebbe of Ropshitz! He left behind him a huge flame!' "

Reb Meir was left with his mystical powers and Reb Uri with his anger.

The second reason for the Seraphin's hostility had to do with . . . materialism.

Whereas Reb Meir forever pleaded with God on behalf of his Hasidim's physical and economical welfare, Reb Uri was concerned with their spiritual development only.

Like the Kotzker Rebbe, the Seraphin categorically refused to intercede with heaven to obtain improved health or material gain for his followers. You wanted him to pray for your soul? With pleasure. For your intellectual growth? No problem. For your share in paradise? Any time. But if you were left with no meat for Shabbat, no credit for clothing and no money for your children's education—you had better not count on the Seraphin of Strelisk!

There exist stories upon stories describing his stubborn refusal to help improve his community's material welfare. Eventually his followers no longer expected him to be their advocate in such earthly matters. They were content with what they had and they loved him for what he was—not for what he gave them concretely but for what he did to elevate their souls.

One day he stopped his morning prayer, turned to his Hasidim and exclaimed, "Whoever, whoever wants money, let him come nearer! Let him put his hand in my pockets; he will find more money than he needs." He repeated his invitation but no one came forward, first, because his pockets were empty, second, because in Strelisk money did not seem to matter to those who had none.

On another occasion, he justified his behavior as he talked with a visiting Rebbe. The visitor wanted to know: "Why aren't you taking care of your people's immediate needs?" "Needs?" said Reb Uri. "You said, 'Needs?' Let us see whether my people need anything." And, during services, he raised his voice and asked, "Who wants me to get him wealth?" No one moved. "Who wants health?" No one moved. "Who wants security?" Still, no one moved. "See?" asked Reb Uri. "Now listen: Who wants fear of heaven?" All responded eagerly. "And who wants fervor?" Again, all responded. "Who needs *Yirat-Shamayim*— fear of heaven?" All needed, all wanted *Yirat-Shamayim*. In Strelisk, they needed nothing else.

Not so in Premishlan.

What Reb Meir's people needed above all was food for the body, a roof over the head, an assured livelihood. And the Premishlaner listened and responded with concern and understanding. Urgent everyday worries were important to him. He did not care much about his own poverty, but that of his fellow men touched him deeply. In this he followed in the footsteps of the Besht and the Maggid of Mezeritch. Just as the Besht was against deliberate self-mortification, the Maggid spoke up against imposed suffering. A small hole in the body turns into a large hole in the soul, the great Maggid had said. To diminish and despise your body is to sneer at God's creation, for the body, too, is part of it—it is in fact its most visible and tangible part. How would man perform His commandments were it not for his senses? Of course, the heart is at the center of man's activities but in order for the heart to live, it needs a healthy body. And the body needs food, not prayer! How did Rebbe Israel Salanter put it? Your *olam-haze* is my *olam-haba*: your earthly needs are my spiritual concerns. What is *Ahavat-Israel*, the basic principle in Hasidism, if not a direct injunction to care for one another in the present? Said Rebbe Aharon of Karlin, "I wish I could love the greatest Tzaddik the way the Almighty, blessed be His name, loves the greatest villain." And this love is not abstract; it is immediate. And real. The love of God is linked to the love of man. One without the other leads to idolatry and inhumanity.

This was—and remains—the teaching of Beshtian Hasidism. Remember his three modes of love? *Ahavat-Hashem*—love of the Almighty; *Ahavat-Torah*—love of study; and *Ahavat-Israel* —love of Israel and mankind. At the time, this formulation of Jewish commitment was called an innovation—why? For centuries and centuries Jews were taught to love God and Torah and Israel—and many sacrificed their lives for that love. But what the Besht did was new indeed: he linked the three modes together in an unbreakable bond. Before him they were separate and divisible. In some circles, only Torah mattered. In others, only God existed. Or only man. The Besht was the first to proclaim for all to hear: The way to heaven leads through this world; the way to divine reward leads through human commitment; the way to God leads through your fellow man.

Fervor? Yes—later. Study? Yes—later. Ecstasy? Yes—later. Not on a hungry stomach. Not with a sick child at home.

But what if you cannot help it? What if you tried everything and misery is still dwelling under your roof? And what if your heart remains shattered? Then—only then—the Tzaddik will teach you how to overcome despair and attain ecstasy through joy and devotion. The difference between Rebbe Meir and Reb Uri of Strelisk? Reb Uri skipped the intermediary stages. He demanded and offered ecstasy right away.

Of course, Reb Uri himself set the example: before his morning prayer, he would bid farewell to his family. So all-consuming was his love of God that he was convinced each time he left that he might not see them again; that while praying in total communion with his Creator, he might die.

Rebbe Meir did not wish to die; he had no time for dying. He had other things to worry about: his helpless Hasidim who had to deal with the village lord and not with heaven, with today and not with eternity.

Of course, both he and his rival from Strelisk loved their poor followers—and they loved them with equal force and passion. But, Reb Uri went one step farther: he loved even their poverty —whereas Rebbe Meir considered poverty outrageous and disgraceful and fought it valiantly throughout his entire life.

When he was only a boy, he was already helping the poor. Every Thursday he would go from house to house collecting money for the town's beggars. Once he returned home empty-handed. In desperation he went to the stable, took his father's only cow, sold it at the marketplace, and, of course, gave the money to the poor.

Then he remembered that the cow was his father's only source of income; he began to cry. He thought of his mother and cried even more. As he stood crying on the road, a man stopped and asked him why he was crying; Meirl told him the truth. "Do not worry," said the stranger. "Here is money, go and buy another cow." But Meirl's mother saw the substitution. "What happened?" she asked her son. "Where is *our* cow?" "She disappeared," said Meirl. "Disappeared?" shouted his mother. "How does a cow disappear?" "Well, she did," said Meirl. "She became charity and went up into heaven. . . ."

To a rich man who refused to give for charity, he once said:

"Before I was born, I was given twenty-five thousand rubles —but I refused to keep them. Already then I wanted to live in absolute austerity. 'Take the money,' my angel insisted. 'It is yours and only yours. If you don't take it, it will stay here in heaven, whereas if you do, you may do something good with it.' 'All right,' I said. 'I have an idea. I shall take the twenty-five thousand rubles and divide them in five equal sums and entrust

them to five Jewish merchants—so whenever I shall need
money for unmarried daughters and imprisoned innkeepers, I
shall know to whom to go . . . to claim my money.' Well," he
said to the rich miser, "you are one of the five. The money you
have is not yours. If you refuse to help the poor—I shall take it
back."

Why shouldn't I pray for money for my Jews? he once asked.
What do they do with their money? Gamble it away? No. Use it
to get drunk? No. They feed their families, they give to charity,
they pay tutors, they support Yeshivot—why then shouldn't I
help them get money?

On another occasion, a preacher asked for his permission to
speak in Premishlan and earn some money thereby. He spoke,
but nobody gave him anything. Later he sat in the Rebbe's
study and saw people come in and put money on the table. "I
don't understand," said the preacher. "Why do they give you
money but not me?" "Simple," said Rebbe Meir. "We all influence our listeners to become more like us. You love money and
therefore, after meeting you, they love it even more. I despise
money and therefore they throw it away, and I am here to pick
it up."

Once he was asked by a disciple, "Why do we put *maror*
(bitter herb) on the table on Passover eve but not gold or
silver? Why must we remember only the bitterness of our Egyptian bondage and not the wealth we took when we left the
country?"

"I'll tell you why," said Rebbe Meir. "Much of the bitterness
is still here—but the money is gone, oh, yes, gone for good."

A storekeeper complained to him that a competitor had
opened a shop too close to his. "What do you want me to do?"
asked the Premishlaner. "Chase him away? And what will he do
to feed *his* children, ha? Listen: have you ever noticed how the
horse behaves at a pool of water? He stamps with his hoof in
the water, right?" "Right." "Do you know why he does that? I'll
tell you why. When the horse drinks, he sees his shadow. So he

thinks that another horse is drinking from the same pool and tries to chase him away. In so doing he stirs up the mud in the water and it becomes undrinkable. . . . You'd better drink and let others drink: there is enough for all the storekeepers in the world!"

We must remember that poverty was considered a virtue in some Hasidic circles. Not only because it was there—and because there was not much they could do about it, except pray— but also because, on a higher level, they felt it was—do not laugh—good for the soul.

They were afraid that money corrupts both those who give it and those who receive it—and that more money engenders more corruption. Better therefore to live without it.

Still others felt that since poverty, too, was willed by God, why then should one reject it?

Just as Reb Nahum of Chernobyl felt sorry for darkness, Reb Meir was moved to pity for poverty.

Poor darkness, Reb Nahum would say. Everybody hates it. Everybody loves light and praises it at the expense of darkness. . . . Well, said he, people are wrong. Between darkness and light the contest is unfair: darkness always loses—but only on the surface. When it yields to light, it does not disappear; it simply goes into hiding. Where? Inside light. . . .

The same could be said of poverty. Everybody is against it—so somebody had to redeem it. Thus Reb Uri—like Reb Nahum of Chernobyl—often praised poverty.

Since poverty was a dominant factor in Jewish life in Eastern Europe, Hasidic Masters had to take a position on it. What could it have been? They had four options: One—to ignore it. Two—to accept it with resignation. Three—to rebel against it and defeat it. Four—to rebel against it by turning it into a virtue.

The Seraphin of Strelisk chose the last option, but Reb Meir of Premishlan would not. He saw in it a hostile presence to be disarmed and vanquished. That is why, in his lifelong battle against his "enemy," he used miracles. So great was his compassion for his people that he even tried to force God's hand. He promised children to childless parents. He offered hope to hopeless farmers. He reassured lonely prisoners everywhere, telling them that God is present to all His creatures, that God listens—and more important, that God can be heard. Even in jail? Even in jail. Even in misery? In misery above all.

True, said Reb Uri. God *is* in misery—in exile—therefore we must do everything on *His* behalf. But what about compassion? Is not a Rebbe, as a human being, as a Jew, as a leader of men, duty-bound to show compassion toward his fellow man? Why did Reb Uri of Strelisk not show any pity for *his* followers? Is it conceivable that he—a pillar of Hasidism—was immune to pity? I do not believe so. The Seraphin of Strelisk was a man of deep feelings. He was possessed and consumed by compassion—but for whom? That is the question.

And that was the issue that divided the two Masters: Rebbe Meir of Premishlan maintained that since man is vulnerable and fragile, forever threatened and hurt, he, as the Rebbe, was duty-bound to feel sorry for his flock. Whereas Rebbe Uri asked: And what about God? What about the Almighty Master of the Universe, who views with sadness what has been going on inside His creation? Who will feel sorry for Him? God suffers because of us—God suffers with us—therefore how can I deny Him my love? My compassion? Condemned to solitude, God is invoked by people only when they need Him—when they want something; what about His demands, His needs? He has given so much—what does He get in return?

One may wonder whether Reb Meir's simplistic miracle-making was really to his taste. After all, he was both lucid and learned; he surely knew that there was much more to Beshtian Hasidism than dealing with the supernatural. Moreover, if he didn't, there were others who forced him to acknowledge it. Reb Uri of Strelisk was not his only antagonist. Reb Meir himself often mentioned his many adversaries, those Hasidic Rebbes and Tzaddikim who objected to his spectacular methods of helping his followers. Then why did he continue? He continued because the welfare of the poor Hasid mattered to him more than the opinion of other Masters. Still, he felt unsure. And what if they were right and not he? And what if he were wrong in using—and displaying—his secret powers?

He was human—profoundly human—and therefore prone to constant introspection and self-doubt.

Actually there remains little by him or about him to support my view, which is mostly intuitive, except for one aspect of his personality . . .

He rarely spoke about himself in the first person. Instead he would say: Meir believes, Meir thinks, Meir sees, Meir says. . . . The word "I" was almost banned from his vocabulary. Whether he addressed himself to God or to people, he would say: Meir implores you, Meir tells you, Meir asks you. . . .

This form of speech must have been motivated, at least partly, by humility. Remember the friend who knocked at the window of Rebbe Aharon of Karlin? "Who is it?" asked Reb Aharon. "Don't you recognize my voice? We studied together at Mezeritch! It is I." "If you say 'I,' that means you have not studied enough; go back to Mezeritch. Only God may say 'I.' "

The other motivation is more complex, for it involves one's attitude not toward God but toward oneself. Since the origins of time, "Who am I?" is the question of questions, the question human conscience cannot avoid. What is the nature of the "I" one refers to? Obstacle or opening? Wall or gate? Sublimation or alienation? In the phrase "I said to myself," who am I? The one who spoke or the one who listened? Who was Rebbe Meir of Premishlan: the character in his tale or its author? Where was Rebbe Meir when Meirl was thinking and pleading and observing and counseling on his behalf? One thing is clear: the miracles were performed by Meirl. Since the Rebbe did not really wish to change the laws of nature by making use of his powers and privileges—but since he did have to use them for the sake of the sick and the hungry—he invented someone to perform his miracles for him: thus Meirl did what Reb Meir would rather not do.

Psychologists may read into this play of words one thing, philosophers another. Both may be right. Or wrong. As for myself, I admire him even for things that may appear childish. Between Meirl and Rebbe Meir I choose . . . both.

The time has come for us to leave Premishlan—for he himself left it. And he did so in a striking and stirring manner.

One day Rebbe Hayim of Sanz came to see him. They talked for a long time; about what, no one knows. All we know is that, at the end of their conversation, Rebbe Meir turned to his guest and said, "Rebbe of Sanz, you are a member of the great rabbinic court. Tell me: Don't you think that it is time for Meirl to leave these tight quarters and move into larger ones?" "Oh, yes," answered Reb Hayim of Sanz. He immediately realized his mistake and tried to retract his statement but it was too late.

The Premishlaner addressed similar questions to other celebrated Masters asking for their permission to depart from this world. Unfortunately their replies were not recorded. He dispatched a special emissary to inform his beloved friend Rebbe Israel of Rizhin that soon he would be left alone. . . .

By then Rebbe Meir was an old man, at the end of his road, and he was no longer the same. He who had sought the company of people now avoided them, he who had given his life and his soul to help others now prepared himself to enter eternity alone. He was sick, tired and disconsolate. During the last week of his life, he let it be known to all his followers gathered under his roof that whoever wished to celebrate Shabbat without disturbance should go home. No one left. He insisted. He wanted everyone to go away. He would have liked to be left to himself and face the inevitable—alone. No one left. And Shabbat went by undisturbed.

That evening, after the last meal in the Rizhiner's palace at Sadgora, a strange incident occurred: the two candles on the royal table were flickering as usual when suddenly the Rizhiner gasped in pain and so did all those who were present. At that moment one of the candles went out.

And it was never lit again.

NAPHTALI
OF ROPSHITZ

It happened on Shabbat Hagadol, the Shabbat that precedes Passover, which is an important holiday, though . . . a costly one. It requires money, a great deal of money, to celebrate it the way it should be celebrated. And the people of Ropshitz had none, or almost none. There were but a few rich merchants; all the others lived from day to day, worrying about every coin, every mouthful that they brought back home. The men were constantly overworked; so were the women. Even the children were pale with fatigue and hunger. That was the picture all year around—which was bad enough. But the week before Passover it became even worse. For at Passover, every Jew must consider himself free and sovereign, free of worries and bonds, like a king.

So on this particular Shabbat, the Rebbe of the community—Rebbe Naphtali—devoted his speech to the theme of *tzedakah* —charity. He quoted parables, invoked the authority of Talmudic sages, added argument to argument, asking those who were well off to share with the have-nots, the victims of providence, the deprived ones, so as not to embarrass them at the Seder, when through the open door the Prophet Elijah would enter and be their guest of honor.

On no other holiday is food that important—on no other holiday is money that important.

Rebbe Naphtali explained, argued, pleaded, ordered. Never before had he spoken with such ardor; never before had he put his entire soul into every one of his words. For this was the time of year when the poor felt even poorer. He had to bring them some joy for the holiday. He had to succeed in convincing his congregation—he *had* to, at any price.

Back home, after services, he fell into a chair, exhausted. His wife asked him how it went. Were there many people? Yes, many; the place was packed. Did so-and-so attend? Yes. And such-and-such? Also. Did you speak? Yes. Were you good? Yes, I believe so. Did you succeed in convincing them? With a smile, Rebbe Naphtali answered: "I only half succeeded, and that isn't bad." And as his wife seemed puzzled, he explained: "I convinced the poor to receive—but not the rich to give."

Original, picturesque, amusing, Rebbe Naphtali was a friend, a peer, of the greatest—with a difference: he dared to antagonize the holy Seer of Lublin, who disliked his sense of humor, and Rebbe Mendel of Riminov, who distrusted his political views. He even dared—albeit respectfully—to mock the founder of a school, the revered Rebbe Elimelekh of Lizensk. He was Hasidism's *enfant terrible.* Most Masters spoke of God; he discussed everyday down-to-earth matters. Most Rebbes cried; he laughed. Better yet: he made other people laugh. Most tended to take life seriously, if not tragically; there were few things *he* took seriously. Laughter was one of them. "Why do you laugh while I am crying?" asked Rebbe Mendel of Riminov. "Because you are crying while I am laughing," he replied. For him, laughter performed a philosophical, quasi-religious function. With him, laughter became an integral part of Hasidic experience and its tales.

Another story:

The celebrated Rebbe Israel, Maggid of Kozhenitz, was said to have such powers that he could be denied nothing in the higher spheres. When the request was simple, he would close his eyes and whisper a prayer. When the request was more difficult to fulfill, he would include it in his thoughts during services. But the most complicated cases he would take up late, very late, at night, surrounded by silence and solitude. For each midnight, sitting on the floor, his forehead covered with ashes, he would mourn over the destruction of the Temple, whose flames still seemed to flicker in his eyes, and he would cry with such intense sorrow that it became impossible—up there—not to lend him an ear. His tears would open all the gates. And then, in the midst of his litanies, he would quickly slip in an urgent plea for this man rotting away in prison, or this other one with a dying wife—and all his wishes would be granted. And he knew it. And he was pleased.

Only once did he encounter a refusal. On one particular night his pleas were not accepted. His prayers were returned; his tears had no effect in heaven. Unhappy, he demanded an explanation. When he received it, he understood—and forgave.

For that same night Rebbe Naphtali of Ropshitz had been on the road, on his way to Kozhenitz. In the inn where he had stopped to rest, a wedding was in full swing; the men and women were drinking and eating and singing. Only the bride was sad, terribly sad. Rebbe Naphtali, who was traveling incognito, wanted to console her.

"Why are you sad?" he asked her.

"Because," she answered, "there is something missing in this wedding, something essential to make it festive and joyous. A jester! There is no jester here to make us laugh—that's why I am sad."

"Is that all?" the Rebbe cried out. "Then stop being sad! For the heavens, may they be blessed, have foreseen this possibility. They have sent me here tonight to dispel your sadness, for I am a *badkhan* by profession, a troubadour and jester—a wedding specialist!"

And he began to compose rhymes about the company, the innkeeper, the Rebbe and the cantor, and he did it with so much talent, so much humor, that all the guests fell under his spell and responded by laughing loud and hard. And the bride, too, was amused. To make her even happier, he sang with great exuberance and told funny stories—and danced—and danced. All around the table the guests were shaking with laughter, and up there, in paradise, the sages and the saints, sitting around their Master and ours, interrupted their studies and listened, and laughed, and laughed. And the angels forgot their nocturnal missions and flapped their wings, and laughed, and laughed. And in the palace of the celestial tribunal, the judges stopped judging and sentencing, and they, too, could not resist laughter. The Supreme Judge Himself stopped receiving His servants' prayers and litanies, including the tears of the holy Maggid of Kozhenitz—for He, too, was listening to the funny stories of Rebbe Naphtali. And He, too, was laughing, He was laughing. . . .

Later the Maggid of Kozhenitz would say to his friend and disciple, "Naphtali, Naphtali, are you aware of your own strength? What I cannot accomplish with my tears, you accomplish with laughter!"

Rebbe Naphtali of Ropshitz was born in 1760 in Linsk, a hamlet in Galicia, the very same day that the Besht died in Medzibozh.

Simple coincidence perhaps? Hasidism denies coincidences. No event is isolated, no encounter deprived of meaning. Some disciples insinuated that, on a very high level, Rebbe Naphtali was the Besht's successor. It is quite possible, since the same could be said—and was—of all great Masters. Except that these particular two personalities had few traits in common: if the Besht was the perfect Master, Rebbe Naphtali was the perfect disciple.

His father, a noted Talmudist, served as local Rabbi and was rather hostile to Hasidism. Not so his mother; she was the one who turned little Naphtali into a Hasid. At thirteen, for his Bar Mitzvah, he went with her to the great Rebbe Mikhel of Zlotchov, a disciple of the Besht and a companion of the Mezeritcher Maggid. Rebbe Mikhel was the one who helped him put on the *tefillin* for the first time, remarking, "I have just tied his soul up there; the knot will be a lasting one."

Shortly thereafter Naphtali was engaged to the daughter of a wealthy Jew, a wine merchant from Brody. The marriage created a sensation—though less than the divorce that followed one year later. The reason? One day he came home and found his young wife primping in front of a mirror. "Don't," he said. "I like you the way you are." "And the others don't count?" she answered. Troubled by such impudence, he fled from the house and took refuge with the Rebbe of Zlotchov, having already made up his mind to divorce.

When he remarried, a year later, he settled in Ropshitz as official Rebbe. Was he happier with his second wife? A witness, Rebbe Yekhezkel of Shineve, says no. And I quote: "Rebbe Naphtali of Ropshitz had the rare and awesome powers to bring the Messiah, but couldn't use them—he was prevented by heaven; he was given as a wife a woman who disturbed him, bored him and annoyed him."

She would often boast about her own erudition and piety, and remarked once that her father regretted that she was born a girl and not a boy, for then his son would have become the greatest of the great scholars alive. "In this case I agree with your father," said Rebbe Naphtali. "I also regret that you were not born a boy."

Was it because he spent so little time at home that she made his life miserable? Or was it, on the contrary, she who made him stay away so much? The fact remains that it was easier to meet him in other people's homes than in his own. Though he was the Rebbe of Ropshitz, and later also of his native town, where he inherited his father's position, he managed to assume and fulfill his official functions in both places—and at the same time roam around the capitals of the Hasidic universe.

He spent one year at the court of Rebbe Mordecai of Neskhiz. Then he spent some time with Rebbe Elimelekh of Lizensk, who at first refused to accept him as disciple: "I don't want celebrities in my house," he said. Crushed, the young Naphtali stretched out on the floor and began to shed bitter tears and even to spit blood. "Is it my fault my father is a Rebbe?" he cried. The Tzaddik of Lizensk finally gave in.

But these were brief attachments. Others, more lasting, linked him to the Seer of Lublin, the Maggid of Kozhenitz and Reb Mendel of Riminov. He sought their company; he admired all three, and all at once, as though to contradict the Lizensker theories of exclusivity. He, Naphtali of Ropshitz, demonstrated that one could have ties to more than one Master; that one could believe in more than one Tzaddik. He believed this so strongly that, while they were alive, he refused to serve as Rebbe himself.

All three died the same year: 1815–1816. He himself died in 1827. In other words, his reign lasted but ten years. Time enough to leave a mark on the life, the ways, and the language of Hasidism.

Time enough, also, to attract and keep disciples such as Rebbe Hayim of Sanz and Rebbe Sholem of Kaminka. They could frequently be found in his kitchen . . . peeling potatoes. Reb Hayim would say about him: "I never called him Rebbe, for I didn't learn anything from him. I couldn't. He was too profound for me. All I took from him . . . is *Yirat-Shamayim*, fear of heaven."

Ten years—time enough to make himself enemies as well— both inside and outside the Hasidic movement. The Mitnagdim —the adversaries—made his life so miserable that he predicted their punishment: after their death they would all return reincarnated as dogs. Inside the movement, his principal enemy was Reb Shlomo-Leib of Lentsheno. But as Hasidic quarrels go, this one was neither too serious nor too fierce. He suffered but didn't show it. Answering his critics, he quoted the Biblical phrase "And the Jews were jealous of both Moses and Aaron"; they resented Moses' solitude and Aaron's sociability. Impossible to please everybody.

Yet he had fewer adversaries, fewer rivals, fewer enemies than most Masters. Even among the Tzaddikim of faraway dynasties, his prestige was great. The Rizhiner praised his intelligence and so did the Premishlaner, and even the Pshiskher. He was invited to all the courts, to all the festivities; he earned his peers' loyalty by being loyal to them—all of them. He saw himself not as prince but as messenger, as link between the various Rebbes. If two Rebbes were rival or enemies, that was no reason for Rebbe Naphtali not to befriend both . . . and he did. Most leaders sought his allegiance, for they considered him not only a valuable friend but also a man of wisdom. In Hasidic literature he is most often described as a wise man—wisdom is his trademark. "Rebbe Naphtali is a *hokhem*," other leaders would say.

A strange description, because he often did not act "wisely" at all. He frequently got himself into trouble because of his humor—and he was always saved by his humor. He loved to tease the Masters he admired. When the Rizhiner paid him a compliment, expecting some words of protest—he did not protest. The Maggid of Kozhenitz, eternally ill, goes to the *mikvah*? Rebbe Naphtali slips into the Maggid's bed. Rebbe Elimelekh insists on remaining in his chambers for an hour of isolation between *Minha* and *Maariv*? Rebbe Naphtali hides under the Rebbe's bed. If that isn't enough, he dares to imitate him in public—leaning on his cane the way he does, frowning in concentration the way he does and even distributing blessings to followers in distress . . . the way he does.

Strangely enough, Rebbe Elimelekh—known for his temper —let him get away with it. "Aha," he said, "I see you have learned my tricks."

Rebbe Naphtali got away with worse offenses, perhaps because they were not directed against any one Tzaddik in particular, but against all. He was, and yet was not, one of them. Other Rebbes attracted admirers by offering them miracles? He offered no miracles and wanted no admirers. He said, "Rebbes usually pray that people should come to see them and be helped. I pray that they should be helped at home."

And . . . he was forgiven. Forgiven his skeptical comments,

his sharp remarks. Forgiven his way of gently mocking his own peers and their habit of taking money for their services. Invited to spend Shabbat at Vielipol, he asked a fee: twenty coins. They promised to pay—and didn't. They couldn't. So he demanded that the synagogue's chandelier be taken down and given to him. Did he need it? Or take it? Of course not; this was his way of refusing all fees. A visitor said, "We are told that the universe was created six thousand years ago, yet astronomers claim that there exists one star which is visible once every thirty-six thousand years!" "So what?" commented the Rebbe. "God can be found in this mystery too. Look for Him—not for the star."

He was forgiven everything—because of his humor. Furthermore, his wit was directed only at the Masters and never at the followers. He loved Rebbes and loved Hasidim. He wanted to be both—and to serve as bridge between them.

"For a long time I refused the role of leader," said he, "because a Rebbe must flatter his followers. I had thought of becoming a tailor, a cobbler, a street sweeper, a bath attendant, even a beadle. And then I realized that the tailor, too, must flatter his customers. And so must the beadle. And the cobbler. So . . . I might as well join the rabbinate."

Even as Rebbe, he adopted an attitude of amused sobriety toward himself. One day he remarked: "In the more distant provinces I am called Rebbe Naphtali of Ropshitz. In Ropshitz, where I am well known, I am referred to as the Rebbe of Ropshitz. But my wife, who knows me best, simply calls me Naphtali." He himself preferred the surname Naphtali *der Belfer*—the tutor.

His very first sermon in Ropshitz made a stir. It is customary on Shabbat that the speaker take into account three principles: the speech must be true, brief, and linked to the Sidra (section of the Torah) of the week. "Well," he said, "I confess I don't know what portion is being read this week. This is true, brief, and to the point." End of speech.

His practical advice to preachers: Make the introduction concise and the conclusion abrupt—with nothing in between.

Another time he ascended the *bimah*, the podium. It was Shabbat Shuva, between Rosh Hashana and Yom Kippur. For what seemed a long time, he silently stared at the congregation. Then he said: "What is man? A worm of the earth—and yet you fear his words." And once more he came down from the *bimah* without another word.

His strong point, however, was not sermons but conversation. His sense of humor was direct, concrete, and showed a swift and sharp mind. Every one of his words hit home.

Even as a child, he baffled adults with his quick replies. A visitor, a friend of his father, turned to him one day and said: "Naphtali . . . if you tell me where God can be found, I'll give you a golden coin." Answered the child: "And I'll give you two if you tell me where He can*not* be found."

A Hasid implored him to intercede in heaven on his behalf, saying, "I study, I learn Torah day and night, and I do not make any progress; I still don't know it." "God didn't ask you to *know* His law, but to study it," was the Rebbe's reply.

Another Hasid, wishing to repent, came to see him—with a story, the classic story about a friend who had committed all the sins enumerated by Torah: sins against God, sins against man, and against himself. But now the friend had seen the light, had repented, and would like to know what to do to expiate his sins. "But he is timid and doesn't dare come himself. What advice would you give him?" "He should come and say that he is speaking not for himself but for his friend," was the Rebbe's tongue-in-cheek reply.

Once, while going around collecting funds to ransom prisoners, he arrived in a small village where there lived a Jew known for his money and for his unwillingness to part with it. Fearing the rhetorical talents of the Rebbe, this Jew hid in the hayloft under a huge bundle of hay. Knowing his man, the Ropshitzer went straight to the hiding place. Face to face with the embarrassed miser, he had this sublime word: "The Talmud claims that to offer hospitality is a deed more important than welcoming the Shekhina. I never understood why; now I do. To welcome the Shekhina, Moses covered his face. You, when you receive guests, cover your entire body."

He hated misers—he hated them almost as much as fools and hypocrites. Hypocrisy was to him the most degrading of sins; he loved to expose it. Nothing made him happier than to unmask self-styled ascetics who wanted only to impress others. "Life is given to man to be lived," he would say. "To mutilate life is to offend its source; to choose suffering is to reject a gift both rare and irreplaceable. The path to paradise leads through the world of reality," he maintained.

He, incidentally, displayed but a very qualified interest in paradise. He affirmed without the slightest hesitation, "Better to go to hell with wise men than to paradise with fools." The Seer of Lublin reproached him with attaching too much importance to intelligence. This is what he answered: "Yes, it is true that the Torah orders man to be naïve, or whole—*tamim*—with God. Only, to be naïve, one must be *very* intelligent." On another occasion he said: "Three principal virtues enable man to comprehend and communicate truth. They are kindness, devotion and intelligence. Kindness alone leads to promiscuity; devotion alone comes close to stupidity; intelligence alone is conducive to crime. So it is essential that the three qualities be present together for man to benefit from them." Well, he possessed them all. But above all, he was known for his wit and intelligence.

However, a question arises: What made him so clever? What exactly did his intelligence consist of? In his two posthumous collections we read his comments on Torah, we repeat his amusing anecdotes. We smile, we laugh—but we do not cry out in wonder. We are struck neither by the depth of his perception nor by his erudition. On the contrary, his metaphors, though brilliant, lack the anguish of a Kotzker saying and the fire of a Bratzlaver tale. Where is his famous *hokhma*, his wisdom, of which one speaks so much in Hasidic literature? In that he managed to serve several Masters at once without arousing their jealousy? Because he enjoyed himself and enjoyed practical jokes? Because he possessed common sense, a talent for practical living . . . and making friends?

We should like to know his own perception of *hokhma*. Unfortunately, it was either not formulated or not transmitted. Was it wisdom? Shrewdness? Intuition? We do know this: that every time his wisdom was mentioned he replied with some witty line—as though to prove that he did not take it seriously. The word provoked a strange reflex in his behavior—a reflex seemingly unrelated to the subject matter.

One day the Rizhiner said to him, "You are considered a sage. So tell us a story." And Rebbe Naphtali obeyed. He told a story, a terrible story, about how a long time ago he had deceived a notorious village miser by impersonating the son-in-law of Rebbe Meir Ba'al Hanes, the famous miracle-maker of the second century. Fooled, the miser gave him money, which he, the Ropshitzer, and his companions, used to purchase some . . . *yash*—liquor. This is wisdom? This is compassion? More surprising is the Rizhiner's comment: "I knew that you were a sage—but not like this!" And both burst out laughing. What were they laughing about? At whose expense?

It would appear that for the Ropshitzer—and the Rizhiner—intelligence and wit were weapons to be used as defense. Rebbe Naphtali loved to tell of his verbal exchanges and in particular he liked to tell about the only three he had lost.

The first time he lost to his son, the future Rebbe Eliezer of Dzikow. Seeing him play one day, Rebbe Naphtali scolded him for wasting precious time, time he could have put to better use—to study Torah, for instance. "It's not my fault," said the little boy. "It's the fault of the *yetzer-hara*, the evil spirit. It's he who led me into sin." "Well answered, son," said the father. "But you should follow the example of the *yetzer-hara*; even he, by inducing you to sin, obeys God's will. Why don't you do likewise?" "For him it's easy," said the little boy. "The *yetzer-*

hara has no *yetzer-hara* to talk him into disobeying God's will!"

The second time he was defeated by a little girl. He had met her in a small village with perhaps ten Jewish men among its few inhabitants. Still, it did have a synagogue and a cemetery. "I don't understand," said the Rebbe to the little girl. "Either the cemetery or the synagogue is superfluous. If one of the ten men dies, there will be no more services in the synagogue. If no one dies, what's the cemetery for?" "Don't worry," said the little girl. "The synagogue will remain open. As for the cemetery, it's for visiting strangers."

The third defeat was inflicted upon him by a coachman. It was on Simhat Torah eve. The Hasidim were rejoicing, celebrating—as one should—the presence and sanctity of the Torah by dancing to the point of drunkenness, by singing to the point of ecstasy. Suddenly the Ropshitzer saw in the middle of the crowd a coachman who was known for his primitive ways and his ignorance. "What?" the Rebbe cried out. "You participate in the festivity? You who never study Torah, you who obey its commandments so badly and so rarely? How does this festivity concern you?" And the coachman replied, "Rebbe, Rebbe, if my brother arranges a wedding, a Bar Mitzvah or any other celebration, am I not allowed to participate?"

This anecdote, which seems cruel, damages him, not the coachman. Yet he himself told it—to show that the coachman was right, that the coachman had a better understanding of things than he.

For this complex and complicated Tzaddik was, in spite of appearances, profoundly humble—and sad. But his humility was hidden under arrogance and pride, just as his melancholy was covered with exuberance.

It is told that one night he was surprised by a visitor from his village who found him sitting on the ground, his face bathed in tears, lamenting the destruction of the Temple in Jerusalem. Yet, lest the visitor take him for a hidden saint, he began to indulge in self-glorification: "Oh," he said aloud, "if the Jews of Ropshitz only knew the true qualities, the rare greatness of their

Rebbe!" He wanted people to take him for a vain person, an actor, anything rather than a Just Man.

He loved to comment on the passage in Talmud in which God showed Moses *Dor dor vedorshav*—the men and women of all future generations and their leaders. "Why," he asked, "did God not start with the leaders? This is why: because of the regression in history. The closer we come to our times, the less striking are the leaders. Imagine Moses resting his gaze on me. He would undoubtedly cry out, 'What? Naphtali, too, is a Rebbe?' But since God would by then have shown him my contemporaries, Moses would understand: 'All right, let it be. He, too, can be a leader . . . alas!' "

To understand him better, we must analyze his attachment to his favorite *mitzvah*: that of dwelling in the *succah*. Like the Berditchever, he said that his very soul was rooted in that commandment. Not one day went by without his mentioning something connected with Succoth, the Feast of the Huts, which lasts only one week. This attachment is symbolic. What is a *succah*? Half tent, half hut, a temporary refuge whose one side remains constantly exposed to rains and winds. It is small, modest and austere—it is meant to remind us of our life in the desert.

Rebbe Naphtali's obsession with Succoth offers the first clue to his hidden image. Only someone who dwells in the desert seeks a tent with such intensity. To rest. To breathe. To dream. What is the *succah* if not the Temple of Jerusalem before Jerusalem—the vision before fulfillment? Only a nostalgic and unhappy visionary would dream of dwelling year-round in his own private *succah*.

The Ropshitzer—sad? Unhappy? He whose gaiety was as legendary as was the Kotzker's melancholy? People saw his laughter but not the torment beneath it; he ranks among the most misunderstood figures in Hasidism.

That is what he wanted: not to be understood. Not to be pitied. He concealed his pain—and that was his wisdom. He laughed so as not to cry; he chose exhibitionism so as to hide his anguish, his lack of confidence in himself, in his own prayers, in his own words.

One Shabbat, surrounded by his followers, he delivered an impressive address. Everyone present listened with bated breath and rose with him to the highest spheres of mystical meditation. He tore away the veils, one after another and one and all could witness creation. After Shabbat was over, Rebbe Naphtali ran to his friend and teacher Reb Mendel of Riminov. "I'm afraid," he said, "I'm afraid I spoke too well; I must have said things I shouldn't have. . . ." Reb Mendel asked him to repeat the address, so he could judge for himself. And I like to believe that Rebbe Naphtali improvised another lecture on the spot.

Was he consoled? Comforted? If so, it didn't last long. It never did. From his early youth he lacked self-confidence, to the point of soliciting blessings from everyone, even from strangers. Before the Jew of Pshiskhe became known, Naphtali Ropshitzer asked for his blessings.

To his disciple Reb Yehuda-Zvi of Razdal he said, "One day you will be Rebbe. You will have to offer blessings to people. So start with me." The disciple refused. "You are wrong," insisted the Ropshitzer. "You see, when I was your age, the great Levi-Yitzhak of Berditchev pleaded with me for the same favor, and I also refused. And I regret it to this day."

Behind the visible Ropshitzer, there was another, invisible one. The first told stories, teased the great and amused them; the second, withdrawn in his own inner tent, lived in silence and torment, aspiring to attain some unattainable truth.

The first was active, militant, gay, exuberant—singing the praises of hope and life in the best tradition of the Baal Shem Tov. His very presence drove away sadness. With one funny remark he disarmed sadness; with one word he brought joy. No matter what the cost, the unhappy Jews in Galicia, who had nobody but their Rebbe in the whole world, needed to laugh, to rejoice, to hold on to existence. In this respect, the Ropshitzer performed a vital function: his combat against despair was a personal one. He didn't trust disciples or messengers; he came alone wherever communities in distress were in danger of giving in to resignation. His weapons? Song and laughter.

One evening of Simhat Torah the news arrived that his friend and disciple Reb Avraham of Ulanov had died. The Hasidim did not have the heart to go on with the festivities. But Reb Naphtali scolded them angrily: "Are we not at war—at war with destiny, with the entire world? What does one do at the front when an officer falls? Does one run away? On the contrary, one closes ranks and fights even harder. So close your ranks and dance, dance, with more vigor than ever; dance like you have never danced before!"

On another occasion he remarked, "What is a Hasid? Someone who possesses a precious key, a key that opens all the doors, even those that God keeps closed. And that key is . . . the *Niggun*, the song of joy that makes our hearts beat faster. The *Niggun* opens the gates of heaven, melancholy closes them."

Dynamic, tireless, the visible Tzaddik participated in Hasidic life. He encouraged, he mediated, he entertained wherever his talents were needed. He visited all the courts to bring them closer to each other. Rather than repudiate the society surrounding him, he worked on it from the inside. He said, "What is the difference between the Prophet and the Tzaddik? The Prophet unveils the future—and the Tzaddik the present. The Tzaddik's task is the more difficult."

Yet he himself accomplished it. He was the wandering minstrel who brought smiles to poor children and memories to their old, tired grandparents. In the famous quarrel between Lublin and Pshiskhe, he vainly urged moderation. Though not publicly, he opposed the messianic conspiracy of his three friends; he was against suffering and war—against using them for any purpose, be it the most sacred of all.

The conspiracy failed, and the three Masters died in the same year. It was Rebbe Naphtali who saw to the holy Seer's burial. Dressed as a gravedigger, his clothes covered with mud, he buried him in Lublin, whispering, "This is how one looks when one buries one's teacher."

He always found the right word for every situation. But behind words, there are other words, inaudible, imperceptible words. And behind them, there is silence.

There was silence in Rebbe Naphtali.

This is a parable he loved to retell: One day the Czar, while inspecting his troops at the front, fails to notice an enemy soldier whose rifle is aimed at him. Fortunately for the Czar, one of his loyal soldiers pulls the imperial horse's reins and so averts tragedy. The grateful Czar says to his savior, "Tell me your secret wish and consider it granted." "Majesty," says the soldier, "my corporal is cruel; send him to another company." "Fool!" the Czar cries out. "Why don't you ask to be made corporal yourself?"

Man's tragedy lies not in what he is denied but in his inability to formulate his desire. He demands too little; he is afraid to set his sights too high; his dreams drag in the dust and his words are empty. That may have been the realization that came to Rebbe Naphtali as he approached the end of his life.

Did he regret his past? Regret that he had not chosen another path? That is possible. Once upon a time, in his youth, he had sought truth in ascetic modes; he had rolled naked in the snow and he had practiced prolonged fasting. He had given all that up—as a Hasid, he had to. Now it was too late to start all over. The traveler had reached the end of his journey. The singer felt no further desire to confront his audience. The minstrel was tired. Now it was the *other* Ropshitzer who emerged and dominated.

Rebbe Naphtali went into seclusion. He stopped entertaining, stopped visiting Rebbes and receiving their disciples; he turned away from his own followers and retired into his own beloved, invisible and haunted *succah*. Surprisingly, and symbolically, he stopped speaking.

For months and months no word left his lips. To the questions of his son, Reb Eliezer of Dzikow, he opposed absolute silence. In the beginning he would explain by gestures that his muteness was due to fatigue, to exhaustion, and ought not be mystically interpreted. Later he stopped explaining altogether. He remained silent. Alone.

Then came the last day. The sick father and his son were alone.

"Speak, Father," begs Reb Eliezer. "Say something, one word." The old Master looks at him and says nothing. "You can," pleads the son, "I know you can. You can speak. Why don't you? Why don't you want to speak, Father?"

The old Master stares at him for a long, long moment and then replies in a hoarse, halting whisper: "I . . . am . . . afraid. Do you . . . understand? Do you understand, Eliezer? I. Am. Afraid."

Afraid of what? Of whom? We shall never know.

THE SCHOOL
OF WORKE

WORKE: another kingdom, a new, enchanting Hasidic adventure—another aspect of Hasidic language, another face of the Hasidic movement.

Worke: a song both humble and powerful—a whisper with profound reverberations of communal life, intense and intriguing alike. Worke: a fervent but restrained prayer—full of ecstasy, but controlled ecstasy. Worke: a journey to the end of language—to the birth of silence.

Silence: that is the seal and distinction of Worke. Elsewhere, Masters and guides talk and make others talk, sing and move others to sing; they shout and are obeyed in this world and in the other. Not here, not in Worke. Here you will meet a silent Hasidism, meant to allow each and every disciple to meditate quietly, though with the Master and through the Master.

Listen to testimony given by Rebbe Berish of Biala:

"It happened during a Shabbat meal. Our holy teacher, the Tzaddik of Worke, was presiding. Lost in thought, he looked at us and at the twilight looming behind us, and said nothing; and we, at his table, listened and said nothing. For a while we could hear only the buzzing of flies on the walls; then we didn't even hear that. We heard the shadows as they invaded the House of Study and brushed the burning faces of the Hasidim; then we stopped hearing even them. Finally, we heard only the silence

175

that emanated from the Rebbe united with our own; solemn and grave, but passionate and vibrant, it called for beauty and friendship. We had rarely experienced such communion. We lost all sense of time; we were living in another sphere, in another universe, where silence was the only language available to man. Then, all of a sudden, the Rebbe shook himself and asked that the *Birkat ha-Mazon* be recited—and that was the end of that."

And the Rebbe of Biala concluded, "Well, let me tell you: what a lesson, what a lesson I received that day. . . . The Master submitted me to a severe and rigorous interrogation that made me shiver. I felt my heart ready to burst—and my arteries too. But I was lucky and the Almighty came to my rescue . . . I passed the test, I knew what to say. What a lesson, what a lesson. . . ."

Actually, to do this the right way and really translate the spirit of Worke, perhaps we ought to bring back Worke in its own style and manner, namely, not with words but with silence.

But we have not yet reached Worke, we have not yet reached that level. We have just set out on our journey. And what do travelers with a long journey ahead of them do? They tell each other stories. So—let us tell each other stories.

The ones about Worke and its leaders are, naturally, endowed with wisdom, charm and depth, although the Masters of the school of Worke, in comparison to their predecessors, are less famous, less important. But then—why compare them at all? Hasidic legends are strikingly singular in that they deny analogies. Every Hasid is called upon to recognize his Master as the greatest—and he will be right. What Hasidism did was to restore to the individual Jew his ability to praise and admire and follow and trust and love. To feel less lonely, less vulnerable, less abandoned, the Hasid had to believe in the strength and wisdom of *his* Rebbe. Each Master was different, as were their followers, but their relationship to their followers was similar: every Rebbe responded to the same need, evoked the same response and told the same tale. There were many Rebbes and many more Hasidim, but all were taught to believe that life has meaning, that words are rooted in a memory older than our own, and that the Hasid's song contains the song of rivers and forests, clouds and fields; all were convinced that man and God are anything but strangers to one another.

In Hasidic terms, every person is unique—but the Rebbe is more so. The Besht was unique—as was his successor, the celebrated Maggid of Mezeritch, the architect and organizational genius of the new movement. And as were his disciples: Rebbe Shneur-Zalman of Lyady with his emphasis on learning and passion; Rebbe Aharon of Karlin with his contagious enthusiasm; Rebbe Levi-Yitzhak of Berditchev with his love, his all-consuming love for Israel; Rebbe Nahman of Bratzlav with his fiery imagination; Rebbe Mendel of Kotzk with his holy anguish. Each had his own vision, each elaborated his own method, each developed his own imprint. Again, it must be stressed, this derives naturally from the basic concept of Judaism: for man, God is one—and for God every human being is one, irreplaceable, never interchangeable: God and God alone may say "I"—but we are all made in His image, we are all part of His "I." Thus all men, including those who oppose Him and contradict one another, meet in God.

Remember the four sons in the Passover Haggada? The Rasha—the wicked one—refuses the tale altogether; he says: *Ma haavoda hazot lackhem*—what is all this to you? What do I have to do with it—or you? The Haggada does not concern me.

And what is our response? We include him against his will! His very opposition to the Jewish tradition becomes part of the Jewish tradition.

How did the Rizhiner put it? If the Rasha, the wicked atheist, were to know that in opposing God he actually obeys Him, he would have a heart attack.

God is everywhere and in all things; this is the basic belief formulated in the Zohar and glorified in Hasidic texts. God dwells in all hearts—God is in everything that brings people together, but also in everything that tears them apart.

Hasidism, therefore, strove not only for harmony but also for variety: all dynasties are interrelated; Hasidism is a tree, and although the branches are separate, they are alive—only because the tree is alive.

Hasidism puts special emphasis on this approach.

Though Rebbe Elimelekh and Rebbe Zusia were brothers, they were different—and Hasidism might well not have been what it was had they been more alike. Was one greater than the other? Was the Tzaddik of Alexander more important than the Tzaddik of Ger? No—such comparisons are unwarranted. A Rebbe is to be compared to himself alone, which means: he is not always equal to himself, which means: he is human.

And necessarily different. Therefore, the leaders of the school of Worke were as essential to the growth and development of Hasidism as any other. True, they are less known. A matter of temperament or luck—or injustice? Some Hasidic Masters are more celebrated than others: Reb Mendel of Vitebsk is better known than Reb Wolfe of Zbarazh; the Shpoler Zeide is less influential today than his adversary Rebbe Nahman.

I confess that I am unable to discriminate among them—I love them all and, at various times, one more than the others. Much depends on my mood. Sometimes I need a Bratzlaver tale, sometimes I need a Rizhiner saying. I particularly love the modest Masters, the humble ones, those who didn't "make it," not really; those who simply wished to be companions or disciples of great Masters and remained reserved and withdrawn; in other words I am fond of the Tzaddikim of the school of Worke, this small village near Warsaw which would have found no place in Hasidic history were it not for the fact that a certain Rebbe Itzhak of Kalish came to settle there.

Let us follow him there—it's worth while. We shall learn the importance of collective silence in Hasidism. Let us go to Worke and witness the metamorphosis of words into other words—and then into something else.

Worke represents an unknown area in Hasidism—unknown

and unsung. No grandiose projects were undertaken there, nor were there any dramatic upheavals to cope with. Its two Rebbes —father and son—were not heroes of any spectacular movements—nor were they victims of any mystical mishap. Worke's originality lies in its modesty—and in the intensity of its particular form of communication.

Worke represents silence—Hasidic silence—which may sound like a contradiction in terms: somehow we do not imagine Hasidim silent; silence is not usually one of their virtues. But then Hasidism never claimed to resolve human contradictions—rather, it assumed they were there. You need an example? Come—let us go to Worke.

Its followers will teach us that silence too has its place in Hasidism. I hope you will find it as attractive as I do. The world has become increasingly noisy. Society has never used so many means to tell, report, investigate, explain, comment, articulate, reveal, expose and criticize; no generation has ever been more talkative—and no generation has managed to say less.

The Torah speaks of God hiding His face. "I am glad it does," said Rebbe Itzhak of Worke. "I am glad that the Torah tells us that there are things we cannot understand—and never will. *Andersh wolt men es nisht oisgehalten*—Were it not for the Torah saying it, we would find it intolerable."

Ancient sages have told us that it takes a person three years to learn how to talk—and seventy years how to be silent. Let us go to Worke: a poetic kingdom is waiting for us there.

Rebbe Menahem-Mendel, the angry old man of Kotzk, once said to Rebbe Mendel of Worke, son of Itzhak, "You seem to have mastered the art of being silent—where have you learned it?" And Rebbe Mendel did not answer.

Clearly, silence can be traced back to the very origins of mankind. If God's word is eternal, so is His silence. But before God spoke, before God did anything—what did He do? He waited? Yes, He waited. For His word to become creation—and for His creation to be expressed in words. God being both source and fulfillment of silence *and* language, there is no conflict between the two—on *His* level. The conflict exists only on the human level, where words form the human language and silence is a form of divine language—or a divine form of language, which is slightly different. For us, both represent a challenge and even a threat: the mystery of one matches that of the other. Adam listened before he spoke—and only God can listen and speak at the same time. For Him, both language and silence point to harmony, and no creation can be accomplished without them.

The theme of silence is rooted in the Bible itself. All those unfinished sentences, all those questions that remain unanswered: God asking Adam, *Ayekha?*—Where are you?—without even waiting for an explanation.

Hence the primary tension in him—and in us—between the human word and the silence of the world. The mystery of the one is matched by the elusiveness of the other. Both are dangerous, therefore attractive vehicles for men of faith, visionaries, poets.

As a child, I yearned for silence—the mystical silence that evokes faraway secrets and forbidden truth. My teachers taught me how to cleanse language and thought by refusing to indulge in language and thought, thereby hastening the coming of the Messiah. Let all men be silent, I thought, and man will be saved.

In Scripture, silence appears on every page, variously as theme, subject, action, illustration of human weakness or its ultimate dénouement.

Silence in man's relations to others, silence in man's attitude toward God, silence enveloping the word of God.

Vayomer Cain el Hevel achiv—and Cain spoke to his brother Abel. . . . And the text does not tell us what he said to him. As though Scripture wanted to let us know that Abel did not listen. And this is perhaps how we are to understand the meaning of the first murder of a man by his brother: one spoke and the other was silent—his silence denied language and was opposed to it; and this kind of silence cannot but end in death.

On that level, silence is sinful, for it means indifference. Why was Job punished? Because in Egypt, as one of Pharaoh's advisers, he chose prudently to remain neutral. He kept quiet. His silence made him an accomplice. Neutrality and silence favor the killer, always; never the victim.

We encounter the same idea in the tragic story of Nadav and Avihu, Aaron's two sons, killed together for having penetrated, desecrated the sanctuary. What was their sin? They were too ambitious, according to Talmudic commentators. They aspired to succeed Moses and Aaron and become Israel's new leaders. One day, Nadav is supposed to have said to his brother Avihu, "When are these old men going to die and let us take over?" That is why they were punished. But there is something wrong with this explanation. We understand why Nadav deserved punishment; he had spoken with arrogance. But his brother had not; in fact he had said nothing—then why was *he* punished? The answer is: That is why. Because he said nothing. He should have protested; his silence made him an accomplice. Even Moses was punished because he failed to object when, in the land of Midian, he was referred to as *Ish mitzri*—the Egyptian.

But then, there are times when silence is interpreted as virtue. When he lost his two sons, *Vayidom Aharon*—Aaron remained mute. He suppressed his pain and his tears. And he is praised for not having spoken.

Before crossing the Red Sea, Moses turned to his people and shouted, "*Adoshem yilachem lachem veatem tachrishun?*—God will fight for you and you will be silent?" What did he want them to do? What could they have done? Fight? With what? No, the sentence has a different meaning. Saul Liebermann, the eminent Talmudic scholar, with his special sense of humor, would simply change the question mark into an exclamation point: God will fight for you, provided you keep quiet!

For God loves silence—or as Rabbi Eliezer of Worms put it: God *is* silence. After the tempest at Sinai, after the thunder and the lightning, there is silence—and that silence signifies that God is present, ready to be heard.

Silence can appease, it can carry melodies and dreams—but it can also open you to anguish and sadness, even to anger. In the Talmud we often meet sages who, in their final hour, do not hesitate to cry out, "But why, why is the Almighty silent?" *Mi kamocha baelim adoshem*—Who among the gods can be compared to you? *Al tikre elim ki im ilemim ki roe beelbon banav veshotek*: Who is as mute as You, God, for You witness the shame and the sorrow of Your children and still You say nothing. . . ."

Said one of the Masters in Worke, "Isaac, son of Abraham, never lost his temper, never got angry—and that is fortunate, for his anger could have destroyed mankind. Instead, his silence saved the world."

So—let us go to Worke and meet its founder, Rebbe Itzhak —or Reb Itzikl, as he was affectionately called.

A disciple and friend of several great Hasidic masters, Reb Itzikl shared in their greatness. He himself has been revered for his saintliness, his knowledge, his humanity, his piety and his modesty.

In Hasidic chronicles we find facts and anecdotes, sayings and episodes that help us reconstruct his portrait.

We know that he was born in 1779 in Zaloshin, a small village near Kalish, in western Poland. His father was affectionately called Reb Shimon Baal-Rachmones: the charitable Reb Shimon. Married at the age of fifteen, Reb Itzikl settled in Zharik, where his wife's family lived.

We know that he was not happy. His wife made too many demands on his time; she treated servants too harshly; she seems to have lacked the sweetly subdued, resigned manner that, in those times, people considered a necessary virtue in a Jewish woman. So miserable was he that he solicited the advice of his first Rebbe, David of Lelov, who gently admonished him not to talk about it—not even to him. And so—he never mentioned it again.

Sources give varying accounts of how he earned his livelihood. In the beginning he was employed by Temerl, the famous woman benefactor whose place in Hasidic legend and lore is often as prominent as that of certain Masters. He was her "regional representative" for a number of years. At one time the government gave him the concession for all local tobacco sales. This we know because we are told that he lacked the funds to pay for the concession. We also know that he owed a certain Reb Hersh Friedman ten thousand golden coins. Before becoming Rebbe he lived in a rented one-room apartment. Even after that, he lived in poverty. An eyewitness relates the following episode: One day, as Reb Itzikl was teaching his afternoon course at the House of Study, his wife came in and angrily interrupted him: "You do nothing but teach," she shouted. "You do nothing but study, and there is nothing to eat at home."

A scholar himself, he was an intimate friend of the first Rebbe of Ger and of the Kotzker, who were both renowned for their erudition. He was also close to the Rizhiner and to Rebbe Yehezkel of Kuzhmir. He traveled frequently. And whenever he went from Zharik to Warsaw he never failed to bring news or messages from their families to the Zharik girls who worked as servants in the capital city. Everybody knew that he was always in a hurry. In fact, he found it necessary to explain why: A Jew is always running, he said. Running *from* sin, running *to* study or pray; a Jew does nothing slowly; he lives fast.

Because of his business activities he had to learn Polish—and he did. He spoke it well, though not as well as Yiddish.

What else do we know? He suffered from insomnia; he would sleep twelve minutes, wake up to study and doze off for another twelve minutes. . . . He was a disciple of more than one Rebbe. Rebbe David of Lelov was one of his teachers, as were the holy Seer of Lublin, Reb Bunam of Pshiskhe and Reb Mendel of Kotzk. He died at the age of seventy, in 1848, on the last day of Passover, having served for twenty years as head of the school of Worke. His two sons continued the dynasty of Worke—the elder as founder of the Amshinov line and the younger as the new Tzaddik of Worke.

In Lublin, he was included in the Seer's private *minyan*. Here is how it happened: When he was first introduced to the holy Seer, Reb Itzikl felt so intimidated that he couldn't utter a word.

"Are you studying?" the Seer asked him. "I am," said Reb Itzikl. "Do you know?" "I try," said Reb Itzikl. "Do you understand?" "I try," said Reb Itzikl. "Have you come up with anything new?" "No," said Reb Itzikl. "All I do is I repeat—I repeat the words and thoughts of our sages—that is enough for me. But today . . ." He stopped in the middle of the sentence and the Seer had to urge him to continue. "Today," said Reb Itzikl, "I studied the question of witnesses who testify before a tribunal. And I do not understand." "What didn't you understand?" "The Talmud stipulates that close relatives may not testify either for or against the defendant. And this I fail to comprehend. I understand why relatives ought not to testify on behalf of a defendant: they are biased. But why couldn't they testify *against*?" "Excellent question," said the Seer. "And what is the answer?" And this is what Reb Itzikl replied: "The Torah says, referring to the witnesses, *Veamdu shnei anashim*—Two persons, meaning two human beings, must testify. Well, a person who would be prepared to testify against a close relative is not human. . . ." The Seer smiled. He enjoyed the question and the answer—and that is how he admitted young Reb Itzikl into his private *minyan*.

Unlike others, Reb Itzikl stayed in Lublin—or rather, Lublin stayed in him—even after he left it. We remember with sadness the break between the Seer and his favorite disciple, Reb Yaakov-Yitzhak of Pshiskhe. Lublin signified miracles, while Pshiskhe meant study. In Pshiskhe they said: "Miracles? Ha! It's much more difficult for a Jew to be Jewish than to perform miracles." Unlike many of his friends, Reb Itzikl chose not to take sides. He admired Pshiskhe and loved Lublin. He himself, as Rebbe, preferred not to impress his followers by dealing with the supernatural.

A story: While he was still working for Temerl, a man came to beg him for three hundred rubles. He needed money desperately to marry off his daughter, who was desperate to get married—she was over eighteen already. "I cannot help you," said Reb Itzikl, who was known never to send visitors away empty-handed. The Jew began to weep: "If you don't help me, who will?" "Well," said Reb Itzikl, "come back tomorrow." Next day he gave him the three hundred rubles. "But why did you wait a whole day?" asked the Hasid. "Why did you let me worry?" "I wanted to teach you," answered Reb Itzikl, "not to rely on men—only on God, on God alone."

A sick man came to him in tears; the doctors had given him up. So Rebbe Itzhak set up a rabbinic court and "sentenced" him to stay alive—and he stayed alive.

We don't know for sure how long he stayed in his position as regional representative for Temerl. What we do know is that he enjoyed it. He talked about it often with relish and humor. Once he observed an inspector doing his work with particular devotion, looking everywhere, checking everything. Reb Itzikl spoke to him. "You know," he said, "perhaps your interpretation of the Torah is too strict; you need not interpret too literally the commandment Thou shalt not steal. You may, you know, yes, you may steal from time to time." "What?" said the overseer, who couldn't believe his ears. "You advise me to steal?!" "No," said Reb Itzikl. "You didn't understand. What I meant was that you may steal a minute here, a minute there, for study and prayer."

In this connection one is reminded of Rebbe Naphtali of Ropshitz, who said, "I read ten brilliant commentaries on the commandment Thou shalt not steal—I almost forgot that it also means simply: 'You shall not steal.' "

We don't know how Temerl, the business tycoon, felt about Reb Itzikl's ideas of labor relations. But we do know that she did not fire him. What is more, he took care of her interests even after he was crowned Rebbe—though not for long.

But perhaps he really did not want to become a Rebbe. Like many of his friends and teachers, he became Rebbe under protest. As they had, before him, he was forced to accept the crown of leadership. More than once, a Rebbe had to be coerced. But, as Reb Itzikl put it, a Hasidic Rebbe doesn't want to become Rebbe; but once he does, he remains Rebbe even in his sleep.

Reb Itzikl would have preferred to live his condition as Hasid and disciple. He would have preferred not to stay in any one place—even his own—but to roam around the courts and centers of Hasidic Masters. And there were many.

For that was the glorious era in Hasidism—an era of heightened hope and exuberance: all things seemed possible within the star-filled movement that had by then reached its climax.

Capitals of study, centers for prayer and meditation, sanctuaries for dreamers and spiritual rebels; they could be found all over, between the Carpathians and the Dnieper; and each bore its particular seal, each developed its distinctive theme. The dream of the Besht, nourished in his mountainous retreat, had blossomed and spread.

Lublin and Pshiskhe, Kotzk and Rizhin, Riminov and Ropshitz, Premishlan and Strelisk: there wasn't a village where the Baal Shem Tov's call for hope and faith was not heard and transmitted from home to home, from heart to heart.

The world outside was caught up in its own destructive and/or liberating upheavals, but the Hasidic movement, drunk with God and transfigured by His mystery, continued to broaden the scope of its conquest and deepen the intensity of its message.

Hasidism had never known such glory. In Kotzk they were busy trying to lift the world by lifting the heavens. In Rizhin they were determined to reinstate the royalty of Jerusalem's kings and princes. In countless courts and centers, men young and old sang and danced, studied and prayed, and everywhere they created bonds to alleviate Jewish solitude, to fight Jewish suffering and dispel Jewish melancholy. There were scores of communities, each with its own customs and melodies, its schools and its Masters—there were so many Masters available that Reb Itzikl refused to be one of them. However this was not a question of preference but of election; he had to yield. And so he used his position, his title, his prestige to help, to reconcile, to appease.

And he was badly needed. Success provokes quarrels, jealousies, among Hasidim. You admire one Master? Then you must fight others. To believe in two Rebbes is bigamy, according to Rebbe Aharon of Karlin. Exclusivity is emphasized in most quarters. Surely that is not only wrong, it's dangerous, but that's how it is, and there is nothing you can do about it. Nothing? Well, you can try to fight it—and Reb Itzikl did. He tried to make peace between the diverse factions and groups, between dissidents and dissidents of dissidents. He spent much time and energy to bring unity to the Jewish people.

Not that he himself escaped the professional scandalmongers. He too was slandered and vilified in old-fashioned rumor campaigns. What people said against him has not been recorded. We are told only that there were rumors.

An episode: One day he was told that one of those rumor-mongers had appeared in Worke, questioning his followers about him in order to smear his name. The Rebbe called in the man and said, "You wish to find out evil things about me—why do you go to others? I know more than they. Sit down and I will tell you worse things about myself than anyone can."

It was characteristic that he did not lose his temper; that he did not protest. Nothing: he remained quiet, friendly, smiling, generous even with an enemy.

While he was still in Pshiskhe, some people tried to provoke him. To this end, they used a simple man, a man without manners, to engage him in conversation while he was praying. "Could you give me some of your snuff?" the man asked. Reb Itzikl interrupted his prayer, gave him some tobacco and went back to his prayer. Three minutes later: "Could you give me some more of your snuff?" Again Reb Itzikl complied and went back to his prayer. Two minutes later: "Could I get some more?" Reb Itzikl smiled, gave him what he wanted—and went back to his prayer, which, because of the interruptions, lasted longer than usual. At the end—because eventually there was an end—he took off his prayer shawl and went over to the man. All those present were convinced that now he would reprimand him. No: Reb Itzikl was still smiling. He took his snuffbox from his pocket and handed it to the man, saying, "I think you need it more than I; when I want some tobacco, I'll ask *you* for it."

Legend has it that he owned a special vest, one he would wear every time he felt himself getting angry. By the time he had put it on, his anger would be gone. Then he would turn to his aide and say, Listen, *you* get angry—I cannot.

In this respect he was totally different from his great and terrible friend Reb Mendel of Kotzk, who elevated anger to the rank of theological principle. In Kotzk, people shouted and howled, shaking heaven and earth and tearing off all masks. In Worke, people meditated—and gathered strength.

There is a story about a Hasid of Worke who happened to arrive in Strelisk just as the followers of Reb Uri the Seraphin were in the middle of their services, singing loudly and shouting even more loudly.

"I understand, I understand," commented the gentle visitor. "You wish to obtain blessings for our people—so do we in Worke. But why are you using force? Have you tried kindness?"

Of his two disciples, who disagreed on everything, Rebbe Bunam of Pshiskhe said, "Both are ascetics and pure; but while Mendel wants to scorch the world with his fire, Itzikl tries to illuminate it with his."

To better comprehend the Masters of Worke, perhaps we ought to return, however briefly, to the Kotzker Rebbe—the solitary visionary who rejected all compromises, weaknesses and failings. Taking a position against the Hasidic establishment, he preached a return to sources, to the early hardships, the pioneering discoveries. The Kotzker felt that, sixty years after the Besht, it had become too easy to be a Hasid: people didn't study enough, didn't pray with enough devotion; they sacrificed truth for comfort and expediency. In Kotzk, he was going to change all that—and his followers trembled in anticipation. They were not many, but to him they were still too many. He disliked crowds; he considered them volatile and servile. He wanted an elite. "If only I could gather ten men to climb to the top of the world and shout that God is God," he would say. Ten? Ten times ten would have followed him. Anywhere. But he chased them away. And the more he chased them, the more they flocked to him to receive his knowledge and learn from him how to discern divine truth in human lies— or, better yet, divine truth in human truth.

For twenty years he lived in isolation and rage. Only three men were allowed into his study: the Gaon of Sochatchov, Rebbe Itse-Meir of Ger and Reb Itzikl of Worke.

When Reb Bunam of Pshiskhe passed away, his followers crowned the Kotzker as their new leader, although there had existed a greater affinity between Reb Itzikl and Reb Bunam. Both loved to travel; the Kotzker did not. Both were interested in secular matters; the Kotzker was not. Both saw themselves as part of society; the Kotzker did not. Both involved themselves in the material problems of their followers; the Kotzker did not. Both wished to change and enrich the world; the Kotzker aspired to escape from it.

But then why was the Kotzker chosen? *Because* he was different from the Master. This was how the disciples wanted to implement their late Master's ideas of rebellion. They applied them even to his succession: they elected someone who was *not* like him.

Reb Itzikl himself described the difference between Worke and Kotzk as follows: "Reb Mendel," he said, "is an express train going nonstop to Leipzig, whereas I am an omnibus; I stop in many places and pick up many passengers, who are permitted to come and go as they please. You see, not everybody is capable of going straight to Leipzig!"

One day, Reb Itzikl returned from a visit to the celebrated Reb Mottel of Chernobyl. "What did you see there?" the Kotzker wanted to know. "Just one thing: the table at which the Besht used to sit and study." "That's all?" commented the Kotzker. "That table is one hundred years old while we here study teachings that are six thousand years old. . . ."

Both were right—both approaches were necessary. *Ele veele*

divrei elokim hayim: God is everywhere—man is not; man is not even where he thinks he is.

Reb Itzikl and the Kotzker represented two opposing views in Hasidism, but they remained friends: both lived and worked *leshem shamayim*, for the sake of heaven.

The Kotzker yearned for solitude, Reb Itzikl opposed it. In Kotzk people believed that Kotzk was the center of the universe; in Worke they learned that the universe has more than one center. Every person is the center of creation—every person is called upon to justify creation.

Form played no role in Kotzk; it did in Worke. The Kotzker was indifferent to things visible, tangible and concrete; only the ineffable attracted him. Reb Itzikl of Worke mingled with his followers, visited their homes, queried them about their worries and preoccupations, shared in their joys as well as in their sorrows; he even took part in the political activity of certain Jewish groups that were working to improve conditions for the Jews. He sometimes went to see influential politicians and social leaders to solicit their help. It is known that he asked for and obtained an audience with the influential Jewish philanthropist Sir Moses Montefiore. We even know where that meeting took place: in the so-called Green Inn near Lomza. What was his request? Better treatment for Russian and Polish Jews—for all Jews, but especially for Hasidim. He wanted permission for Hasidim to dress as they chose. And to obey the *Shulkhan Arukh*, which the authorities, according to rumor, intended to burn. And it is said that Montefiore told Reb Itzikl, "If only the Jews could have their *own* little state, all Jews would be happier, and safer, everywhere."

One day Reb Itzikl tried to convince an important Jew to go to the governor on behalf of the community. The Jew was afraid: How could he go alone? Then the Rebbe of Worke said, "It is written in Scripture that God told Moses, *Bo el Paaro*, come to Pharaoh. Come? He should have said: '*Go* to Pharaoh.' But—when someone goes to intercede on behalf of his community, God is with him. God precedes him. God is there to meet him."

. . .

Man is never alone. This idea, conceived by Judaism and glorified by Hasidism, dominated the mood in Worke. Even if man wished to be alone, he could not. Man cannot detach himself from his Creator. God is in His creation—God is present, God is presence. It is up to man to be present, too—present to God, to himself, and to his fellow man.

Unlike Kotzk, which provided the framework for Worke just as Pshiskhe did for Kotzk, and Lublin for Pshiskhe, Worke stressed the humanist implications of Hasidism. In Worke friendship was as important as study—even more important than the attachment to the Tzaddik.

Biglal Kamtza u-Bar-Kamtza nechreva Yerushalayim; remember the Midrash? Jerusalem was destroyed because of human hatred. There was a man who had a friend named Kamtza and an enemy named Bar-Kamtza. One day he organized a dinner and told his servant to invite Kamtza; the servant invited Bar-Kamtza instead. The host was furious, and after insulting Bar-Kamtza publicly, chased him out of his house. But Bar-Kamtza took revenge: he denounced the Jews to Rome and, as events unfolded, Jerusalem was ultimately reduced to ashes. "I can understand the guilt of Bar-Kamtza," said Reb Itzikl of Worke. "But Kamtza? How can he be guilty since he wasn't even present at the dinner? *That* was his guilt," commented Reb Itzikl. Kamtza's friend gave a dinner party to celebrate an occasion, and he—his best friend—did not attend? What kind of friend was he? All right, he wasn't invited; never mind! As a friend he should have come—even without an invitation!

Popular belief has it that true friendship can be ascertained only in times of need. Not so: there are Hasidim who maintain that only in happiness will you recognize your true friends. They alone will not be envious. You will usually find friends to feel sorry for you. But rare are those who will be happy simply because you are happy.

Said Reb Itzikl of Worke: "The Talmud tells us that Rebbe Zeira lived long because he never rejoiced over the defeat of his colleagues. What kind of praise is this? Is it conceivable that a sage like Rebbe Zeira could rejoice over his friends' misfortunes? No, the text must be read differently: as long as his colleagues were unhappy, he was unable to rejoice."

From his sayings and teachings, from anecdotes about him, we learn that the founder of Worke was modest, unassuming, simple, warm, often choosing to stay in the shadow, doing everything in his power to honor his teachers and then his companions. Though he was a Rebbe, he fled the limelight. Though he was a Rebbe, he behaved as a Hasid, endlessly searching for continuity and fidelity. After Rebbe Bunam died, he remained loyal to the Rebbe's son, Rebbe Avraham Mordecai, whereas most disciples followed Reb Mendel to Tomashov and then to Kotzk.

Rebbe Bunam's death occurred on a Friday evening, according to Hasidic tradition. A few days earlier the Master had been reciting *Maariv*, the evening prayer, in bed. His son, who was standing at his bedside, was surprised to hear him suddenly say the morning prayer. "Father," he exclaimed, "it's still evening." Without a word of reply, Rebbe Bunam then began to recite the afternoon prayer—*Minhah*. That was too much for Reb Avraham Mordecai; he lost consciousness and was carried into his chambers. When he came to, he ordered his friends to leave him alone, and forbade them to allow anyone into his room. "You keep the door closed," he told his servant, Reb Yiddel, "even if they try to break it down." A day went by. Another one. Three days went by. In the meantime Rebbe Bunam's condition worsened. People came to warn the son and take him to his father's bedside. He refused to let them in. Then his mother came to beg him: "You must be there, your father is dying. . . ." "I cannot," he answered. "I don't have the strength." She asked Reb Itzikl of Worke to plead with her son. He refused, saying, "This matter is too serious; I have no right to interfere."

Later, years later, when Reb Itzikl himself was on his deathbed, his son, Reb Mendel, withdrew into his private chambers and gave orders not to disturb him. He too felt he didn't have the strength to face the loss of his father. As for the Hasidim of Worke, they had to face the loss of their Master—and of their friend. Rebbe Itzikl was more than a friend; he was a brother to his disciples. Every person, he said, must see in the other a Sefer Torah—a Holy Scroll. Every human being is sacred; every creature deserves respect. Man's body itself reflects divinity. Once he scolded a Hasid who had mortified himself: "You are selfish," he told him; "selfish and possessive." "I?" wondered the man. "But I have nothing." "Precisely: you have nothing and yet you behave as though you do; you punish your body—is it yours alone? It belongs to God, to God too."

Another disciple told him of his custom to fast from Sunday to Friday. Reb Itzikl scolded him too: "This is not the Hasidic way," he said. "But it was the Besht's way," said the Hasid. "Didn't *he* live in the mountains, didn't *he* fast from Sunday to Friday?" "No comparison," said Reb Itzikl. "On Sundays the Besht left his family, taking with him food for the entire week— but he forgot to eat it. You go without food but you don't forget it; your mind is on food all week long."

A woman in Worke misbehaved, and as a result, people ostracized her. He defended her, saying, "If everything I hear about her is true, then she deserves pity, not insults."

Ahavat-Israel cannot go hand in hand with self-hate, according to Worke. Dignity, respect and self-respect are principles to be adhered to. Why do we recite the *Viddui*—the confession— alphabetically? "So we know when to stop," said Reb Itzikl. "To cry and moan endlessly is wrong; it is not the way that leads to God. Joy and gratitude are also part of life. *Banim atem laadoshem*, we are all God's children," said Reb Itzikl: "to forget it is the worst of sins." Quoting the Song of Songs, which describes King Solomon sleeping in a bed made of gold, he wondered aloud, "But how can one sleep in a bed made of gold? Read what follows," said Reb Itzikl, answering himself: " '. . . and the inside thereof was inlaid with love'—where there is love, one can sleep even on gold."

Reb Itzikl's son, Reb Mendel, told the Rebbe of Kotzk that he had seen his late father in a dream: he was leaning on a cane, near a river. "Yes," said the Kotzker. "And do you know what the river was? It was a river of tears—tears of all the Jews persecuted everywhere."

True: all his life, Reb Itzikl tried to collect the tears of his tormented people. His son said of him, "Throughout his life, my father would repeat over and over one verse of the Torah: *Veahavta*—and you shall love your God with all your heart, and you shall love, and you shall love. . . ."

Yet, at the same time, Reb Itzikl displayed a marvelous sense of humor. Once he was told that thieves had broken into his son's store and had carried away much of his merchandise. On the following night they returned for what they had left. "Poor thieves," Reb Itzikl remarked, "they didn't sleep two nights in a row. . . ."

Why isn't hospitality included among the six hundred and thirteen commandments of the Torah? he wanted to know. "I'll tell you why," he said. "If it were, people would force strangers not to go home but to come and eat with them, sleep with them, live with them. . . . True hospitality means," he said, "to let your guests leave when they want to leave—and not later."

His older son—a Talmudic scholar—would study aloud in his presence. "Good, good," the father would say, "but you must want to study." So his son studied harder. "Good, good," Reb Itzikl said, "but you must want to study." So his son studied even harder—until he neither slept nor ate, doing nothing but study. "Good, good," said his father, "but you must want to study." "But I have been doing nothing else!" cried the son. "Not entirely true," said Reb Itzikl. "One must want to study to study—and not to impress."

The Kotzker asked him why he had hired a cynic as his private secretary. "I'll tell you," said Reb Itzikl. "All private secretaries become cynical—so why wait?"

He used to say: "One can be alone with people, one can fast while eating; and true silence can be obtained inside words."

It is this silence that, under his younger son, Reb Mendel, was to become the emblem of Worke. He was called Reb Mendel der Schweiger—the silent one. He welcomed silence into Hasidism as a force both disturbing and creative.

In many ways, Reb Mendel, who was born in 1819, is more striking than his father. Philosophically he is closer to Kotzk than to Worke. He too seeks solitude; he too is fascinated by what remains unsaid, unseen, inaccessible.

At the age of three, he was introduced to Rebbe Bunam, who gave him a glass of beer. "Do you like it?" "Yes," said the child. "It tastes bitter but good." "He will be a Rebbe," said Rebbe Bunam.

He married, but soon after left his business and his family and, together with a few friends, went to live in the forest. What they did there has not been revealed. Hasidic tradition has it that they indulged in certain mystical experiments with joy rather than mourning. They sang, they danced, they laughed, they played—but in appearance only. What they hoped to achieve we don't know. We do know, however, that they didn't achieve it—and that Reb Itzikl tried unsuccessfully to convince his son to return to a normal life.

Reb Mendel refused. When his father fell ill, instead of fasting and praying, he went from one inn to the next, drinking one *Lehayyim* after the other in the company of friends whom he called his bodyguards.

Rebbe Berish of Biala followed them secretly one evening. It was Shavuot eve, when one is supposed to spend the whole night in study and meditation. Well, Reb Mendel and his friends spent the night . . . drinking. Reb Berish was indignant, but he contained himself. He watched the scene and waited. Reb Mendel and his friends continued drinking, and after a while Reb Mendel stood up and began talking quietly, almost in a whisper. Reb Berish couldn't hear a word but he saw Reb Mendel burst into tears. Later he begged the group to accept him as a member, and he was admitted but only after a long initiation period.

When Reb Itzikl died, his orphaned followers insisted on crowning Reb Mendel as his successor rather than his elder brother, Reb Yaakov-David of Amshinov. But Reb Mendel refused. Like his father, like the Kotzker and other great Masters, he wanted to follow rather than be followed, leave the title, the responsibilities to someone else. "I am not a Rebbe," he told the Kotzker; "I don't feel that I am one." "It's not up to you to make that decision," answered the Kotzker. "Hasidim make the Rebbe, not the other way around." "No," said Reb Mendel cryptically. "I refuse to be a beggar."

Was it a lack of self-confidence? Possibly. Excessive humility? Probably. "The proof that vanity is bad," he used to say, "is that it can be found in mean people." He was afraid of becoming a leader because leadership implied the possibility of vanity—if not vanity itself. He preferred to be away from crowds—not to show them his true face, not to allow them to come too close. God's command to Abraham: *Lech lecha*—go away, go to another land—is interpreted by Reb Mendel as *Lech lecha*, go toward yourself. This is how he explains the Talmudic expression "Tzaddik-Hasid": an average man is ordered not to fool others, while a Tzaddik-Hasid is called upon not to fool himself. "From my father," he said, "I learned two things: not to tell lies, and not to be a fool." Another version of the same idea: "You cannot fool God," he said; "you cannot even fool people; you can only fool yourself." To the Kotzker he said: "What did King Solomon teach us? That man's intelligence is powerless without God."

Like the Kotzker Hasidim, the followers of Reb Mendel of Worke are encouraged to accept that while life is not made of joy and ecstasy alone, and also contains fear and trembling, and anxiety and sadness—fear and trembling, anxiety and sadness, too, can lead to truth. And God. "To avoid sin," he once said, "is easy, and even simple: when you lie in your bed, imagine that you are lying in your grave."

Contrary to his father, he paid no attention to the routine worries of his followers. My father, he explained, interceded for them with kings; I plead on their behalf before the King of all kings.

And yet, Hasidim flocked to him in great numbers; they revered him, they loved him. He was strange? Surely he had his reasons. He did not talk? Silence too can become a link, a link stronger than the spoken word.

He *was* strange—he resembled the Kotzker, except that he went further than his father's friend. The Kotzker was angry— but present. He shouted. He admonished. He thundered. But he was there. Even when he was in his room, alone, he was there: his Hasidim felt his presence, his closeness. With Reb Mendel it was different. He was there—but not really, not entirely. He was present but not all the way.

He delivered no sermons, gave no courses, avoided offering commentaries on the weekly portion of Scripture, revealed no mystical secrets—in fact, more often than not he said nothing. People came to Worke simply to be silent. To discover living silence—the newest and most disturbing aspect of the Hasidic experience.

He would spend sleepless nights sitting around his table with fervent disciples. The silence would be overwhelming, total. Soon there was nothing else in creation but this silence, and soon it reached farther still, higher still. A primary force, it would grow more and more intense and pure and true. Time stood still, for it had not been disrupted by words. One morning, at sunrise, Reb Mendel shook his head and said in a clear resonant voice, "Happy is the person who knows that the one is one—always one."

Silence has virtues that words cannot have. He explained: "Silence is good even if it is empty—not so with words. When they are empty, they remain empty."

Once he quoted a passage from the Psalms—*Eenkha beseter raam*—God says: "I shall answer you from inside thunder." And Reb Mendel exclaimed, "*Brider Yidden*, brother Jews, *lomir dunnern shtilerheit*—let us all thunder silently."

"These are the three principles I want you to follow," he told his disciples: "Learn how to kneel and stand erect; to dance and remain motionless; to shout and be silent—all at the same time."

Other Hasidic masters have extolled the virtues and powers of silence, but none practiced it as he did.

There were times when the Baal Shem Tov asked his disciples to contain their ecstasy—or their laughter—and keep quiet, and turn the absence of sound into something creative, and enter silence.

There were times when the great Maggid Reb Dov-Ber of Mezeritch would listen, listen to his disciples without offering them a reply.

There were times when Rebbe Elimelekh of Lizensk would withdraw, for hours or days, into a state of muteness.

There were times when Reb Levi-Yitzhak of Berditchev would speak in whispers, so that no one could hear him. He too was intrigued by silence. "When the Messiah will come," he once said, "it will be given to man to understand not only the words of the Torah but also the empty spaces between them."

As for the Kotzker, he taught us that certain truths can be transmitted by words, others by silence, and still others cannot be communicated at all, not even by silence.

Yes—many Hasidic masters felt, at one point in their lives, the compulsion to confront the problem—the mystery—of silence. Rabbi Nahman of Bratzlav, for instance, demanded of his disciples that they live one hour every day in solitude and silence. In his tales we often meet characters—poets, orators and minstrels—unable or unwilling to speak.

But no Master spoke of silence—no Master put silence into words—as did Rebbe Mendel of Worke. With him, it became a world to explore, a major theme to dwell upon, a way of life.

He loved to explain the Biblical verse *Vayishma adoshem et kol hanaar*—And God heard the complaints of Ishmael in the desert. He commented: "There is no mention that Ishmael cried or even moaned. This means," he continued, "that Ishmael, Hagar's tragic son, cried silently—and that is why he was heard by God."

The same, he felt, was true of Hannah, mother of the Prophet Samuel, who prayed in silence—the highest form of prayer, according to Reb Mendel. Once he spoke of Batya, Pharaoh's daughter, who noticed the child floating on the Nile and saw him crying. She *saw* him crying? Didn't she hear him? Can a child cry inwardly? "Yes—a Jewish child can," said Reb Mendel of Worke, "at times, a Jewish child must."

One day he met Rebbe Eliezer, son of the Maggid of Kozhenitz, to discuss an urgent matter. They withdrew into a room, sat down facing one another, looked at one another for a long while but said nothing. Then they opened the door. "We have finished," said Reb Mendel to his Hasidim waiting outside.

Why this obsession with silence? Was it because Reb Mendel distrusted the spoken word, too often and too successfully misused by man? Was it that he longed for the silence that the Besht had absorbed in the Carpathian mountains before it was turned into tales and sayings, teachings and precepts? Was it something else, something more? Was his purpose not to withdraw from language but to amplify and deepen it with silence? Perhaps he meant to innovate, to invent, to create something new in Hasidism. Perhaps he felt that everything had been said: that he could only repeat what others had said before him. That he could never live up to his forerunners.

There is another possibility. His actions may have derived from higher, more spiritual impulses—perhaps even theological considerations. Since God dwells in silence, why not seek Him out there? Why not challenge Him there?

The nineteenth century witnessed new bloodshed and justified new fears. Outside the Hasidic kingdom, the world was preparing the abyss for future generations of Hasidim and their Masters. New wars were erupting, preparing the way for the most cruel of all. And God was silent? Satan howled and God did not respond? Evil spread throughout creation and the Creator said nothing? Since He remained silent, what could man possibly do?

One Passover evening, a week before he died, at the age of forty-nine, Reb Mendel was singing the Haggada—the beautiful story of our exodus from Egypt—when he stopped in the middle. He paused and then he whispered, "In truth, there exist in this world Tzaddikim, Just Men, who possess the powers to bring the Messiah. But they choose not to use their powers. Why? I shall tell you why: Since God is silent, they choose to remain silent too."

When divine silence is answered by human silence—it is tragic for both.

But then—where is hope to be found? The two silences *can* merge, *can* grow one through the other, one in the other. That is sufficient—that *must* be sufficient. One can purify and free the other, and that is sufficient, that *must* be sufficient.

For ultimately the choice is a limited one: We can answer God's silence with human words—or respond to God's words with human silence. But there too the road is not without obstacles: What if the silence of the one is the language of the other? How are we to know? Is it at all possible to know?

These are disturbing questions, especially for my generation. We have so far failed to decipher or even to confront God's silence in a universe empty of God—or worse: filled with God.

Now, in this generation, we have learned at least one lesson: that some experiences lie beyond language, that their language *is* silence. For silence does not necessarily mean absence of communication.

Imagine a great dancer motionless—for one hour—on stage; imagine a gifted painter staring intently—for one day—at the white canvas; imagine a forceful sculptor with her fingers riveted to the stone—her fingers becoming stone. Imagine them and you may be able to capture the evocative, descriptive silence of the artist.

For the poet, the artist, the mystic and the survivor, silence has many facets, zones and shades. Silence has its own texture, its own spheres, its own archeology. It has its own contradictions as well. The silence of the victim is one thing, that of the killer, another. And that of the spectator, still another. There is creative silence, there is murderous silence. To a perceptive human being the universe is never silent—but there exists a universe of silence, and only perceptive human beings are aware of it.

Now—I confess that I feel close to Worke because of its silence—it symbolizes to me another universe, one that *was* dominated by silence. There, during the eternity of one night, endless nocturnal processions of men and women and children, crossing a continent in flames, went to meet their executioners and death—and God—silently whispering age-old prayers, the Kaddish, the *Viddui*, the *Sh'ma Israel*, and nothing else, as though they too had despaired of language.

More than the hunger of the hungry, more than the agony of the tormented, more than the flames over the mass graves, it is the silence of the victims that is haunting us—and will haunt us forever. The quiet, fearless Rebbe and his frightened community. The teacher and his disciples. The dreamers, the workers, the rich and the poor, the learned and the ignorant, they did not cry, they did not shout, they did not protest; they walked and walked into death and left their silence behind them. And if ever silence attained the level of absolute, it was then. It was there.

And so, let us go back—back to Worke—and stay there, lest we go mad, mad with pain and anguish and yearning.

I remember silence in Worke—I remember silence away from Worke.

And now we know what it was: an appeal, an outcry to God on behalf of his desperate people and also on His behalf, an offering to night, to heaven, an offering made by wise old men and quiet children to mark the end of language—the outer limits of creation—a burning secret buried in silence.

AFTERWORD

It is only reluctantly that the teller of tales considers leaving these great Masters whom we have just encountered in their very own capitals of the Hasidic universe; their hold on him has never been stronger.

Such is the power of their legends; their intensity, their beauty stay with you and involve you—almost against your will, almost against your better judgment.

Somewhere, a Master spoke to one or many of his followers about their fears and doubts and what to do to alleviate them, and his message was heard then, and today, for their exchange is also about us; there is a curious immediacy to their stories, a timeless application to their sayings.

A Hasidic story is to be told, not studied. It is to be lived, not analyzed. The anger of Rebbe Barukh, the compassion of Rebbe Moshe-Leib, the melancholy visions of the Seer of Lublin: they teach Hasidim how to live, not how to reflect.

A Hasidic story is about Hasidim more than about their Masters; it is about those who retell it as much as about those who experienced it long ago, in a time of both physical and spiritual hunger and solitude.

Rebbe Pinhas and his wisdom, the Besht and his warmth, Rebbe Naphtali and his humor: to their followers they appeared as kings, judges, prophets. There are intimations of royalty in their vocabulary: notables are "appointed" to positions, Rebbes are "crowned" and ascend "thrones."

How can the attraction they held for their contemporaries be comprehended today? They were as close to God as to those who were seeking Him. Though they differed considerably in their outlook, in their life styles, their education—some were more learned than others, more renowned than others—they were all endowed with mystical powers and they used them not to isolate themselves but rather to penetrate and enrich their communities.

They were inspired, and they inspired others. They communicated joy and wonder, and fervor too, fervor above all, to men and women who needed joy and fervor to live, to survive. These teachers brought warmth and compassion to followers in the Ukraine, in Poland and in Lithuania. For Jews who felt abandoned, forsaken, there was always a Master somewhere who incarnated an irresistible call to hope and friendship.

Friendship, *Dibuk-haverim*, is a key word in the Hasidic vocabulary. For the disciple it is as important as *Ahavat-Israel*, love of people, is for the Master.

To follow a certain Rebbe means also to relate to his pupils and admirers. A Hasid alone is not a true Hasid. Solitude and Hasidism are incompatible. What was the Hasidic movement in its origins if not a protest against solitude? The villager left behind his farm, his daily misery and uncertainties, and went to spend the High Holidays, or a simple Sabbath, with his Master—not just to see and hear him and pray and study with him, but also to meet his fellow Hasidim, his friends. And over and over again, they would celebrate their reunion, their common faith and their dream.

And yet, and yet . . . all these great spiritual leaders and guides, who somehow, somewhere, managed to move so many others to joy and ecstasy, often seemed to struggle with melancholy, and at times even with darkest despair.

The holy Seer of Lublin, the famous Jester of Ropshitz, the Sage of Koretz, the wanderer from Zbarazh: what was this sadness they had to engage in combat—and why?

Intercessor rather than mediator (the Jewish tradition rejects the concept of intermediaries in the relations of man to his

Creator), the Rebbe often is bound to feel inadequate: all these vigils, all these prayers, all these promises, all these appeals, yet the Messiah does not come. All these trials and sufferings, and heaven remains closed. And the Shekhina remains in exile. As do the people of Israel. What must one do to keep from losing hope, what can one do? Said Rebbe Aharon of Karlin: "Either God is God and I do not do enough to serve Him, or He is not and then it is my fault." Who is responsible for all the wars, the persecutions, the long nights of fear? Who is to blame for all the hatred, the torment, the massacres, the pogroms? Hunger, thirst, death: Who can acquiesce? Who can justify? The Master listens and listens to his followers' tales of woe and eventually cannot ignore the signs of approaching melancholy.

Every Master—whether in Mezeritch or Sassov, in Rizhin or in Premishlan—is vulnerable. The problem is inherent in his functions. He must go on listening to his followers. He must go on being available to them—always and in everything. He has no right to abandon those who believe in him. The Master is responsible for his Hasidim.

And so he controls himself. Surmounting all obstacles— rational doubts, irrational fears—he liberates in himself and in his followers a kind of joy that will be justified only retroactively. He combats sorrow with exuberance; he defeats resignation by exalting faith. He attempts to create happiness so as not to yield to the sadness around him. He tells stories so as to escape the temptations of irreducible silence.

To express my admiration and my love for all these Hasidic Masters whose portraits I have tried to draw is repetitious. But then, repetition is part of the Hasidic tradition.

Naturally, I stressed some themes more than others. I probably spoke too much of certain Rebbes and not enough of others—Rebbe Shneur-Zalman deserves a volume to himself—but there too, I only did what the Hasid in me has always done— and what all Hasidim are still doing. Hasidism has never claimed to oppose subjectivity.

Afterword

In retelling these tales, I realize once more how much I owe these Masters. Sometimes consciously, sometimes not, I have incorporated a song, a suite, an obsession of theirs into my own fables and legends. For me, the echoes of a vanished kingdom are still reverberating. And I have remained the child who loves to listen.

While listening I see myself with my grandfather at various "courts." We laugh with the Rebbe of Ropshitz, we tremble in the presence of the Seer of Lublin, we dance with Rebbe Moshe-Leib of Sassov. Somewhere, a Master is singing, and we feel compelled to join him and learn his song.

Elsewhere, in a novel, I imagined a man who one day finds himself sharing a cell with a madman. After a while, he realizes that slowly, inevitably, he too is losing his mind. Having been exposed to madness, he will in time become its victim. And so, in order not to go mad, he sets out to cure his mad fellow prisoner. The hero of my tale did not know, could not know that he was only following in the steps of Rebbe Nahman of Bratzlav, Rebbe Pinhas of Koretz, Rebbe Mendel of Worke and their peers whom I have evoked in this volume.

Did I say that the teller of tales would soon leave his old Masters? In truth, he will not. For even if he wanted to, he could not; they surely would not willingly recede into the shadows of his burning memory.

More than ever, we, today, need their faith, their fervor; more than ever, we, today, need to imagine them helping, caring —living.

GLOSSARY

ALIYAH (literally "Ascent"): Usual meaning is emigration to Israel.

BAAL SHEM (literally "Master of the Name"): Title attributed since the Middle Ages to men who know the true name of beings and things, recognize their secret and can act upon them, through them. By naming the forces, such a man masters them; his knowledge is power. Were he to use this power to attain immediate or profane gains, he would be nothing more than a miracle-maker. But if he chooses to bring the names closer to the Name, and unite beings and things with God, he becomes Master of the Good Name, Baal Shem Tov.

BEADLE: The equivalent in the synagogue to a church sexton.

BEIT MIDRASH (literally "House of Study"): In order not to interrupt meditation and discussion on the sacred Word, the rabbinical academies chose to remain there for services rather than move to the Beit Knesseth, the assembly house (synagogue). The two "Houses" often became one, or at least were made to adjoin, with services extending into study and study culminating in prayer. "At the hour of prayer and study" is a frequently recurring expression in Hasidic texts.

According to Haggada, the first Beit Midrash was founded by Sem on the morrow of the Deluge. When Isaac was freed of his bonds and left the altar, that is where he retired to study.

THE BESHT, or Rebbe Israel Baal Shem Tov (1700–1760): The founder of the Hasidic movement.

DAYAN: Judge of the rabbinical tribunal, arbiter.

DIN: Judgment, legal decision; *midat hadin*: divine rigor and severity.

FRANK, JACOB (1726–1791): Last of the "great" would-be Messiahs. A disciple of Shabtai-Tzvi, he tried to "rehabilitate" Christianity for the Jews, ultimately converting amid great pomp in the Warsaw cathedral with Emperor Augustus III as his godfather. Later he spent thirteen years in prison for heresy. Retired to the Rhineland with his daughter Eve, famous for her beauty, he taught and practiced the "rehabilitation" of sexuality by unrestrained indulgence in its every form.

GAON OF VILNA, or Rabbi Elijah ben Salomon Zalman (1720–1797): The most exalted rabbinical figure of Eastern European Jewry, a man of outstanding moral stature and quasi-encyclopedic learning. The unchallenged master of Halakha, he also had a profound knowledge of Kabbala. Leader of the Mitnagdim, he vehemently opposed the Hasidic movement and vigorously fought its expansion in Lithuania.

GOG AND MAGOG: The opponents of the Messiah. In the great eschatological battle against the righteous host, they are to head the forces of evil. In rabbinic literature, the rebel people who rise up against God and His anointed.

HAGGADA: Parables, commentaries, legends, proverbs and fables, most often deriving from Biblical texts, expounding on their complexities and constituting one of the aspects of Talmud and Midrash. Whereas Halakha enjoins conformity by tracing guidelines to a way of life, Haggada, less severe and less coercive, and even at times and as circumstances require, mischievous or poetic, awakens thought, meditation or prayer, and brings into focus the foundations of a system of ethics and faith.

HALAKHA (literally "walk, way, rule"): That which in Talmud and rabbinical literature concerns itself with the ritual, social and economic life of the community and the individual. Like the texts of Haggada, with which they overlap, the texts of Halakha are generally based on Biblical exegesis. They constitute the basis of an ample body of laws regulating every aspect of the life of a practicing Jew.

HASID (literally "fervent, pious"): One who acts out of love, with tenderness. Derived from *hesed*, grace, one of God's attributes complementing *din*, strict justice. God's grace calls forth the fervor, the piety of man, his love for God and all His creatures.

In the Psalms, Hasid (plural, Hasidim) often denotes the faithful, the lover of God. In the Talmud (Pirkhe Aboth, V, 13–16), Hasid is "he who says: what is mine is yours and what is yours is yours; he who is slow to anger and quick to relent; he who enjoys giving and likes others to give"—and again, "he who, even before he prays, turns his heart to God—for at least one hour" (Ber. 30b)—and even "the Hasidim among the Gentiles will have their share in the world to come" (Toss. Sanh. 13; Mishne Torah, Melakhim 11).

In the second century B.C. a Jewish sect, the Hasidim or Assideans, "valiant men whose hearts were bound to the Law," fought with the Maccabees against Antiochus Epiphanus. But refusing all compromise on religious law and unwilling to become involved in politics, they broke away from the Hasmonean dynasty after victory had been achieved. The Talmud refers to them as "the Hasidim of yore."

In the thirteenth century of the Common Era, there flourished in the Rhineland an important school called the Hasidim of Ashkenaz, the Holy Men of Germany; they created a trend of thought that found wide acceptance. Their major work, the *Sefer Hasidim*, the Book of the Devout, rooted in Jewish mystical tradition, stresses the majesty of God but also the mystery of oneness, elaborating a veritable philosophy of history and man's relationship to man, emphasizing the importance of silent piety, of prayer, and of a system of ethics based on renunciation of earthly matters, spiritual serenity, total love of one's fellow man culminating in the expression of the fear and the love of God in "the joy that scorches the heart."

HEDER: An elementary religious school of the type prevalent in Eastern Europe, often situated in a single room in the teacher's home.

HILLEL AND SHAMMAI: Respectively president and vice-president of the Sanhedrin in the first century B.C. They are the last and best known of the "couples" of rabbis whose opinions challenge and complete one another. The School of Shammai, more concerned with principles and ultimate goals, was the more severe, the more rigorous of the two; the House of Hillel, mindful of the lessons of the past, leaned toward a gentler approach.

KAVANA (literally "intention"): Spiritual concentration on prayer or the religious act to prepare for *dvekut*—compliance with the Divine Will. The Talmud stresses the need of directing one's thoughts toward God, not only while praying but also while obeying the Commandments. The "mystics" of the Middle

Ages, and later the Hasidim, insisted on this form of contemplation, and composed *Kavanoth*, "prayers—or poems—of intention," to prepare and assist in the transition into ritual service.

LAMED VAVNIK: "The world," says the Talmud, "must not contain fewer than thirty-six Just Men" who have been allowed to contemplate the Divine Presence. It is thanks to them that the world subsists. Popular imagination took hold of these Lamed Vavnik (the numerical value of the letters *lamed* and *vav* is thirty-six), gave them a background of poverty and obscurity and described them as leading hidden lives, revealing their qualities and powers only in cases of need, when the survival of the community, the people, or the world is at stake.

LURIA, ISAAC, also referred to as the Ari, the Holy Lion of Safed (1534–1572): He was born in Jerusalem, lived in Cairo and died in Safed; one of the most mysterious, complex and popular masters of Kabbala. His strictly oral teachings owe their dissemination to notes taken by his disciple Hayim Vital. His thoughts on *Tzimtzum* (the withdrawal of God into Himself to leave room for human groping and error); on the *Shevirat Hakelim*, the "broken vessels" of Primary Light whose sparks subsist even in the infernal regions; on the *Tikkun* (the "bridging" of gaps, the in-gathering of sparks, "restoration" as a historical objective); on the Messiah in chains awaiting the redemption of our every deed, all strongly influenced Hasidism.

MAARIV: Evening service, also called *Arevit*, recited daily after nightfall and named after one of the opening words of its first prayer.

MAGGID: A popular preacher. The Maggid became a characteristic feature of the Russian and Polish Jewish communities. It was mainly by means of these wandering preachers that Hasidism was spread in the eighteenth century.

MASKIL: A title of honor for a learned man.

MELAMED: A teacher who supervised the single-room *heder*.

MEZUZAH (literally "doorpost"): A small tubular case, usually of metal or wood, containing a tightly rolled piece of parchment inscribed with verses 4–9 of Deut. 6 and 13–21 of Deut. 11 on one side, and *Shaddai* (a name applied to God) on the other, the latter visible through an aperture in the case. The mezuzah is traditionally attached to the right doorpost of the Jewish home. The great philosopher-legislator of the Middle Ages, Moses ben Maimon (Maimonides), expressed its meaning this way:

"By the commandment of the mezuzah, man is reminded, when entering or departing, of God's Oneness, and is stirred into love for Him. He is awakened from his slumber and from his vain worldly thoughts to the knowledge that no thing endures in eternity like knowledge of the 'Rock of the World.' This contemplation brings him back to himself and leads him unto the right path."

MIDRASH: From a Hebrew verb meaning to expound, to interpret, to deduce; specifically to expound the precepts and ethical dicta of Scriptures; in fact, a large body of Talmudic literature that developed during the Tannaic and Amoraic periods (second century of the Common Era).

MIKVAH: Ritual bath for immersion to wash every uncleanness.

MINHAH: The second of the two statutory daily services. It is recited anytime during the afternoon until sunset and corresponds to the daily "evening" sacrifice in the Temple.

MINYAN: The ten male Jews required for religious services.

MISHNAH (literally "study"): Compendia of tradition compiled in Palestine ca. 200 C.E.

MITNAGDIM (literally "adversaries"): They opposed the "new Hasidic sect," judging it revolutionary, dangerous, heretic.

QUEEN SHABBAT: The Sabbath is welcomed as a bride and a queen and the end of the Sabbath is marked by the festive meal *melave-malka*—"accompanying the Queen."

RABBI: Literally "master" or "teacher."

REB: Mr.

REBBE: Term used for Hasidic leaders and spiritual guides. The Rebbe or Tzaddik is not necessarily a halakhic scholar and teacher, but guides his followers by virtue of his spiritual power and holiness.

Glossary

SHABBAT: The Sabbath, the weekly day of rest, observed from sunset of Friday until nightfall Saturday.

SHABTAI-TZVI (1626–1676): The most prestigious of the false Messiahs. Born in Smyrna, well versed in Talmud and practical Kabbala, he wandered from Salonika to Jerusalem, enticing crowds and attracting wrath, teaching a doctrine in which are evident elements of the school of Luria. In 1665 he proclaimed himself Messiah. The news spread like wildfire and aroused indescribable enthusiasm and exultation in the Jewish world; people everywhere prayed for "our Master, the Anointed of the Lord"; some even sold their property, expecting an imminent miraculous departure for the Holy Land. In 1666 he expressed the wish to meet the Sultan so as to request recognition of his sovereignty over the Land of Israel. Instead he found himself in prison. Then, one day, the Sultan summoned him; we don't know what took place, except that soon thereafter Shabtai-Tzvi converted to Islam—only to be exiled to Albania, where he ended his days in obscurity.

    Yet the most fervent among his disciples saw in his conversion but another step in a divine pattern; his cult subsisted until the twentieth century in the East, and at least one hundred years in the West, where he provoked controversies and suspicions, heresy and excommunications.

SHAVUOT: Holiday in late spring, commemorating the gift of Torah at Mount Sinai.

SHEKHINA: The Divine Presence. Tradition has it that the radiance of the Shekhina with its many blessings accompanies those who are pious and righteous.

SH'MA ISRAEL (literally "Hear O Israel"): A liturgical prayer, prominent in Jewish history and tradition, recited daily at evening and morning services, "you will say them when you lie down and when you rise" (verse 7, Deut. 6); it brings together three passages of the Pentateuch, all expressing Israel's ardent faith in and love of God. The important place it holds in Jewish consciousness has made it into a veritable "profession of faith" that is repeated by the dying man and the martyr.

SHIMON BAR YOHAI (second century of the Common Era): Famous Master whose teachings are frequently quoted and expounded in the Talmud. He was condemned to death for having criticized the Roman occupiers but succeeded in escaping. With his son, he took shelter in a cave, where he spent thirteen years. There are numerous legends woven around this period in his life: it was said that he explored the mysteries of Kabbala during his reclusion and laid the foundations of the Zohar. To this day, there are considerable numbers of faithful who visit his grave in Meron, near Safed, on the thirty-third day after Passover, the anniversary of his death.

SHOKHET: One trained and ordained to perform the ritual slaughter used to supply kosher meats.

SHTETL: A very small town.

SHTIBL: House of Prayer of Hasidim, usually extremely small with only one or two rooms.

SHULKHAN ARUKH: A compendium of Jewish law compiled in the sixteenth century C.E. by Joseph Caro.

SIMHAT TORAH: Festival of the Law in the autumn; the last day of Succoth celebrating the end of the yearly cycle of reading the Torah.

SUCCAH: A temporary, wooden hut covered with branches, in which all meals are taken during Succoth.

SUCCOTH: Feast of Tabernacles; begins four days after Yom Kippur.

TALLIT: Prayer shawl.

TALMUD (literally "learning"): Mishnah plus Gemara, the commentary on the Mishnah produced in rabbinical academies from ca. 200–500 C.E.

TANYA: The basic work of the HaBaD movement within Hasidism which produced the school of Lubavitch. Authored by the founder of HaBaD, Rebbe Shneur-Zalman of Lyady (1747–1813), the Tanya consists of two parts: the first shows the way to "those who are neither perfect Just Men nor evil outcasts," in other words those who may, through study, prayer and meditation, attain the love of God; the second, the Book of Unity and Faith, is a commentary on the *Sh'ma*.

TEFILLIN: Phylacteries; two leather cases which are bound by straps attached to the forehead and the left arm during the morning prayer.

Glossary

TORAH (literally "teaching"): Can refer to the Pentateuch, or to all of Scripture, or to all revelation, written or oral, in Judaism.

TZADDIK: Just Man, ideal of moral, social and religious perfection, he is a man "who lives by his faith," and to whom God responds. In the Hasidic movement the Tzaddik rapidly became an institution, but though a "spiritual model," when exposed to temptation, he was not always able to resist, going as far as to proclaim himself intermediary between his disciples and God, presiding over veritable courts and founding dynasties.

YOHANAN BEN-ZAKKAI, also called Rabban, our Master: One of the key figures in the elaboration of the Talmud. In order to protect the continuity of studies, he fled a Jerusalem occupied by Vespasian and founded the Academy of Yavneh, which succeeded the Sanhedrin and guaranteed the survival of the tradition. After the destruction of the Temple, Rabbi Yohanan Ben-Zakkai compiled all that was known of sacrificial ritual, down to the smallest details, in expectation of messianic restoration. At the same time he stressed the important place held, in the absence of the Temple, and to this day, by study of the holy texts and the synagogal cult.

ZOHAR: The "Book of Splendor," principal work of Kabbala, esoteric commentary on the Pentateuch, traditionally attributed to Shimon bar Yohai.

SYNCHRONOLOGY

ISRAEL BAAL SHEM TOV (THE BESHT) (1700–1760)	
DOV-BER OF MEZERITCH (THE MAGGID) (1704–1772)	
ELIMELEKH OF LIZENSK (1717–1786)	1720 In Lowicz (Poland), the clergy decides to prohibit the building of new and the restoration of old synagogues.
PINHAS OF KORETZ (1728–1791)	1727 First Jews naturalized in American colonies.
AHARON OF KARLIN (THE GREAT) (1733–1772)	1730 Founding of the first synagogue in New York.
WOLFE OF ZBARAZH (–1802?)	1738 Public execution in Stuttgart of Joseph Susskind Oppenheimer (Jud Süss).
LEVI-YITZHAK OF BERDITCHEV (1740–1809)	
MOSHE-LEIB OF SASSOV (1745–1807)	1745 Empress Maria Theresa orders the expulsion of Jews from Bohemia and Prague.
THE SEER OF LUBLIN (1745–1815)	
	1750 Stringent anti-Jewish legislation adopted in Germany: limitation on marriage and increased taxation.

IN THE WORLD AT LARGE	IN THE ARTS
	1726 Swift's *Gulliver's Travels*.
1733–1735 War of the Polish Succession.	1733 J. S. Bach's B-Minor Mass.
1740–1748 War of the Austrian Succession.	1740 Hume's *Treatise on Human Nature*. 1742 Handel's *Messiah*.
	1748 Montesquieu's *Spirit of the Laws*.

IN THE JEWISH WORLD

BARUKH OF MEDZIBOZH (1757–1811)	1753 British Parliament rejects a proposed law granting certain civic rights to Jews.
	Major trial of Polish Jews accused of ritual murder. (More than twenty such trials took place in Poland alone between 1700 and 1760.)
NAPHTALI OF ROPSHITZ (1760–1827)	
BUNAM OF PSHISKHE (1762–1827)	
	1763 The twenty-five-year-old philosopher Moses Mendelssohn receives the first prize of the Prussian Academy of Sciences for an essay on metaphysics.
	1764 "Council of the Four Lands" dissolved. Polish Jews are left without any central organization.
NAHMAN OF BRATZLAV (1772–1810)	1772 The Mitnagdim, gathered in Vilna, excommunicate the "new sect," the Hasidim.
YAAKOV-YITZHAK OF PSHISKHE (THE JEW) (1776–1813)	1775 Pius VI's edicts condemn the seven thousand Jews of Rome to misery and public disgrace.
ITZHAK OF WORKE (1779–1848)	1779 Lessing publishes his apologia of Judaism: *Nathan der Weise.*

Synchronology

IN THE WORLD AT LARGE	IN THE ARTS
1756–1763 Seven Year's War. Russia, Austria, France and others against Prussia and Great Britain.	
1759 Public debate in Lemberg between Frankist renegades and prominent rabbis.	1759 Inauguration of the British Museum. —— Haydn's First Symphony performed. —— Voltaire's *Candide*.
1760 Beginnings (in England) of the Industrial Revolution.	
1762–1796 Reign of Catherine II (the Great) of Russia. In the name of the Enlightenment she encourages art, education and letters, and instigates political and social reforms—yet she does nothing to abolish serfdom.	1762 Rousseau's *Le Contrat Social* and *Émile*. —— Gluck's *Orfeo ed Euridice* performed.
1764–1795 Reign of Stanislas II (Poniatowski), last king of Poland. The country is dismembered by Russia, Austria and Prussia during the first (1772), the second (1793) and the third (1795) partitions. Having no country left to govern, he resigns in 1795.	
1772 First partition of Poland.	1771 First publication of *Encyclopaedia Britannica*. 1772 Diderot publishes last volume of *Encyclopédie*. 1774 Goethe's *Werther*.
1775–1783 American War of Independence.	
1778–1779 War of the Bavarian Succession.	
	1779 Lessing's *Nathan der Weise*.

IN THE JEWISH WORLD

MEIR OF PREMISHLAN (1780–1850)	1781 First Jewish Free School opened in Berlin, marking the breakthrough of Jewish *Aufklärung*: Enlightenment. 1784 Beginning of publication in Berlin of *Hameassef* (The Gatherer), devoted to rationalist Judaism.
MENAHEM-MENDEL OF KOTZK (1787–1859)	
ISRAEL OF RIZHIN (1796–1850)	
AHARON OF KARLIN (1801–1872)	
	1812 Napoleon's invasion of Russia brings about the emancipation of its Jews.

IN THE WORLD AT LARGE	IN THE ARTS
	1781 Kant's *Critique of Pure Reason*.
	1785 Mozart's *Marriage of Figaro*.
1789–1799 The French Revolution.	1790 Goya's *Caprichos*, works of social satire. Goethe's *Faust*.
1793 Second partition of Poland.	
1793–1794 The Reign of Terror. Robespierre massacres opposition; Marie Antoinette is guillotined.	
1794 Polish national uprising led by Thaddeus Kosciusko crushed by combined Russian and Prussian armies.	
1795 Third partition of Poland. Russia, Prussia and Austria absorb the last Polish territories.	
1796 Napoleon Bonaparte embarks on a series of victories.	
	1797 Chateaubriand's *Essays on Old and Modern Revolutions*.
1799 Napoleon and his army reach the Holy Land.	
	1800 Schiller's *Marie Stuart*.
	1807 Byron publishes his first poems; Fichte, his *Sermons to the German Nation*; Hegel, his *Phenomenology of the Mind*.
	1808 Beethoven's Pastoral Symphony.
1812 Napoleon invades Russia.	
1813 Battle of Leipzig—Napoleon defeated.	
1814–1815 Congress of Vienna ends wars of Napoleonic era.	
1815 Waterloo. Napoleon defeated and exiled.	

IN THE JEWISH WORLD

	1815 Pius VII reinstitutes the Inquisition. The constitution of Poland—finally formulated—denies civic rights to Jews.
MENDEL OF WORKE (1819–1868)	1819 Beginning of movement "Wissenschaft des Judentums" in Germany; it will expand to all of Western Europe. 1824 Mass persecution of Jews in Russia.

IN THE WORLD AT LARGE	IN THE ARTS
1815 The Holy Alliance is signed by all European rulers except the King of England, the Pope and the Sultan. Alexander I is the most active sponsor of this agreement, which allies Christian principles with politics and which generally represents a reactionary policy against liberal ideas.	
	1820 Keats publishes his major poems, the *Odes*; Shelley, his *Prometheus Unbound*.
1825–1855 Reign of Nicholas I of Russia is marked by autocracy and repression of all liberal tendencies.	1827 Heine's *Das Buch der Lieder*.

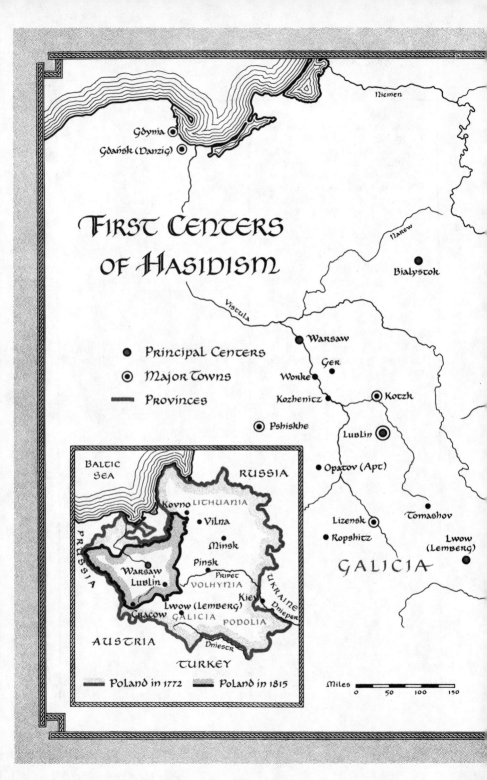

FIRST CENTERS
OF HASIDISM

- ● **Principal Centers**
- ◉ **Major Towns**
- ▬ **Provinces**

Niemen

Narew

Gdynia ◉
Gdańsk (Danzig) ◉

Białystok ●

Vistula

Warsaw ●
Ger ●
Worke ●
Kozhenitz ●
Kotzk ◉
Pshiskhe ◉
Lublin ◉
Opatov (Apt) ●
Tomashov ●
Lizensk ◉
Ropshitz ●
Lwow (Lemberg) ●

GALICIA

BALTIC SEA
RUSSIA
Kovno ● LITHUANIA
● Vilna
● Minsk
Pinsk ●
PRUSSIA
Warsaw ● PRIPET
Lublin ● VOLHYNIA
Lwow (Lemberg) ● Kiev ●
Cracow ● GALICIA
UKRAINE
Dnieper
PODOLIA
AUSTRIA
Dniestr
TURKEY

▬ **Poland in 1772**   ▬ **Poland in 1815**

Miles
0   50   100   150

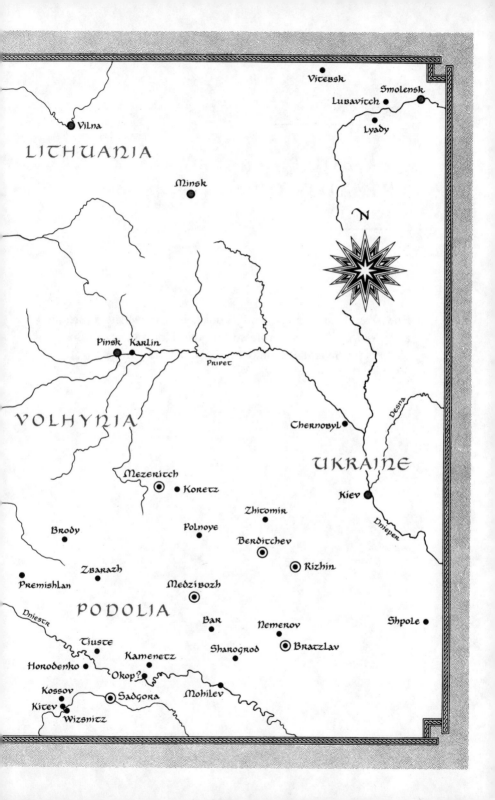

ABOUT
THE AUTHOR

Elie Wiesel, author of twenty books, is a university professor
and Andrew Mellon Professor in the Humanities at Boston
University. He and his family live in New York City.